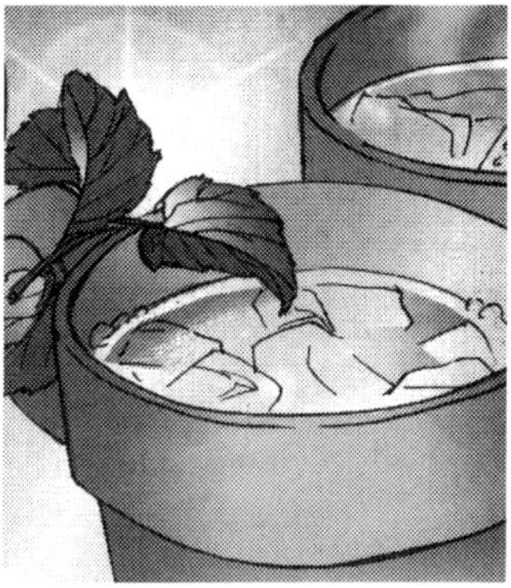

DELICIOUS SEASONS

Delicious Seasons

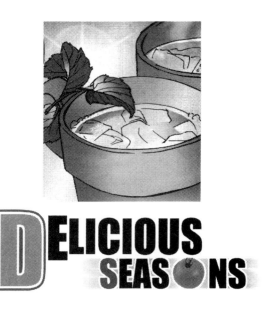

Delicious Seasons

STORY AND ART BY
RAINBOW BUDDY

Editor in Chief/ Angela Wenjia Wang

PARENTAL ADVISORY
Delicious Seasons may contain violence, language and alcohol or tobacco usage. It is rate "T" for teens.

Printed in U.S.A.
Published by Silicon Times, Inc.

Delicious Seasons

《美味季节》—Buddy—

Vol.1 SPRING'S COMING

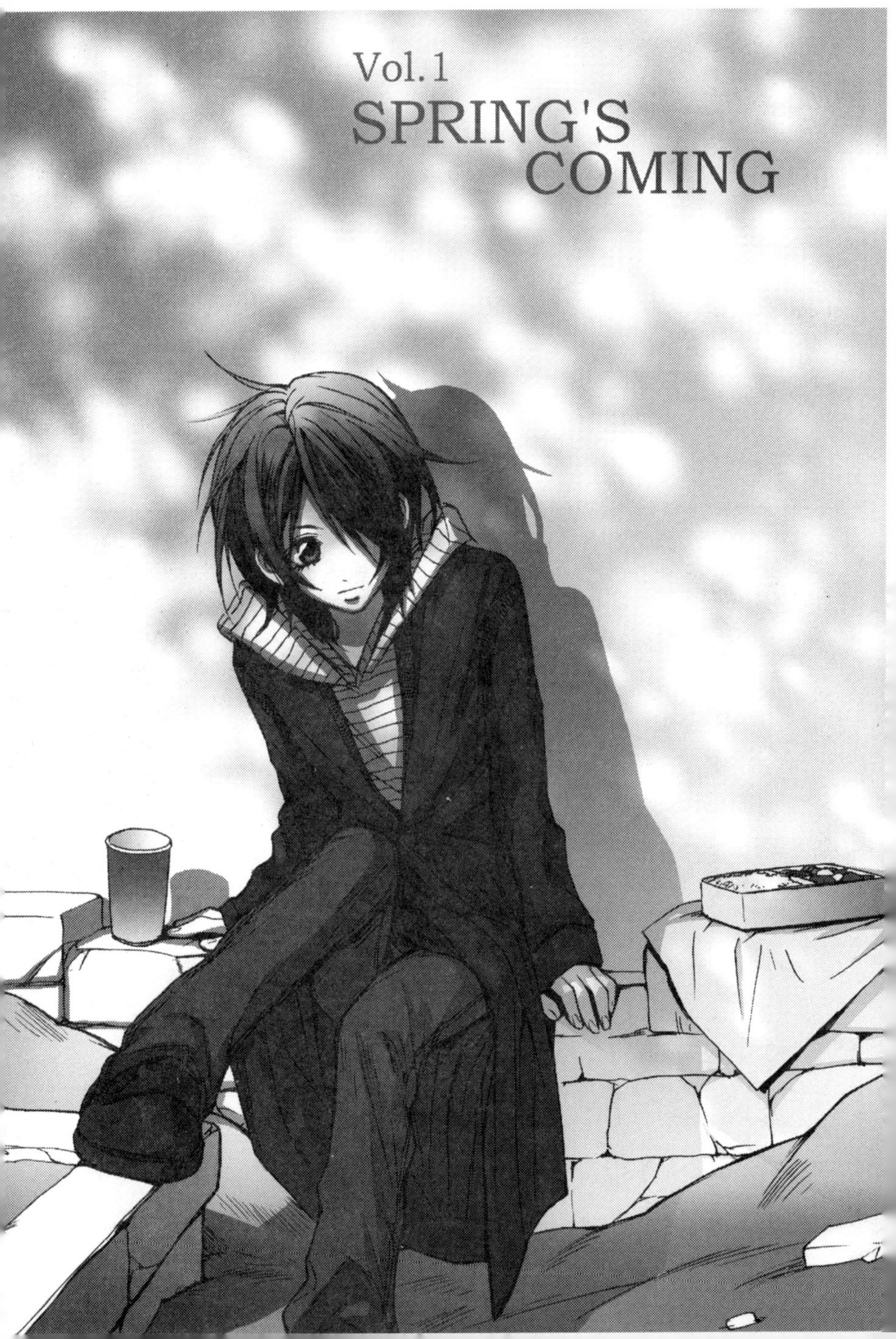

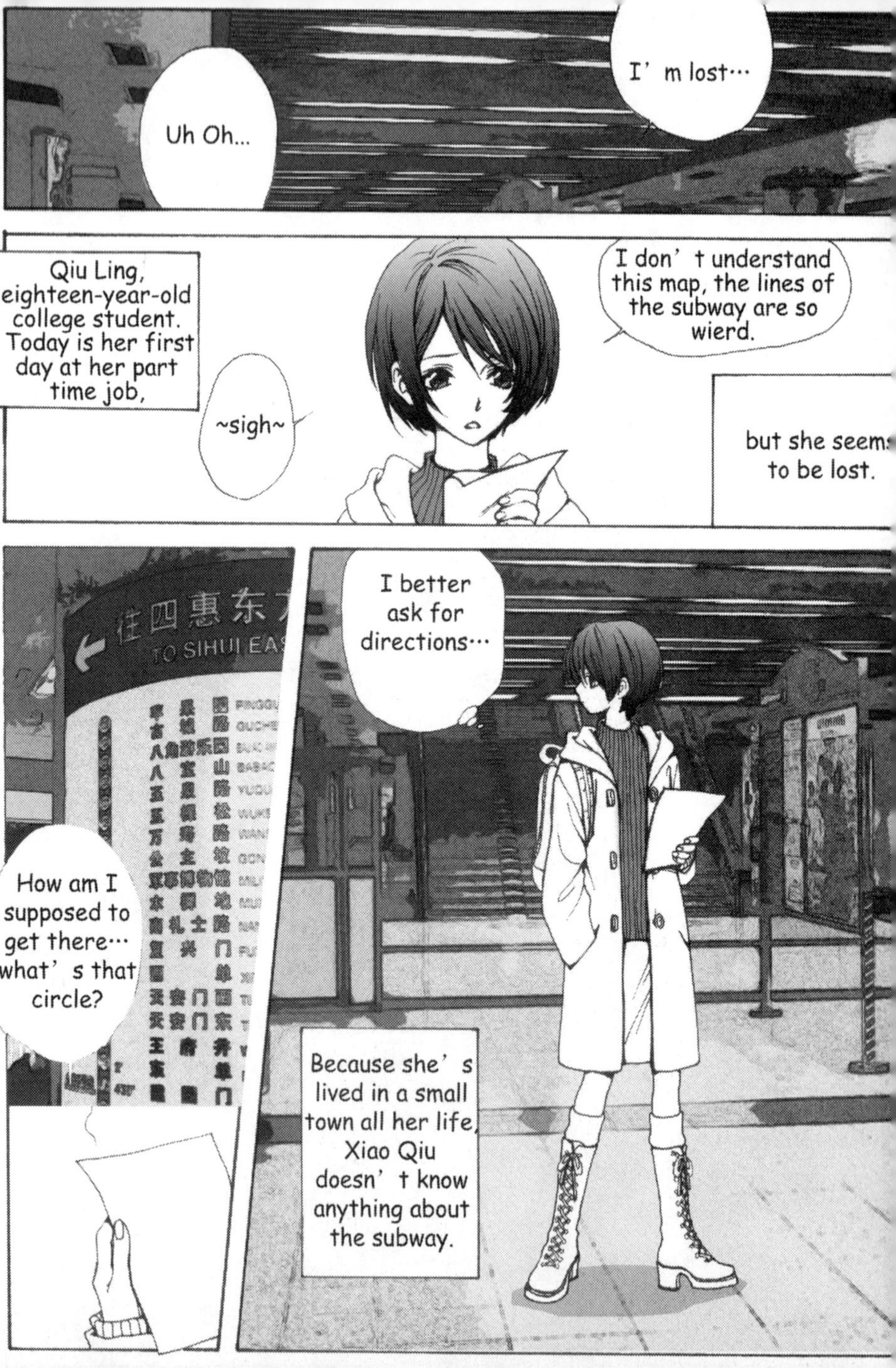
Uh Oh...
I' m lost···
Qiu Ling, eighteen-year-old college student. Today is her first day at her part time job,
~sigh~
I don' t understand this map, the lines of the subway are so wierd.
but she seems to be lost.
往四惠东
TO SIHUI EAS
How am I supposed to get there··· what' s that circle?
I better ask for directions···
Because she' s lived in a small town all her life, Xiao Qiu doesn' t know anything about the subway.

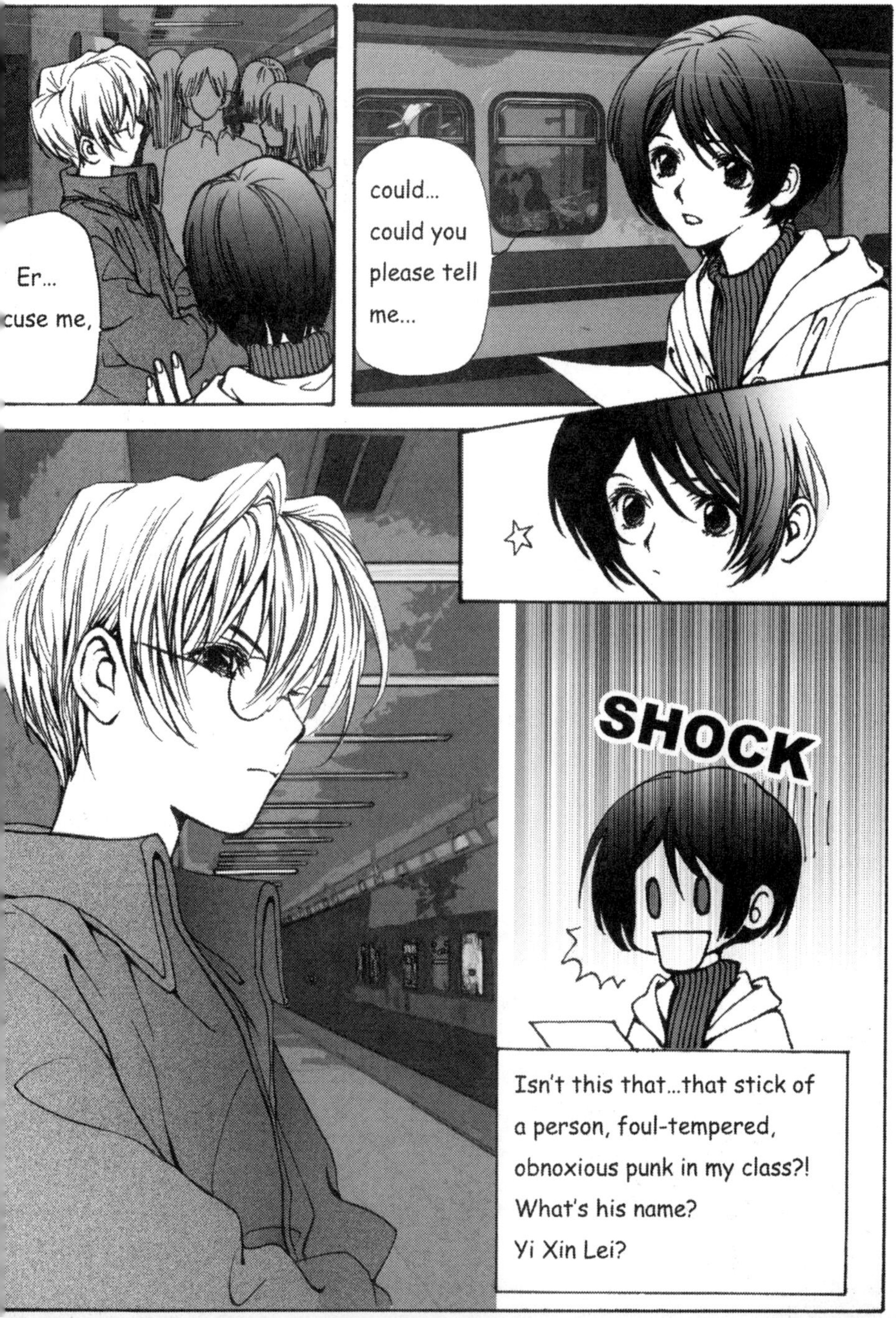

Er...
cuse me,
could...
could you
please tell
me...
SHOCK
Isn't this that...that stick of
a person, foul-tempered,
obnoxious punk in my class?!
What's his name?
Yi Xin Lei?

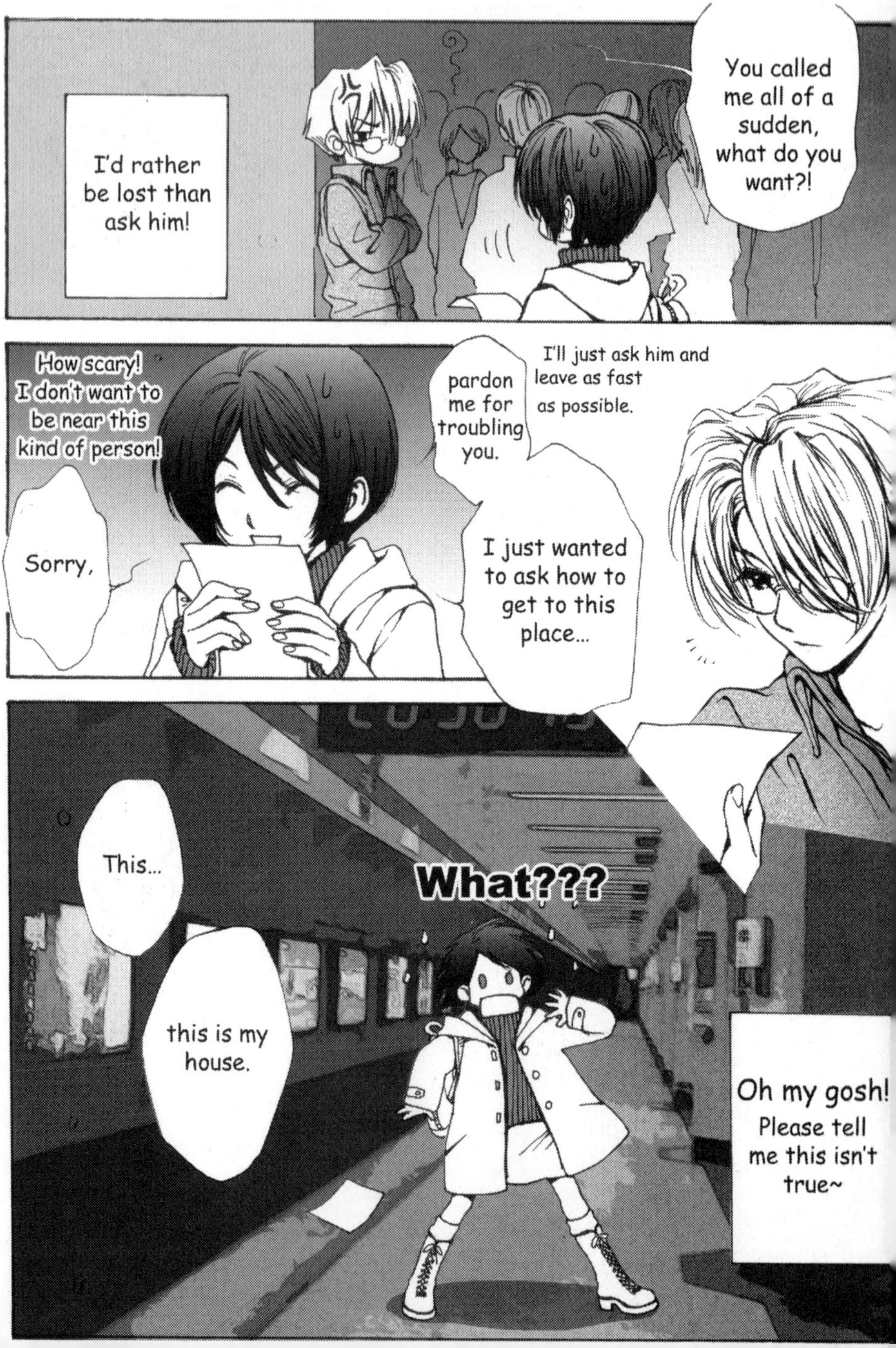

You called me all of a sudden, what do you want?!
I'd rather be lost than ask him!
How scary! I don't want to be near this kind of person!
I'll just ask him and leave as fast as possible.
Sorry,
pardon me for troubling you.
I just wanted to ask how to get to this place...
This...
this is my house.
What???
Oh my gosh! Please tell me this isn't true~

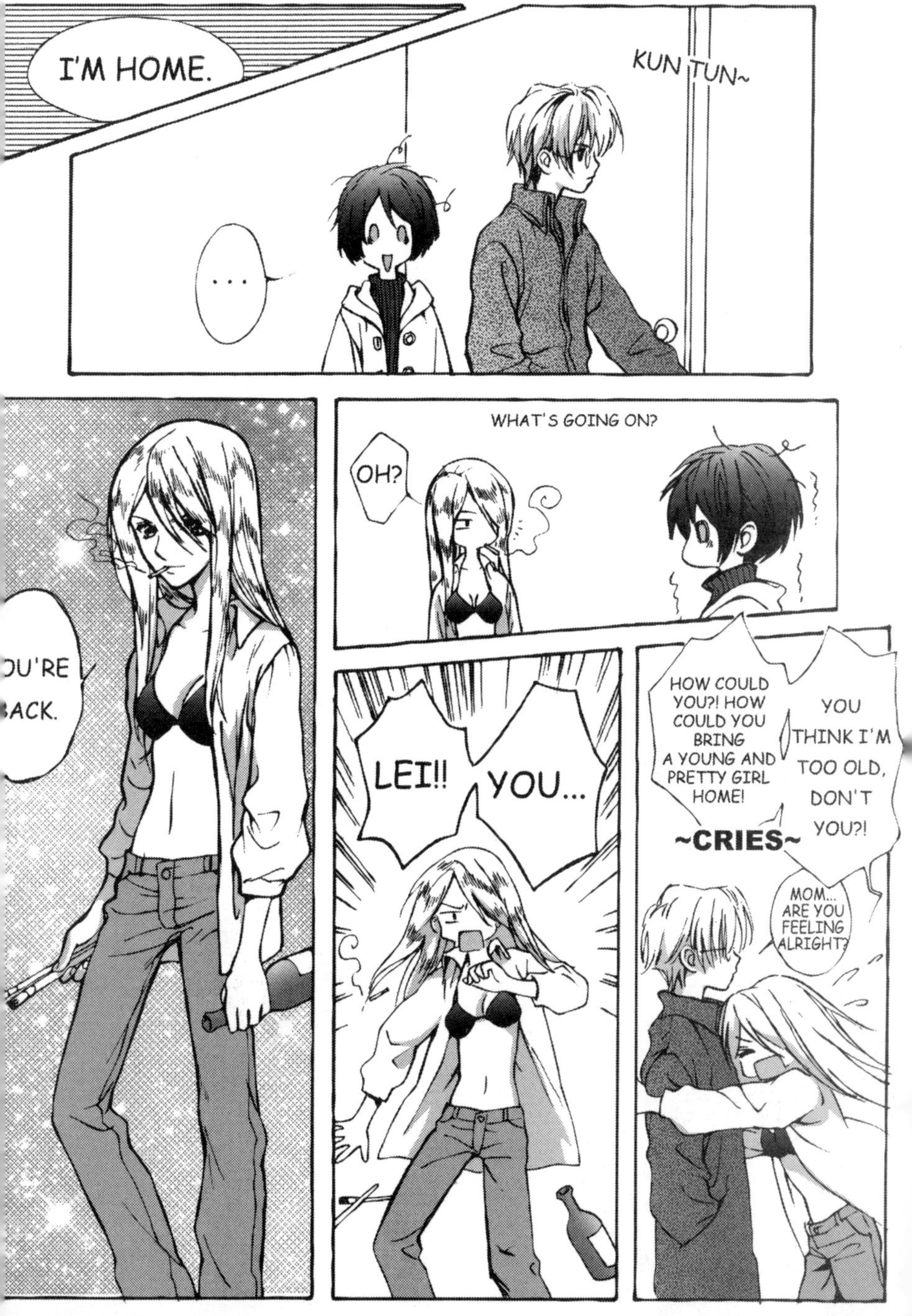
I'M HOME.
KUN TUN~
. . .
OU'RE
ACK.
WHAT'S GOING ON?
OH?
LEI!!
YOU...
HOW COULD YOU?! HOW COULD YOU BRING A YOUNG AND PRETTY GIRL HOME!
YOU THINK I'M TOO OLD, DON'T YOU?!
~CRIES~
MOM... ARE YOU FEELING ALRIGHT?

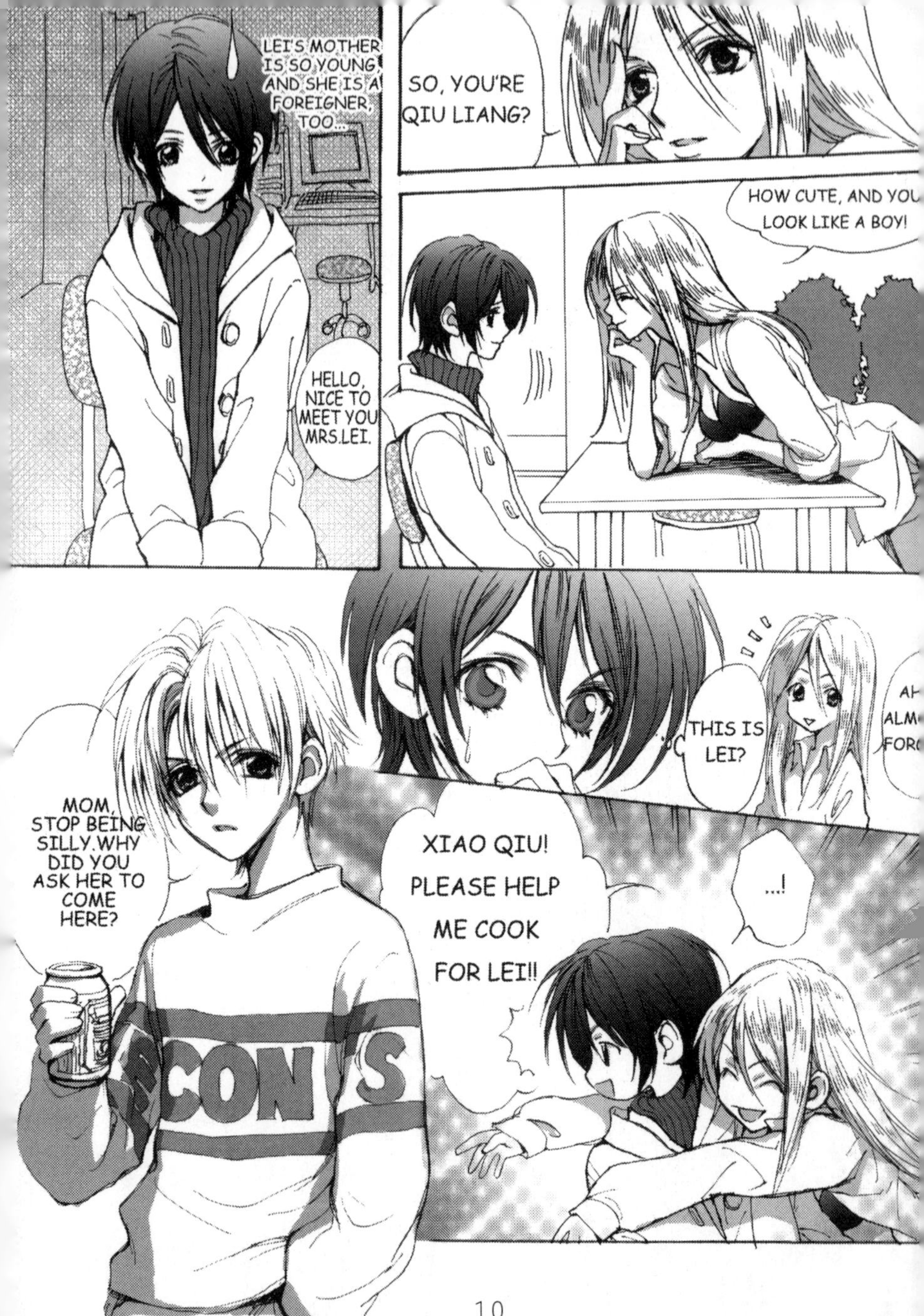
LEI'S MOTHER IS SO YOUNG, AND SHE IS A FOREIGNER, TOO...
HELLO, NICE TO MEET YOU MRS.LEI.
SO, YOU'RE QIU LIANG?
HOW CUTE, AND YOU LOOK LIKE A BOY!
THIS IS LEI?
MOM, STOP BEING SILLY.WHY DID YOU ASK HER TO COME HERE?
XIAO QIU! PLEASE HELP ME COOK FOR LEI!!
...!

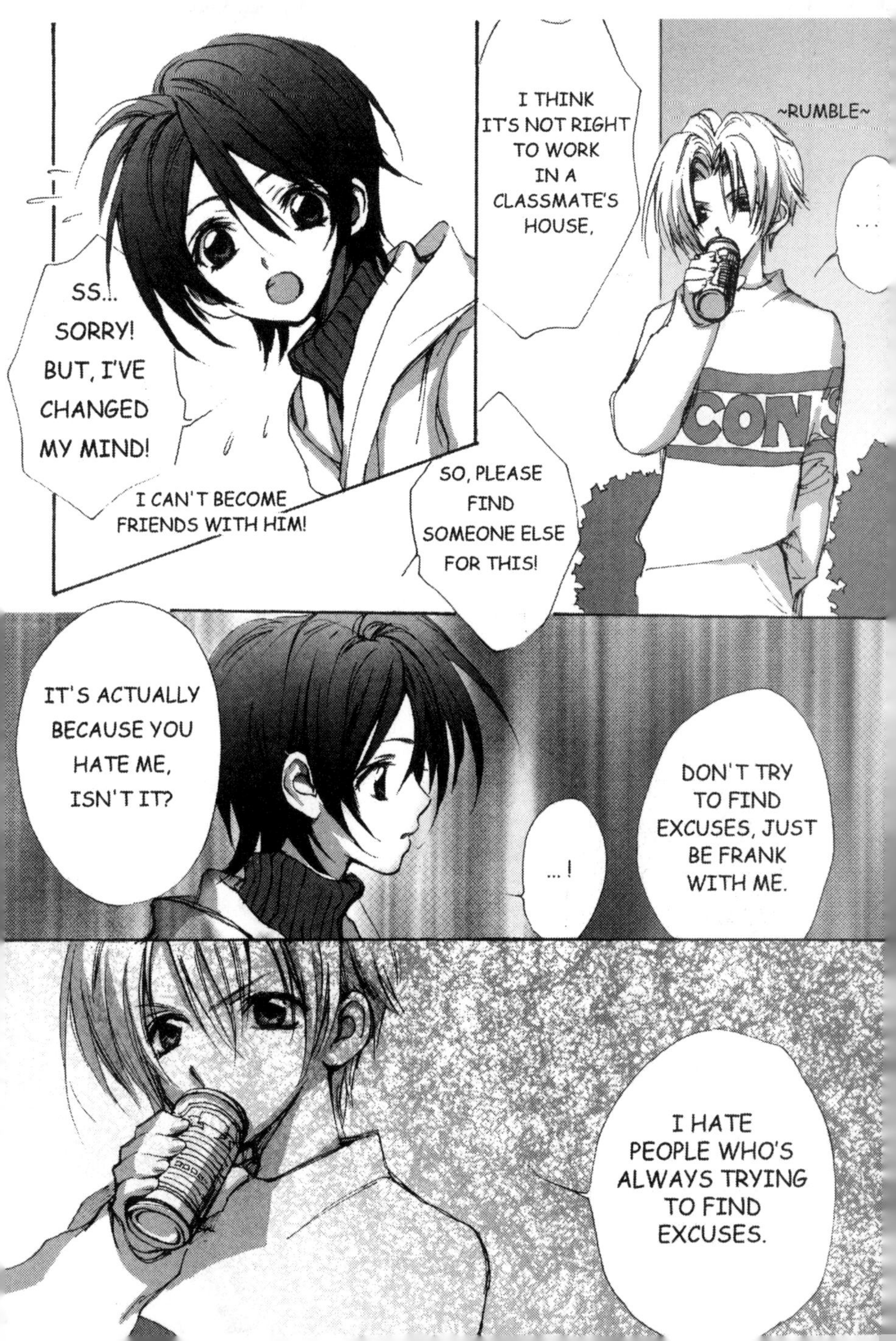
SS... SORRY! BUT, I'VE CHANGED MY MIND!
I CAN'T BECOME FRIENDS WITH HIM!
I THINK IT'S NOT RIGHT TO WORK IN A CLASSMATE'S HOUSE,
~RUMBLE~
...
SO, PLEASE FIND SOMEONE ELSE FOR THIS!
CON
IT'S ACTUALLY BECAUSE YOU HATE ME, ISN'T IT?
...!
DON'T TRY TO FIND EXCUSES, JUST BE FRANK WITH ME.
I HATE PEOPLE WHO'S ALWAYS TRYING TO FIND EXCUSES.

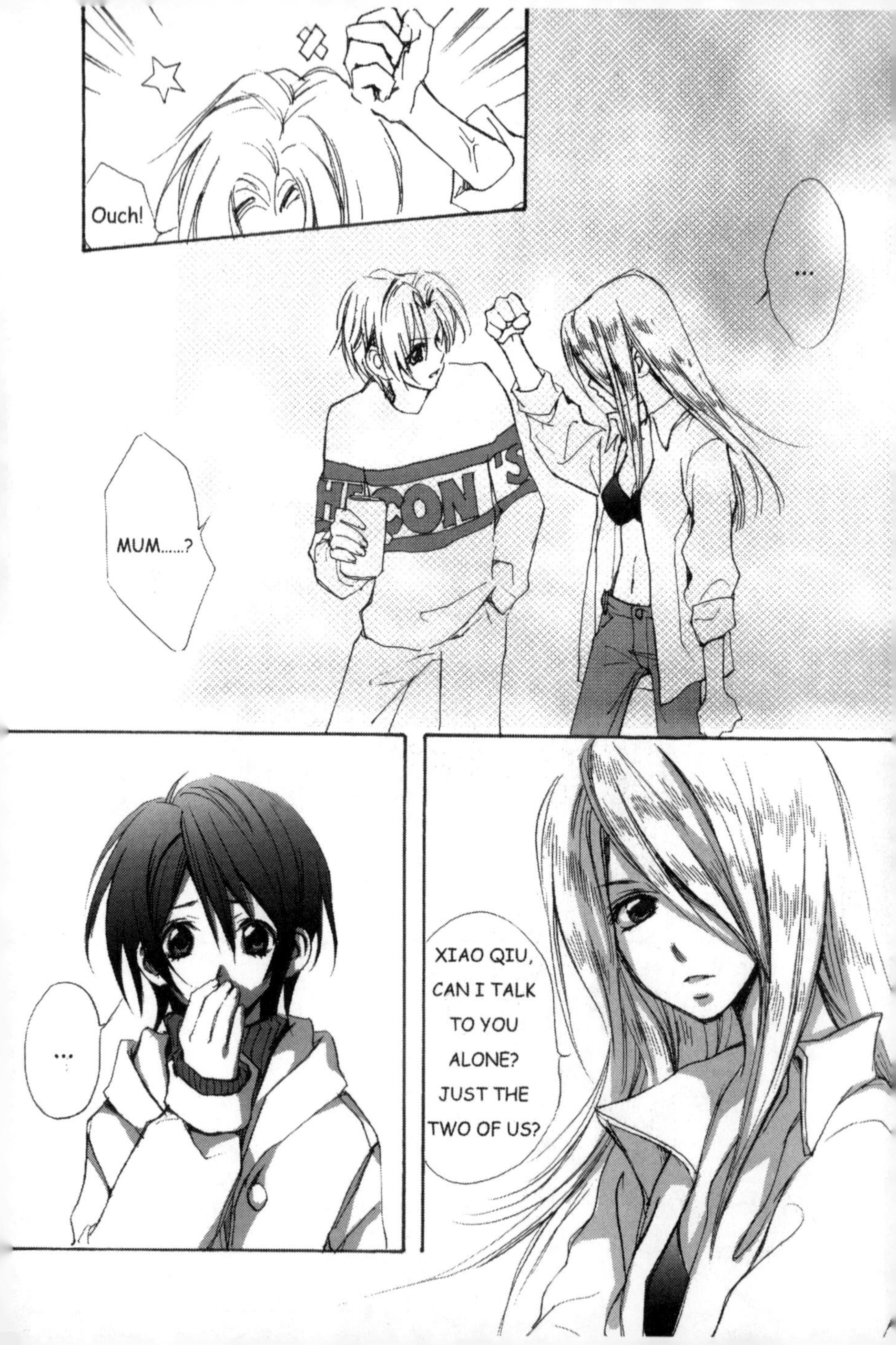
Ouch!
...
MUM......?
...
XIAO QIU, CAN I TALK TO YOU ALONE? JUST THE TWO OF US?

~SIGH~ THERE ARE SOMETHINGS I DON'T WANT TO SAY IN FRONT OF LEI.

WE CAN FINALLY TALK NOW.

EN?

XIAO QIU, COME SEE THIS.

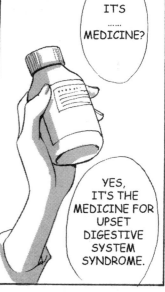

IT'S ...... MEDICINE?

YES, IT'S THE MEDICINE FOR UPSET DIGESTIVE SYSTEM SYNDROME.

13

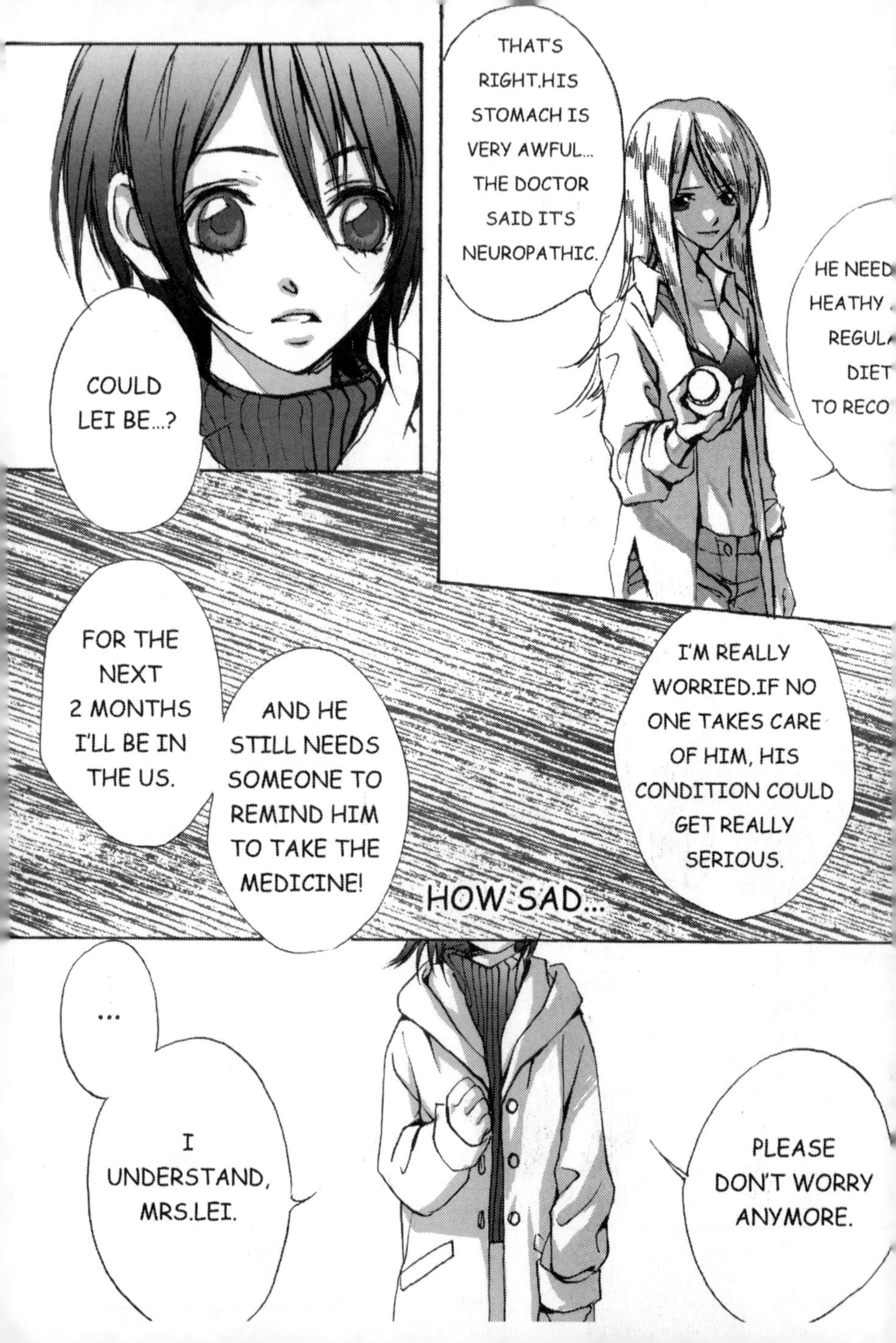
COULD LEI BE...?
THAT'S RIGHT.HIS STOMACH IS VERY AWFUL... THE DOCTOR SAID IT'S NEUROPATHIC.
HE NEED HEATHY REGUL DIET TO RECO
FOR THE NEXT 2 MONTHS I'LL BE IN THE US.
AND HE STILL NEEDS SOMEONE TO REMIND HIM TO TAKE THE MEDICINE!
I'M REALLY WORRIED.IF NO ONE TAKES CARE OF HIM, HIS CONDITION COULD GET REALLY SERIOUS.
HOW SAD...
...
I UNDERSTAND, MRS.LEI.
PLEASE DON'T WORRY ANYMORE.

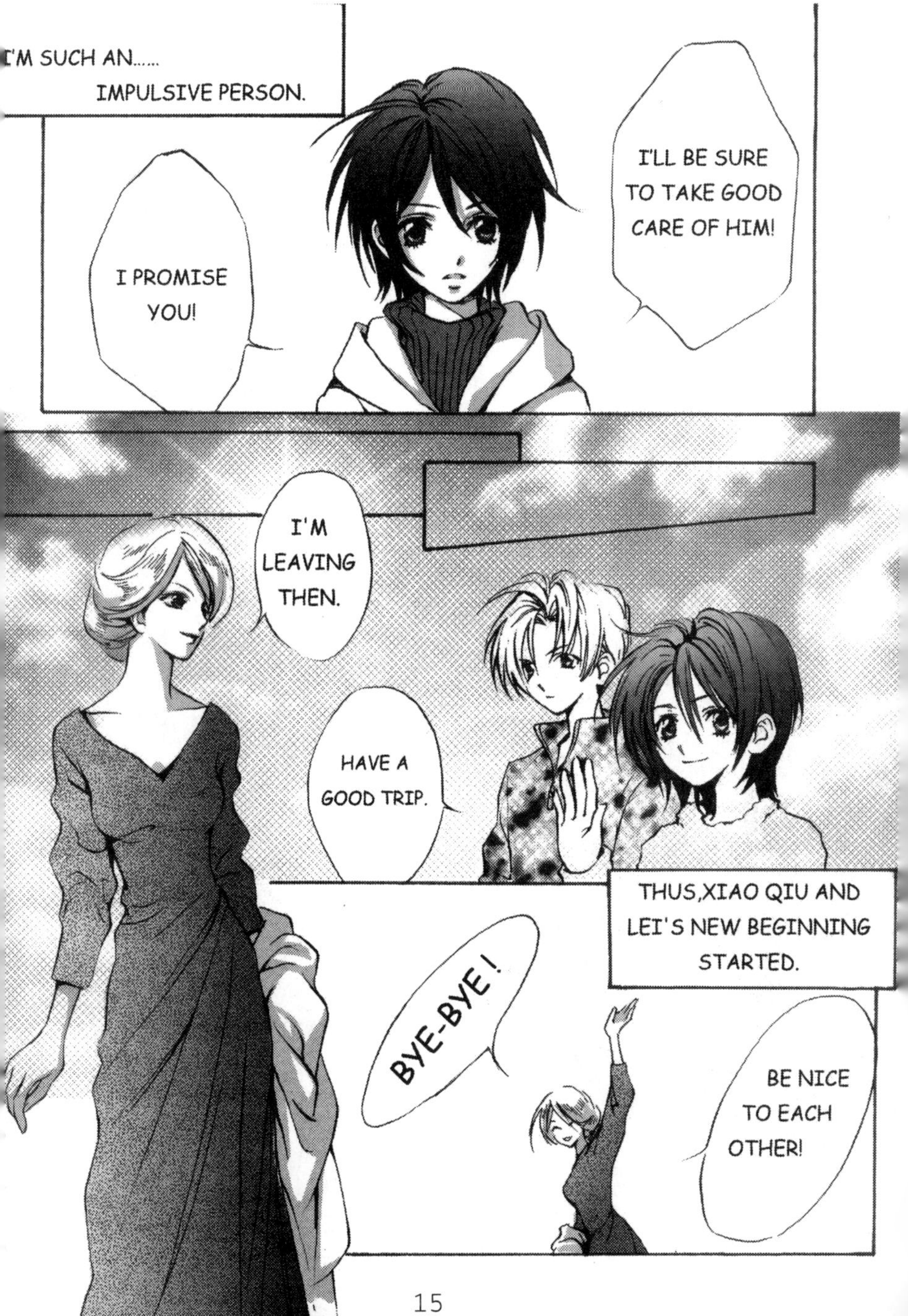
I'M SUCH AN......
IMPULSIVE PERSON.
I PROMISE YOU!
I'LL BE SURE TO TAKE GOOD CARE OF HIM!
I'M LEAVING THEN.
HAVE A GOOD TRIP.
THUS,XIAO QIU AND LEI'S NEW BEGINNING STARTED.
BYE-BYE!
BE NICE TO EACH OTHER!

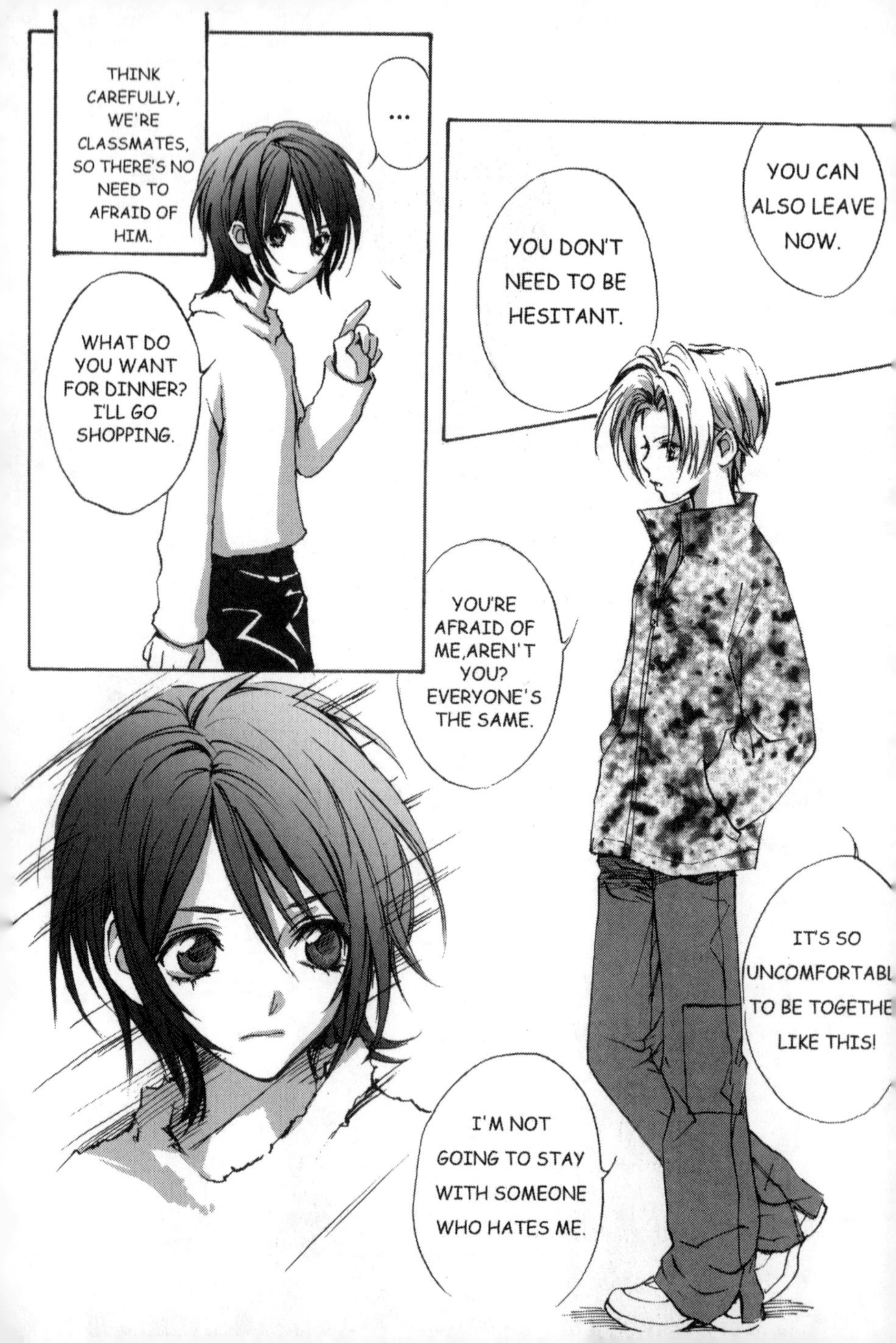
THINK CAREFULLY, WE'RE CLASSMATES, SO THERE'S NO NEED TO AFRAID OF HIM.
WHAT DO YOU WANT FOR DINNER? I'LL GO SHOPPING.
...
YOU DON'T NEED TO BE HESITANT.
YOU CAN ALSO LEAVE NOW.
YOU'RE AFRAID OF ME,AREN'T YOU? EVERYONE'S THE SAME.
I'M NOT GOING TO STAY WITH SOMEONE WHO HATES ME.
IT'S SO UNCOMFORTABL TO BE TOGETHE LIKE THIS!

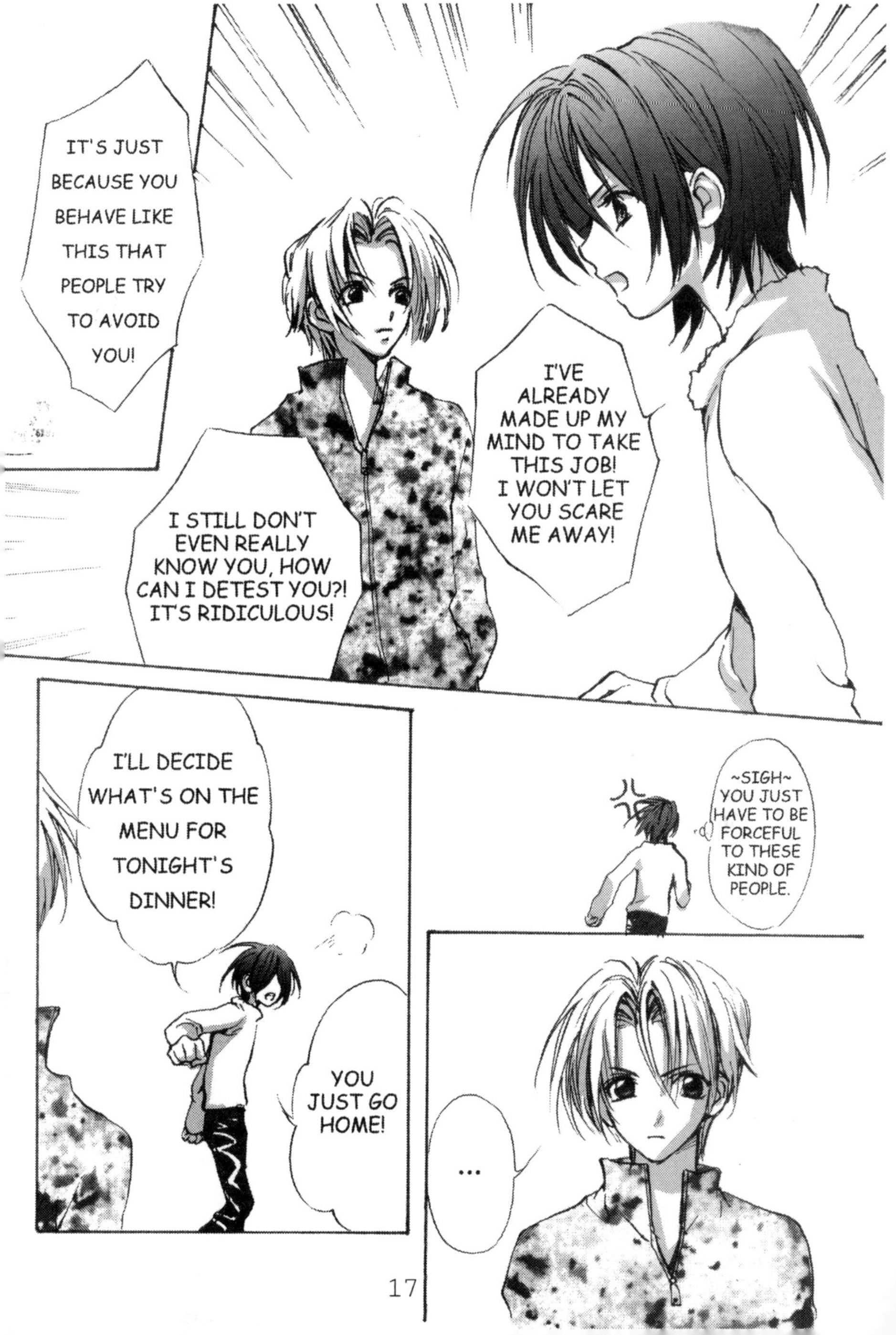
I STILL DON'T EVEN REALLY KNOW YOU, HOW CAN I DETEST YOU?! IT'S RIDICULOUS!
IT'S JUST BECAUSE YOU BEHAVE LIKE THIS THAT PEOPLE TRY TO AVOID YOU!
I'VE ALREADY MADE UP MY MIND TO TAKE THIS JOB! I WON'T LET YOU SCARE ME AWAY!
~SIGH~ YOU JUST HAVE TO BE FORCEFUL TO THESE KIND OF PEOPLE.
I'LL DECIDE WHAT'S ON THE MENU FOR TONIGHT'S DINNER!
YOU JUST GO HOME!
...

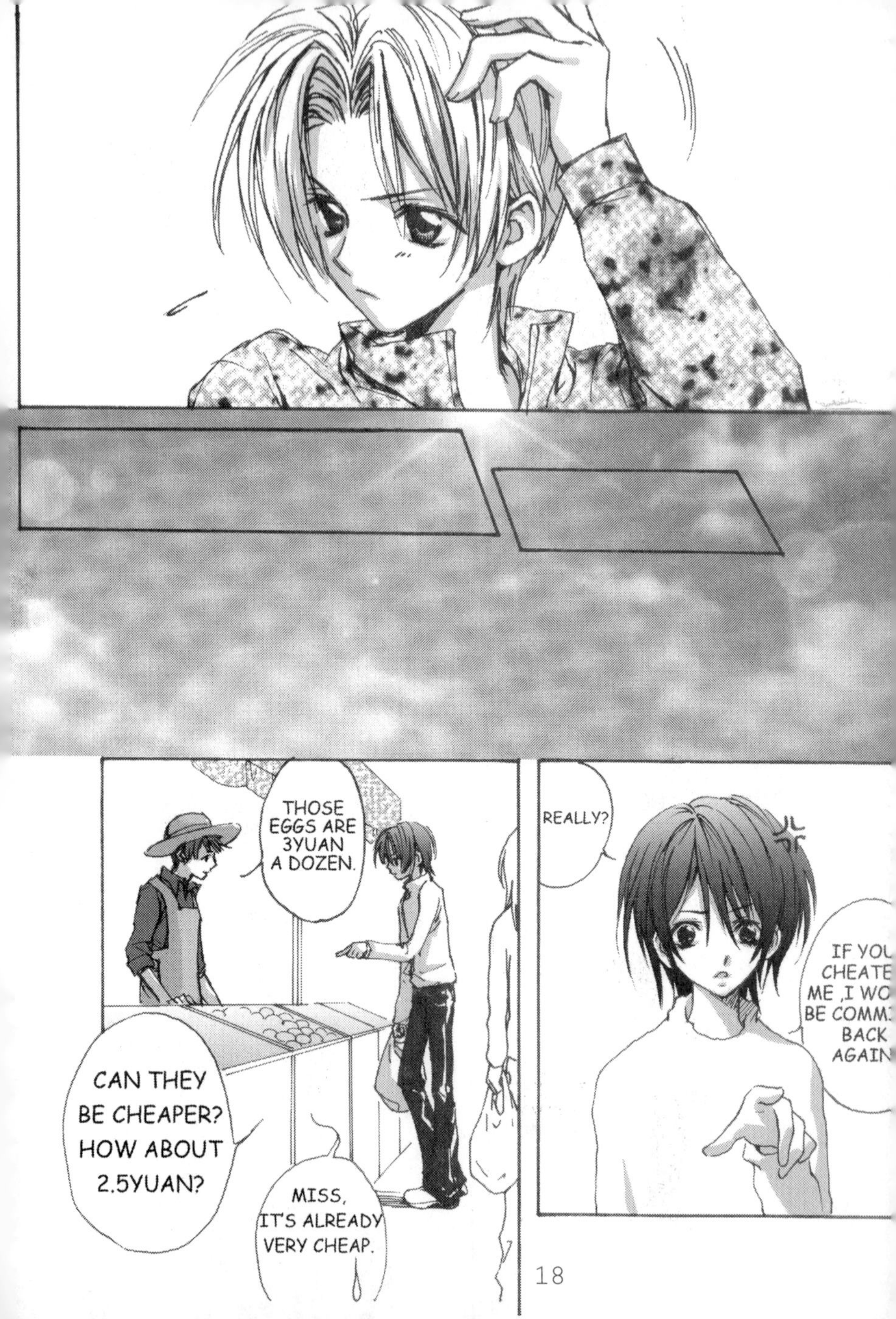
THOSE EGGS ARE 3YUAN A DOZEN.
CAN THEY BE CHEAPER? HOW ABOUT 2.5YUAN?
MISS, IT'S ALREADY VERY CHEAP.
REALLY?
IF YOU CHEATE ME ,I WO BE COMMI BACK AGAIN

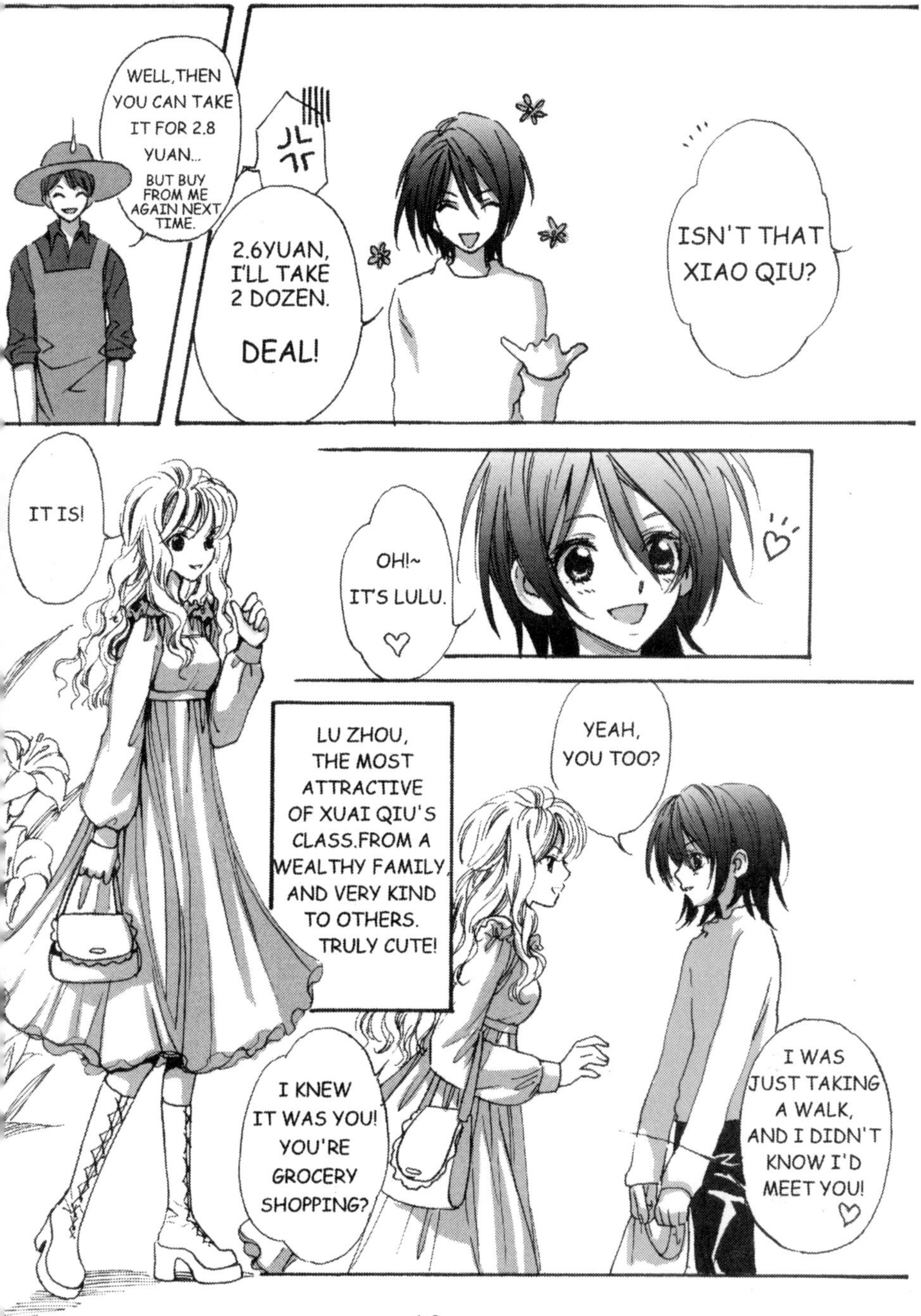

WELL, THEN YOU CAN TAKE IT FOR 2.8 YUAN... BUT BUY FROM ME AGAIN NEXT TIME.
2.6YUAN, I'LL TAKE 2 DOZEN. DEAL!
ISN'T THAT XIAO QIU?
IT IS!
OH!~ IT'S LULU. ♡
LU ZHOU, THE MOST ATTRACTIVE OF XUAI QIU'S CLASS.FROM A WEALTHY FAMILY, AND VERY KIND TO OTHERS. TRULY CUTE!
YEAH, YOU TOO?
I KNEW IT WAS YOU! YOU'RE GROCERY SHOPPING?
I WAS JUST TAKING A WALK, AND I DIDN'T KNOW I'D MEET YOU! ♡

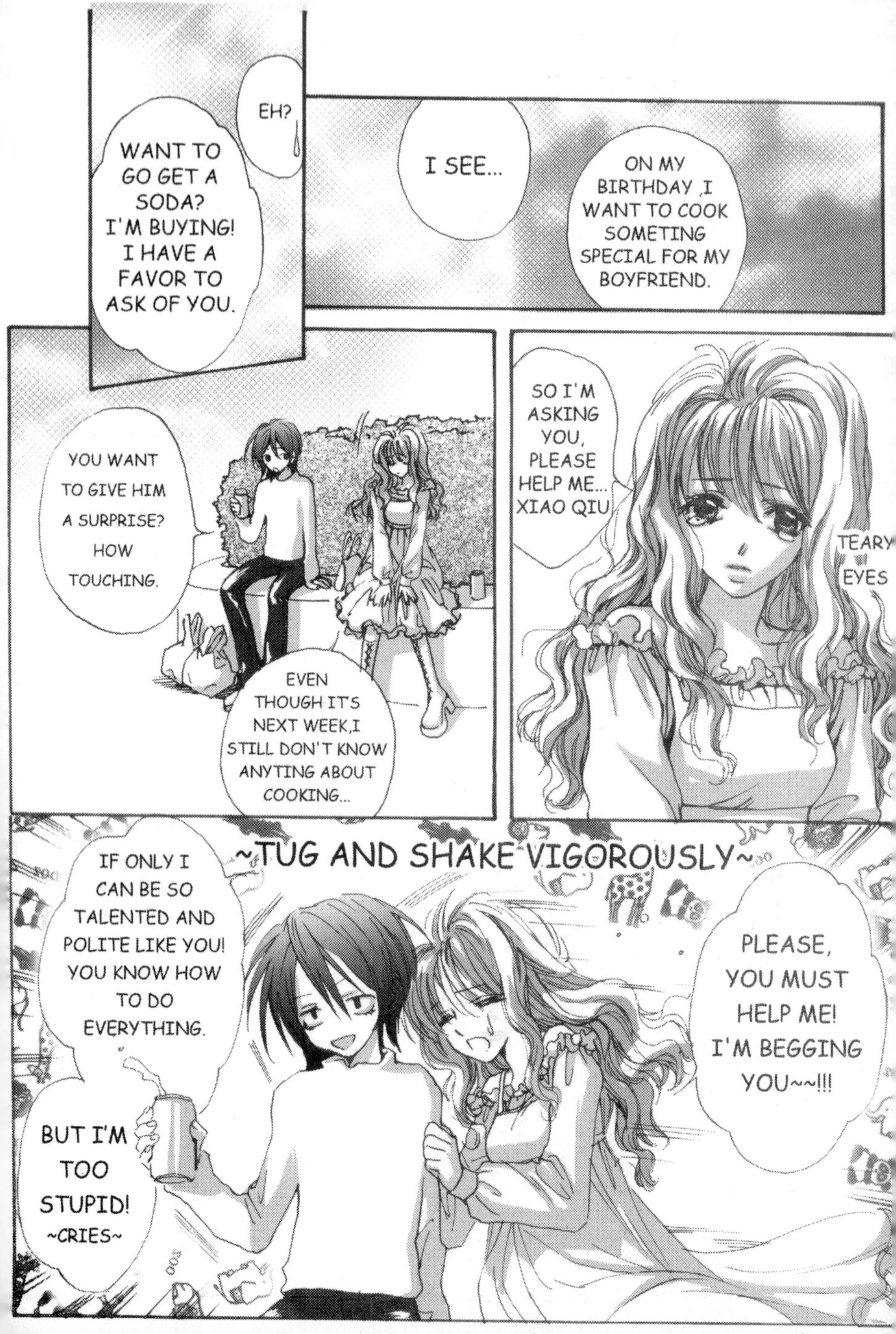
WANT TO GO GET A SODA? I'M BUYING! I HAVE A FAVOR TO ASK OF YOU.
EH?
ON MY BIRTHDAY ,I WANT TO COOK SOMETING SPECIAL FOR MY BOYFRIEND.
I SEE...
YOU WANT TO GIVE HIM A SURPRISE? HOW TOUCHING.
EVEN THOUGH IT'S NEXT WEEK,I STILL DON'T KNOW ANYTING ABOUT COOKING...
SO I'M ASKING YOU, PLEASE HELP ME... XIAO QIU
TEARY EYES
~TUG AND SHAKE VIGOROUSLY~
IF ONLY I CAN BE SO TALENTED AND POLITE LIKE YOU! YOU KNOW HOW TO DO EVERYTHING.
BUT I'M TOO STUPID! ~CRIES~
PLEASE, YOU MUST HELP ME! I'M BEGGING YOU~~!!!

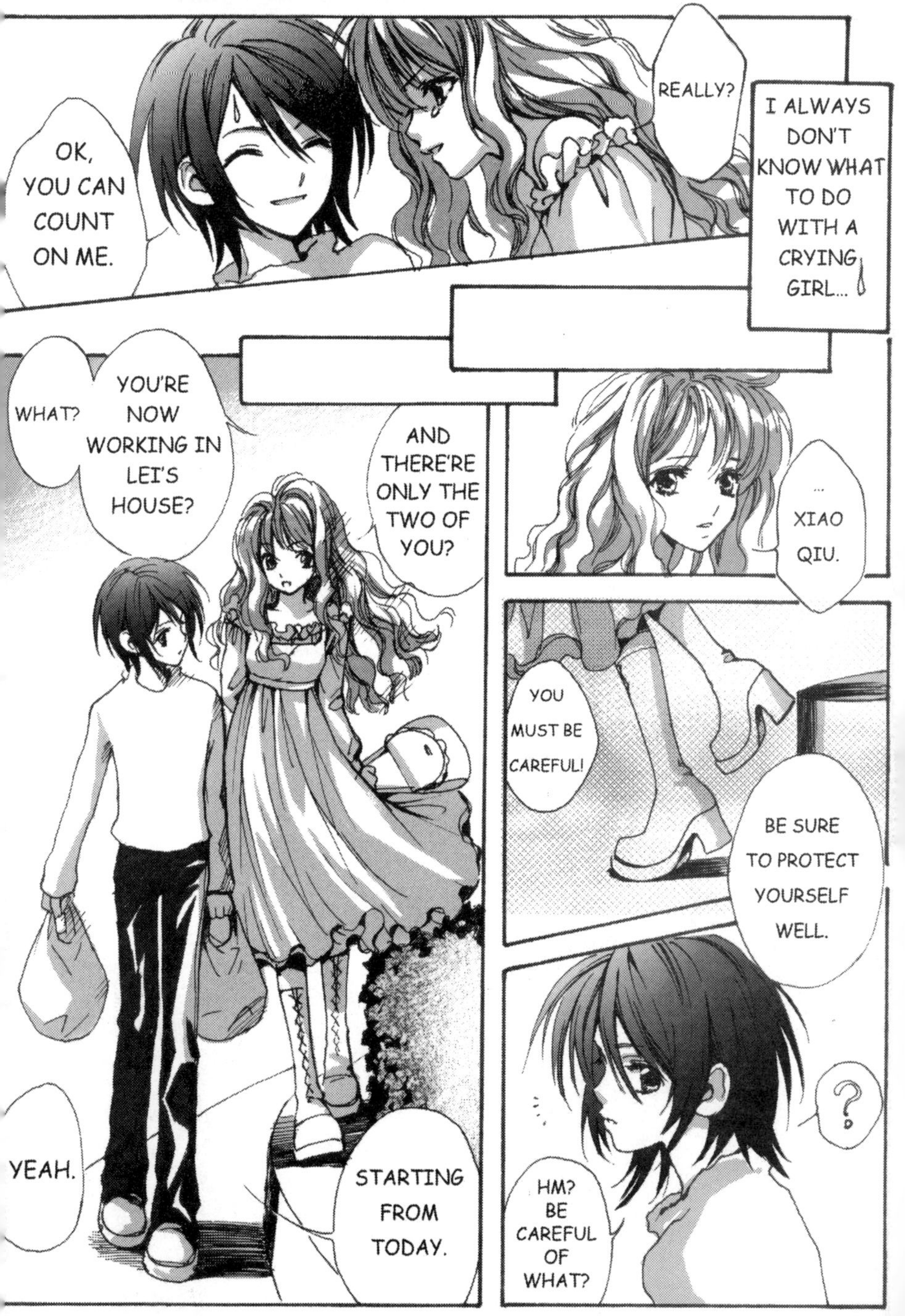
OK, YOU CAN COUNT ON ME.
REALLY?
I ALWAYS DON'T KNOW WHAT TO DO WITH A CRYING GIRL...
WHAT?
YOU'RE NOW WORKING IN LEI'S HOUSE?
AND THERE'RE ONLY THE TWO OF YOU?
YEAH.
STARTING FROM TODAY.
... XIAO QIU.
YOU MUST BE CAREFUL!
BE SURE TO PROTECT YOURSELF WELL.
?
HM? BE CAREFUL OF WHAT?

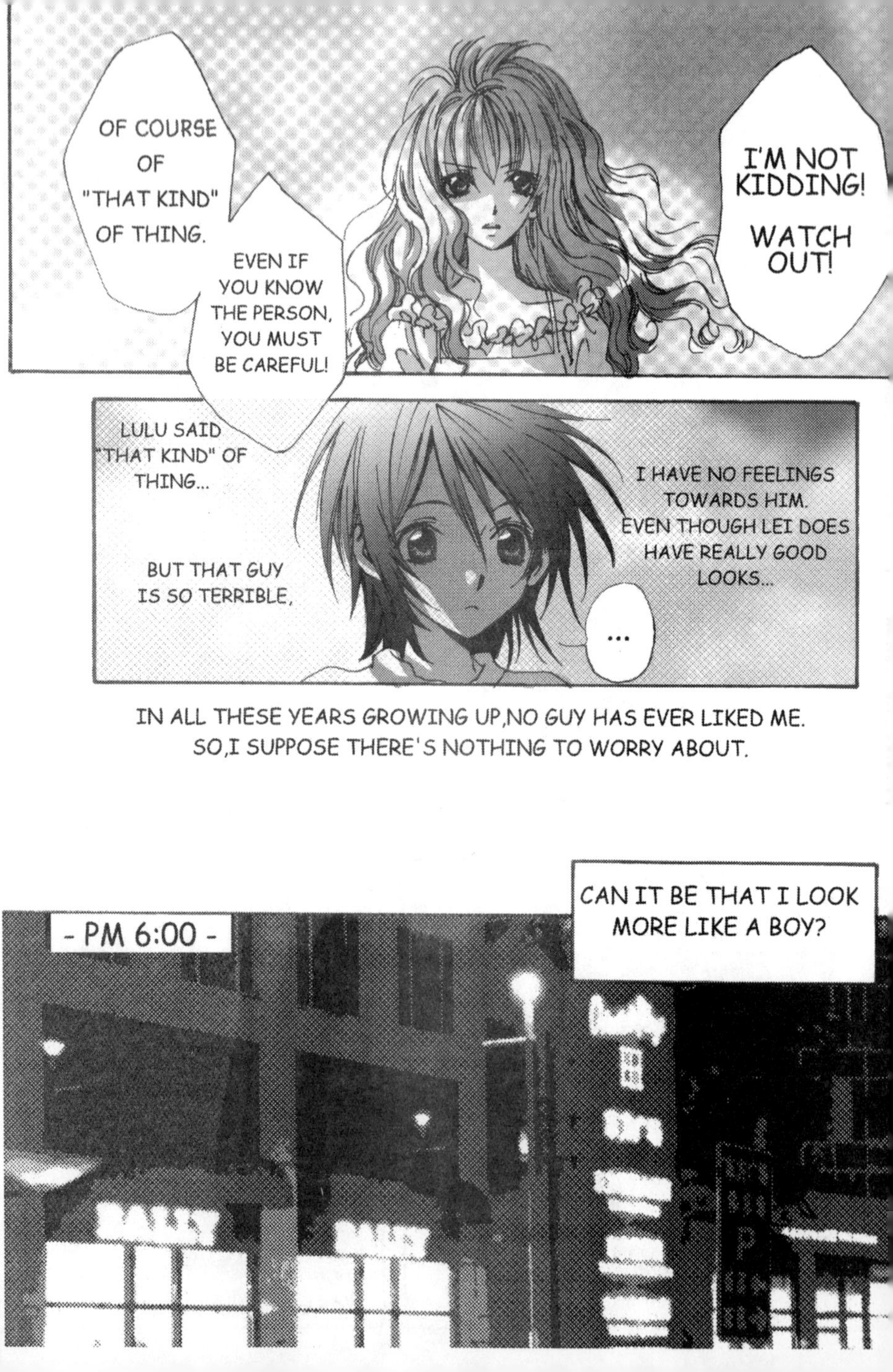
I'M NOT KIDDING!
WATCH OUT!
EVEN IF YOU KNOW THE PERSON, YOU MUST BE CAREFUL!
OF COURSE OF "THAT KIND" OF THING.
I HAVE NO FEELINGS TOWARDS HIM. EVEN THOUGH LEI DOES HAVE REALLY GOOD LOOKS...
LULU SAID "THAT KIND" OF THING...
BUT THAT GUY IS SO TERRIBLE,
...
IN ALL THESE YEARS GROWING UP,NO GUY HAS EVER LIKED ME.
SO,I SUPPOSE THERE'S NOTHING TO WORRY ABOUT.
CAN IT BE THAT I LOOK MORE LIKE A BOY?
- PM 6:00 -

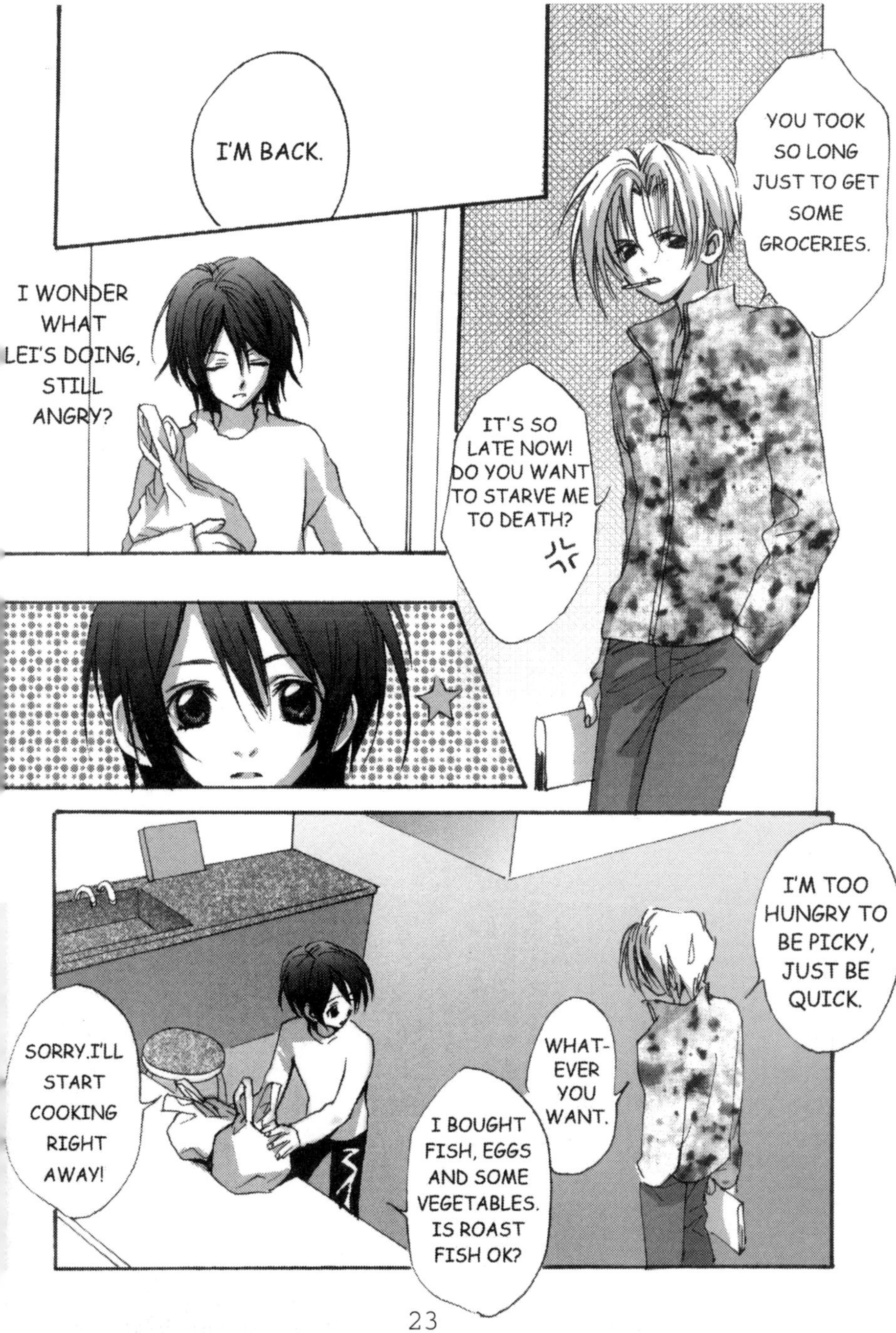
I'M BACK.
I WONDER WHAT LEI'S DOING, STILL ANGRY?
YOU TOOK SO LONG JUST TO GET SOME GROCERIES.
IT'S SO LATE NOW! DO YOU WANT TO STARVE ME TO DEATH?
SORRY.I'LL START COOKING RIGHT AWAY!
I BOUGHT FISH, EGGS AND SOME VEGETABLES. IS ROAST FISH OK?
WHAT-EVER YOU WANT.
I'M TOO HUNGRY TO BE PICKY, JUST BE QUICK.

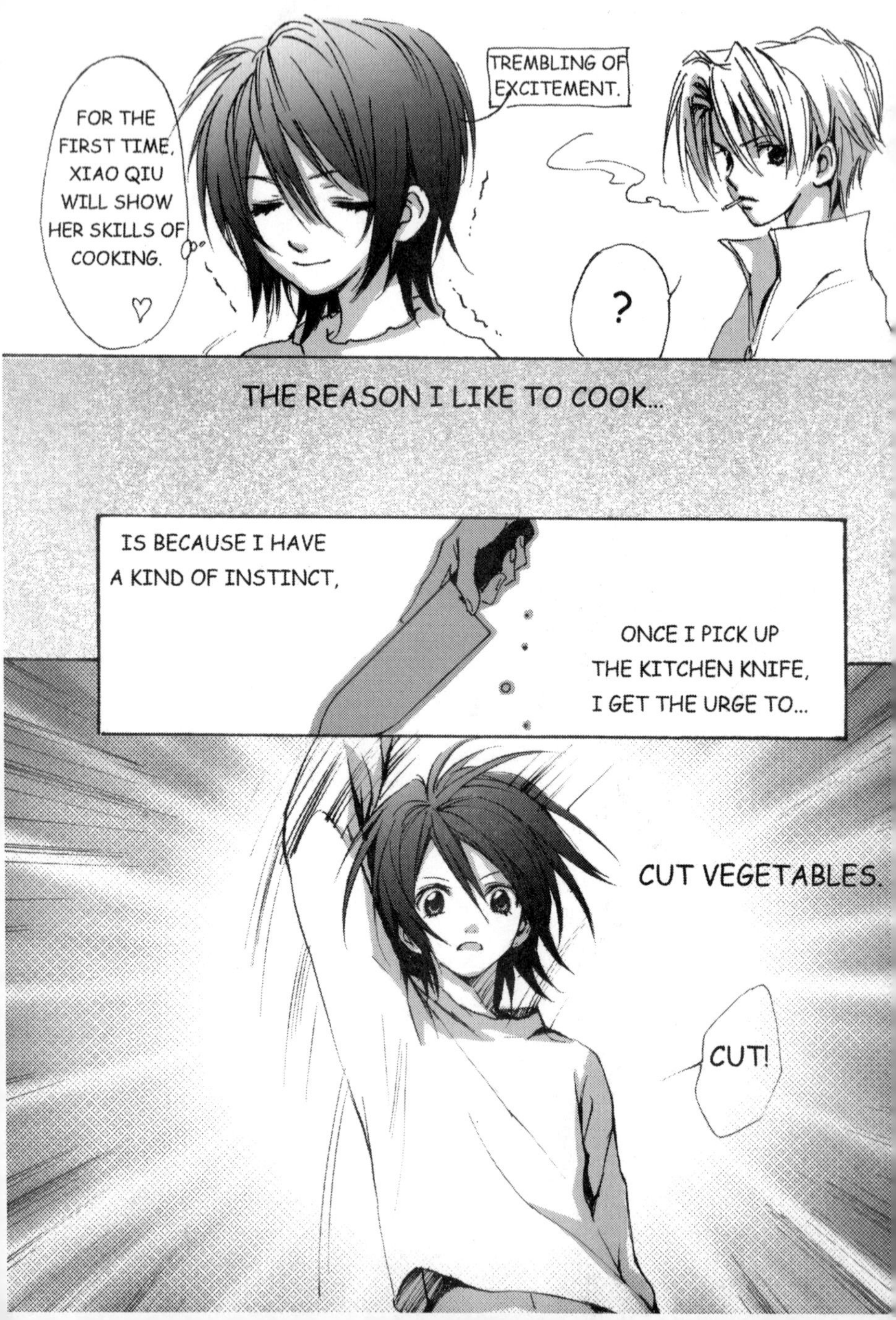

FOR THE FIRST TIME, XIAO QIU WILL SHOW HER SKILLS OF COOKING. ♡
TREMBLING OF EXCITEMENT.
?
THE REASON I LIKE TO COOK...
IS BECAUSE I HAVE A KIND OF INSTINCT,
ONCE I PICK UP THE KITCHEN KNIFE, I GET THE URGE TO...
CUT VEGETABLES.
CUT!

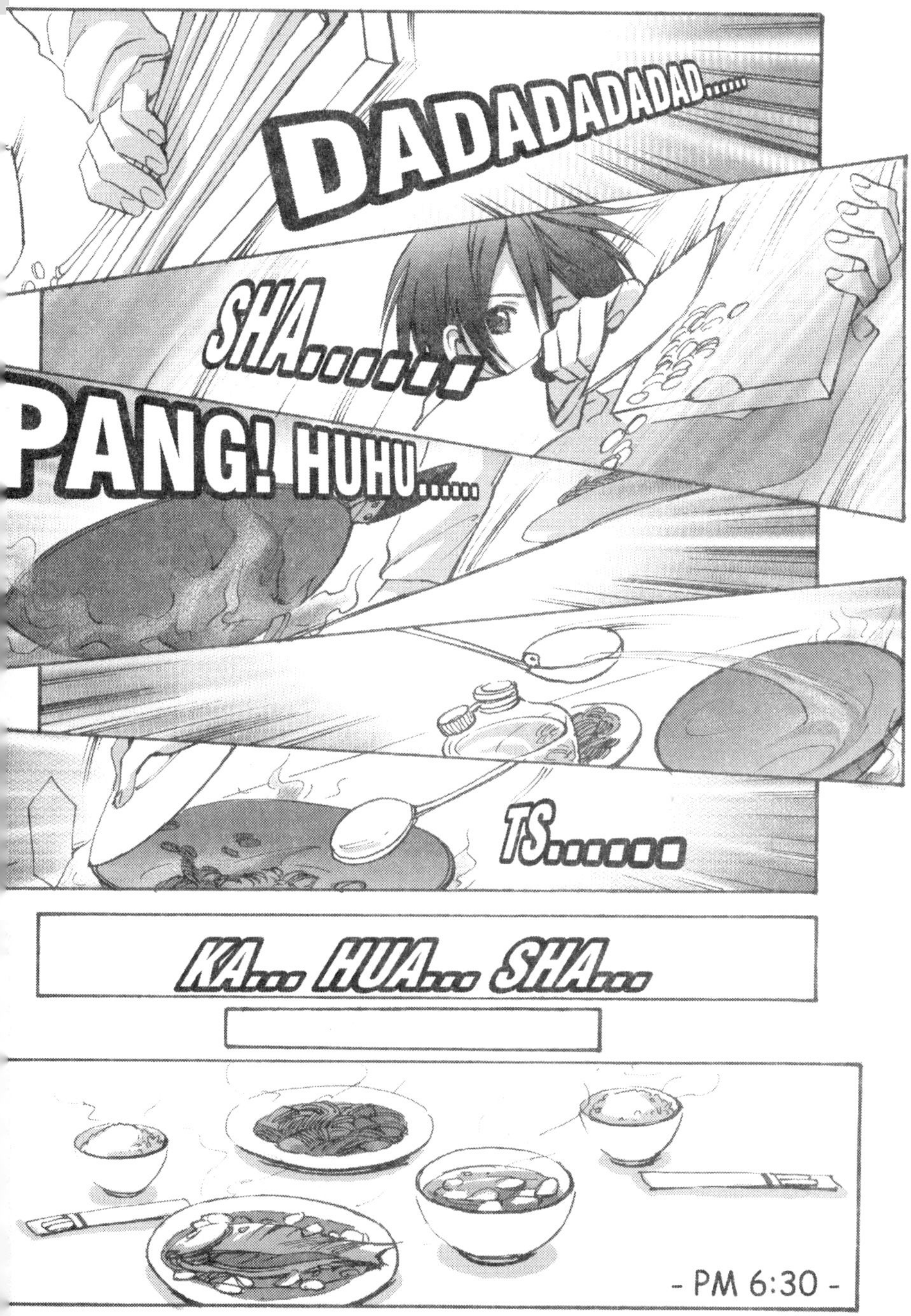
DADADADADAD......
SHA........
PANG! HUHU......
TS.......
KA... HUA... SHA...
- PM 6:30 -

SHOCK ...

...

SORRY TO MAKE YOU WAIT THAT LONG. ♡

PLEASE WASH YOUR HANDS BEFORE YOU EAT.

WHAT'S WRONG? DIDN'T YOU SAY YOU WERE ALMOST DYING OF HUNGER?

SO COMMANDING...

AH, YOU CAN'T DRINK BEER WHILE YOU'RE EATING.

UH?

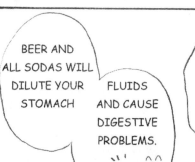

BEER AND ALL SODAS WILL DILUTE YOUR STOMACH

FLUIDS AND CAUSE DIGESTIVE PROBLEMS.

BUT I'M USED T DRINKIN BEER A DINNE

26

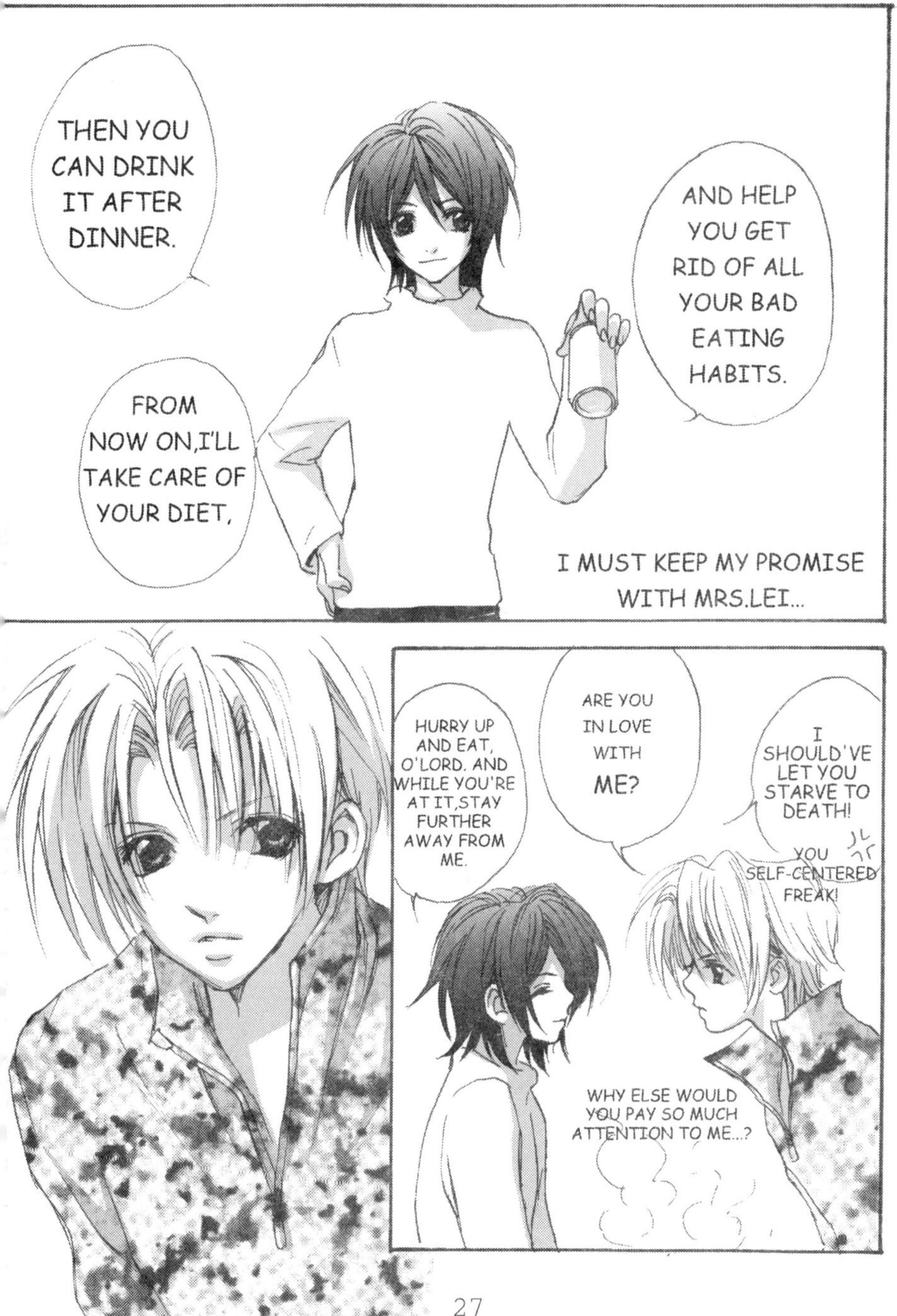
THEN YOU CAN DRINK IT AFTER DINNER.
FROM NOW ON,I'LL TAKE CARE OF YOUR DIET,
AND HELP YOU GET RID OF ALL YOUR BAD EATING HABITS.
I MUST KEEP MY PROMISE WITH MRS.LEI...
HURRY UP AND EAT, O'LORD. AND WHILE YOU'RE AT IT,STAY FURTHER AWAY FROM ME.
ARE YOU IN LOVE WITH ME?
I SHOULD'VE LET YOU STARVE TO DEATH!
YOU SELF-CENTERED FREAK!
WHY ELSE WOULD YOU PAY SO MUCH ATTENTION TO ME...?

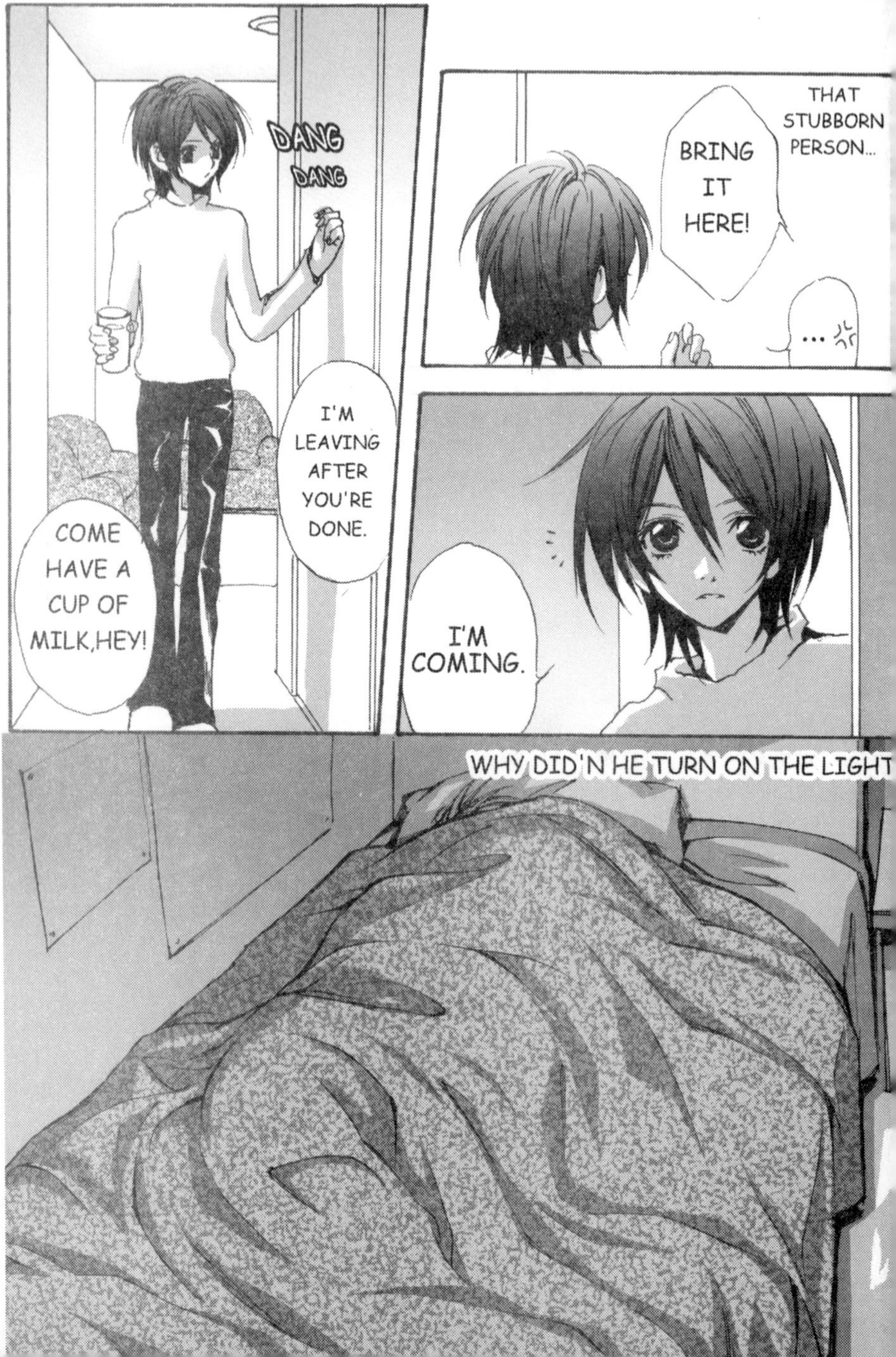

THAT STUBBORN PERSON...
BRING IT HERE!
...
I'M COMING.
DANG
DANG
I'M LEAVING AFTER YOU'RE DONE.
COME HAVE A CUP OF MILK,HEY!
WHY DID'N HE TURN ON THE LIGHT

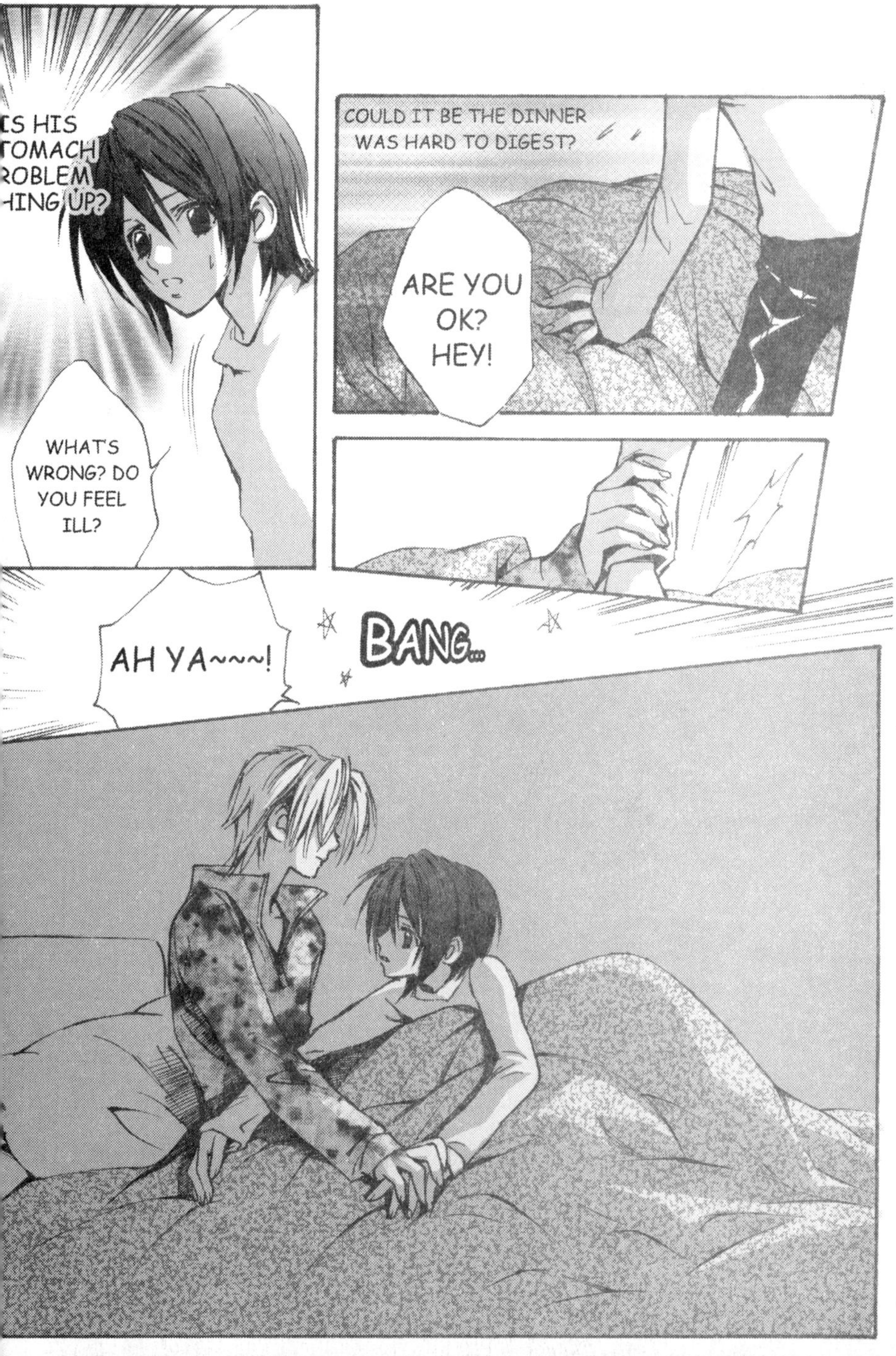
COULD IT BE THE DINNER WAS HARD TO DIGEST?
ARE YOU OK? HEY!
IS HIS TOMACH ROBLEM HING UP?
WHAT'S WRONG? DO YOU FEEL ILL?
AH YA~~~!
BANG...

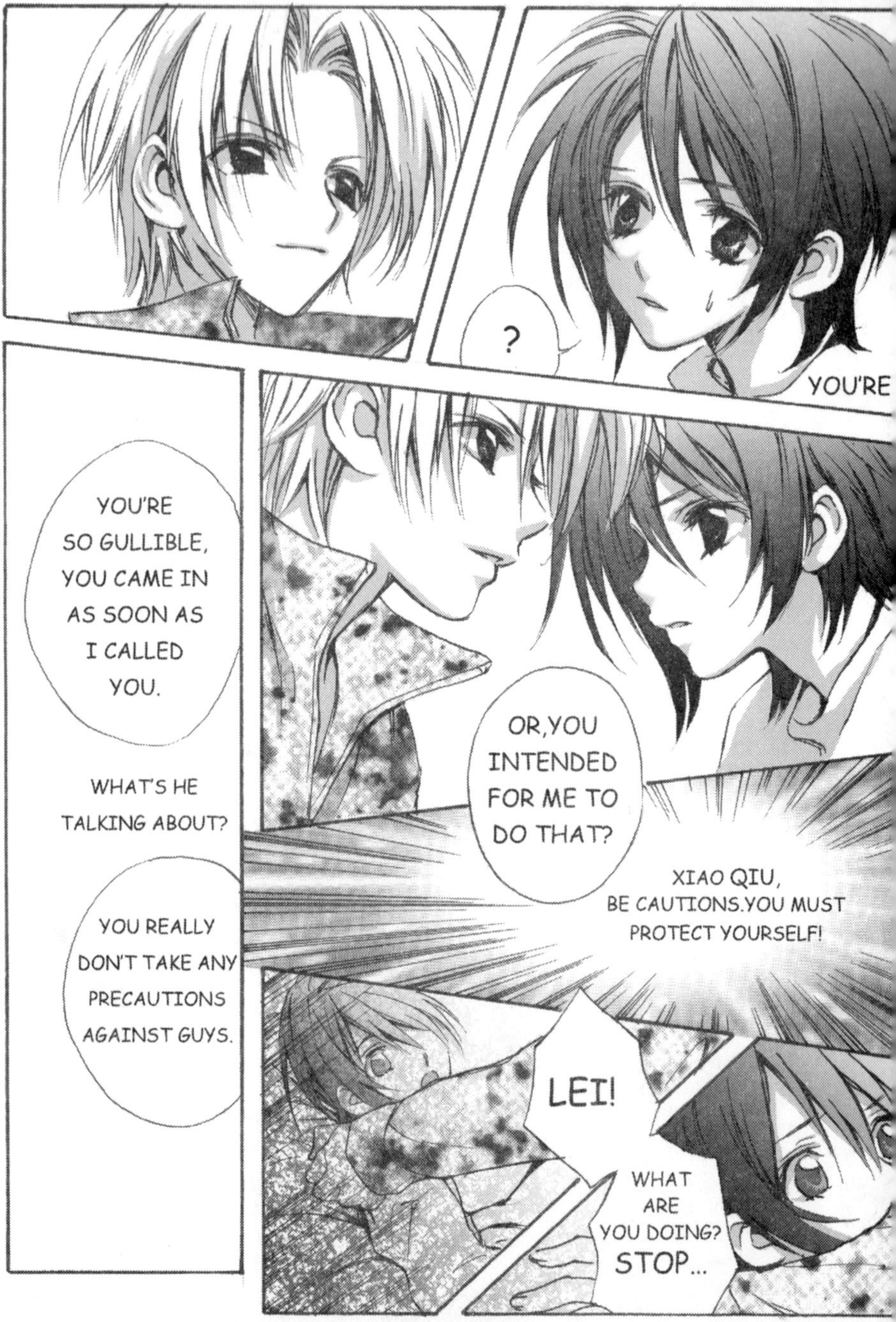
?
YOU'RE
YOU'RE SO GULLIBLE, YOU CAME IN AS SOON AS I CALLED YOU.
OR,YOU INTENDED FOR ME TO DO THAT?
WHAT'S HE TALKING ABOUT?
XIAO QIU, BE CAUTIONS.YOU MUST PROTECT YOURSELF!
YOU REALLY DON'T TAKE ANY PRECAUTIONS AGAINST GUYS.
LEI!
WHAT ARE YOU DOING? STOP...

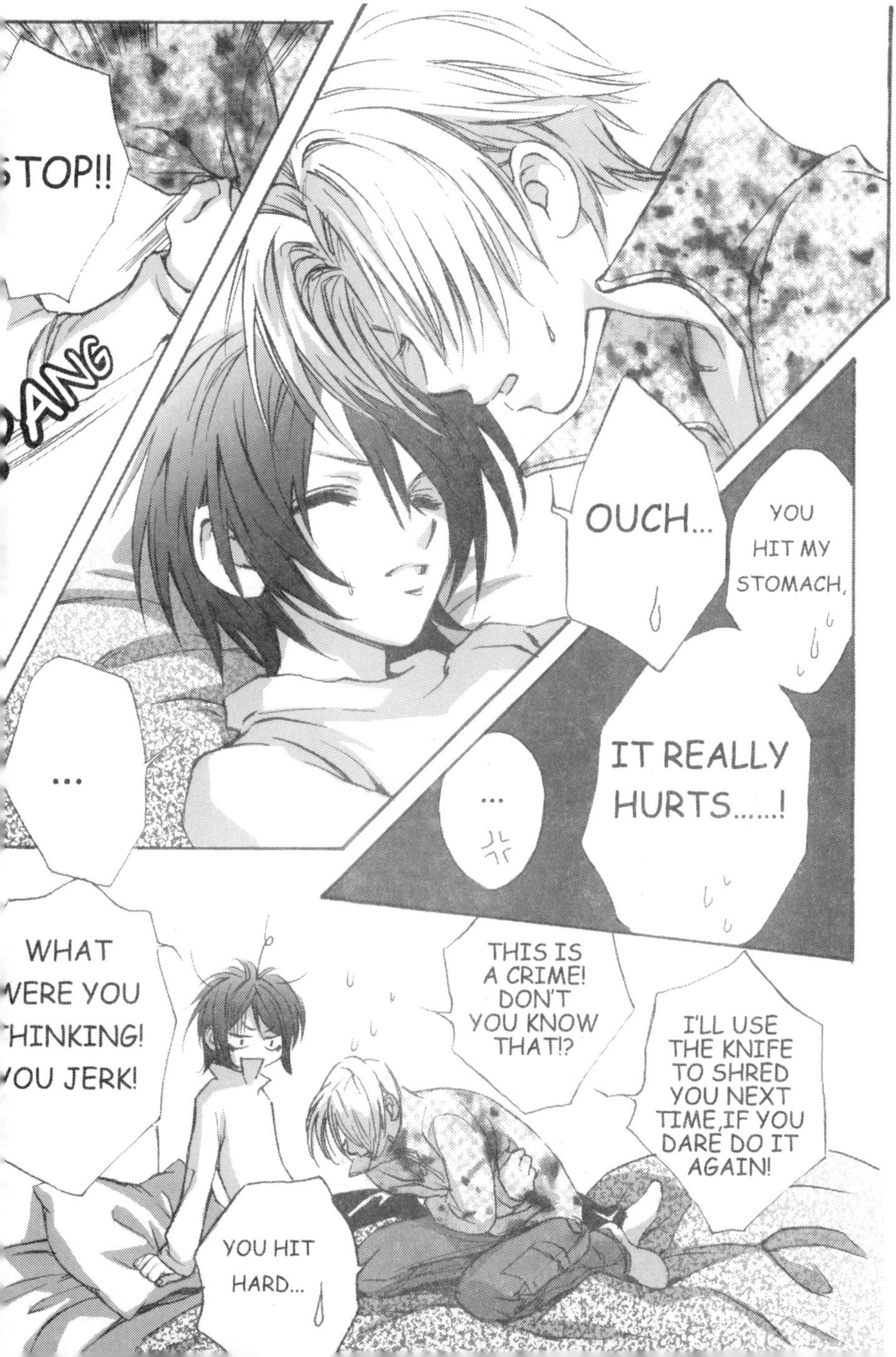
STOP!!
DANG
OUCH...
YOU HIT MY STOMACH,
IT REALLY HURTS......!
...
...
THIS IS A CRIME! DON'T YOU KNOW THAT!?
WHAT WERE YOU THINKING! YOU JERK!
I'LL USE THE KNIFE TO SHRED YOU NEXT TIME,IF YOU DARE DO IT AGAIN!
YOU HIT HARD...

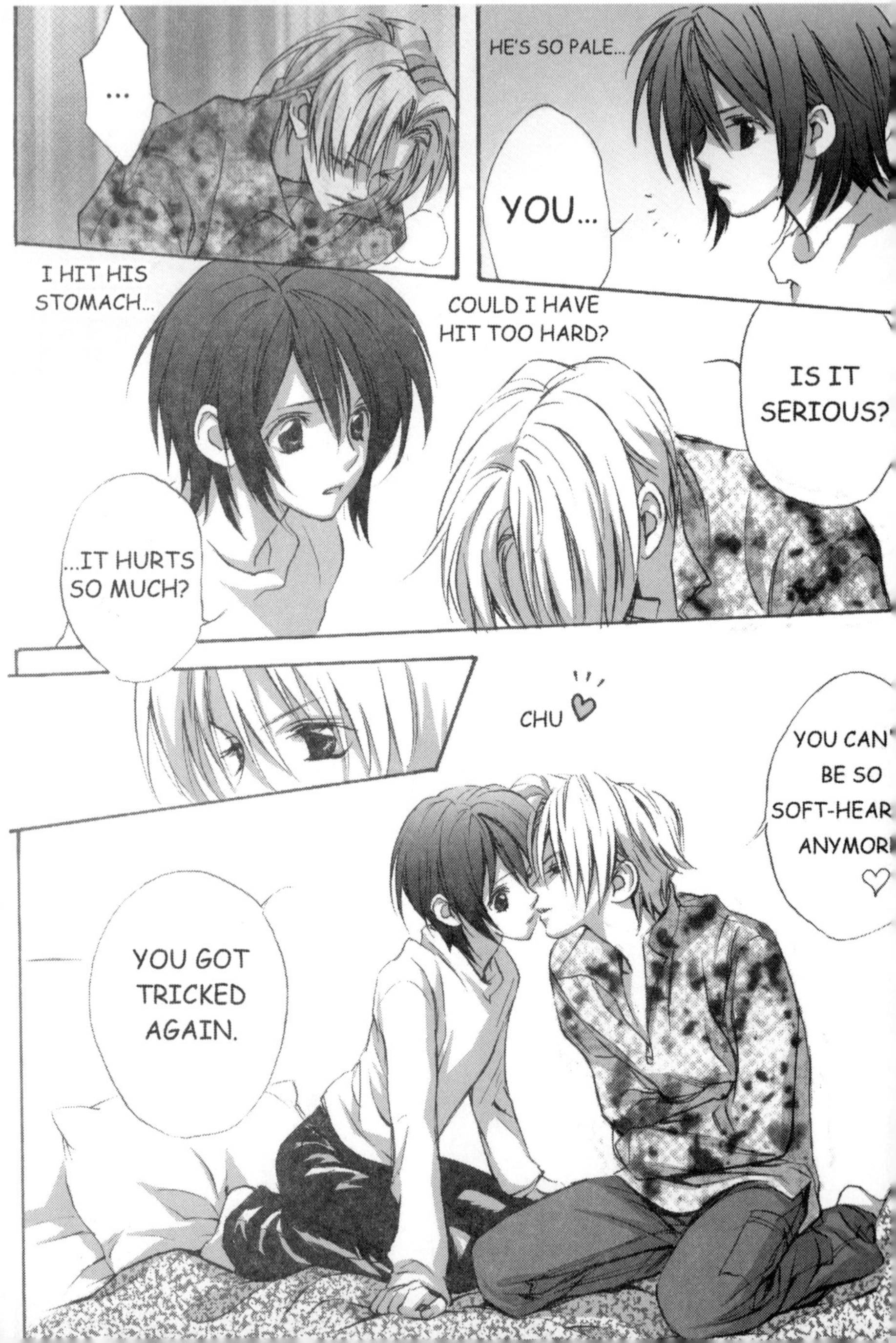
HE'S SO PALE...
YOU...
...
I HIT HIS STOMACH...
COULD I HAVE HIT TOO HARD?
IS IT SERIOUS?
...IT HURTS SO MUCH?
CHU
YOU CAN' BE SO SOFT-HEAR ANYMOR
YOU GOT TRICKED AGAIN.

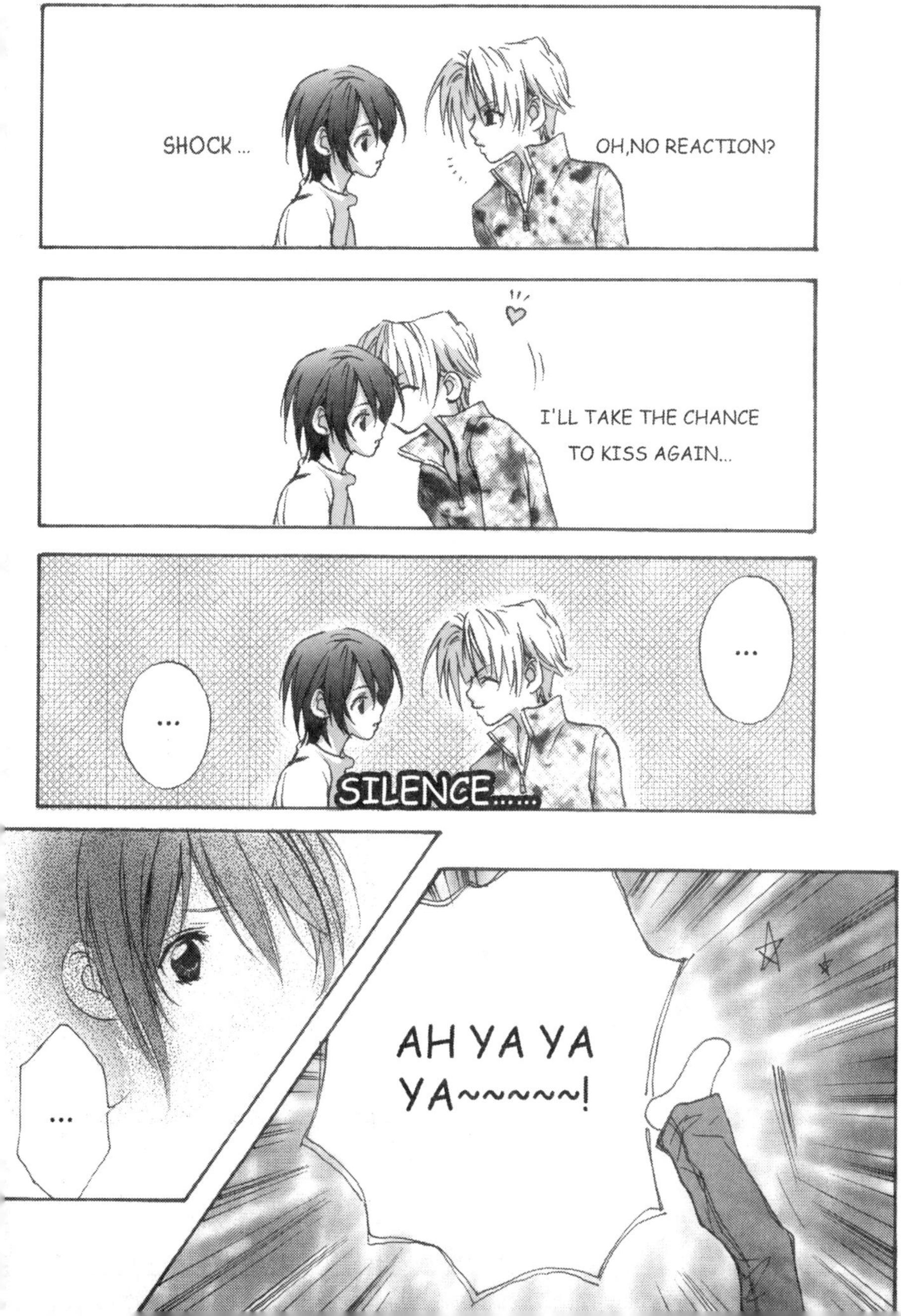
SHOCK ...
OH,NO REACTION?
I'LL TAKE THE CHANCE TO KISS AGAIN...
...
...
SILENCE......
...
AH YA YA YA~~~~~~!

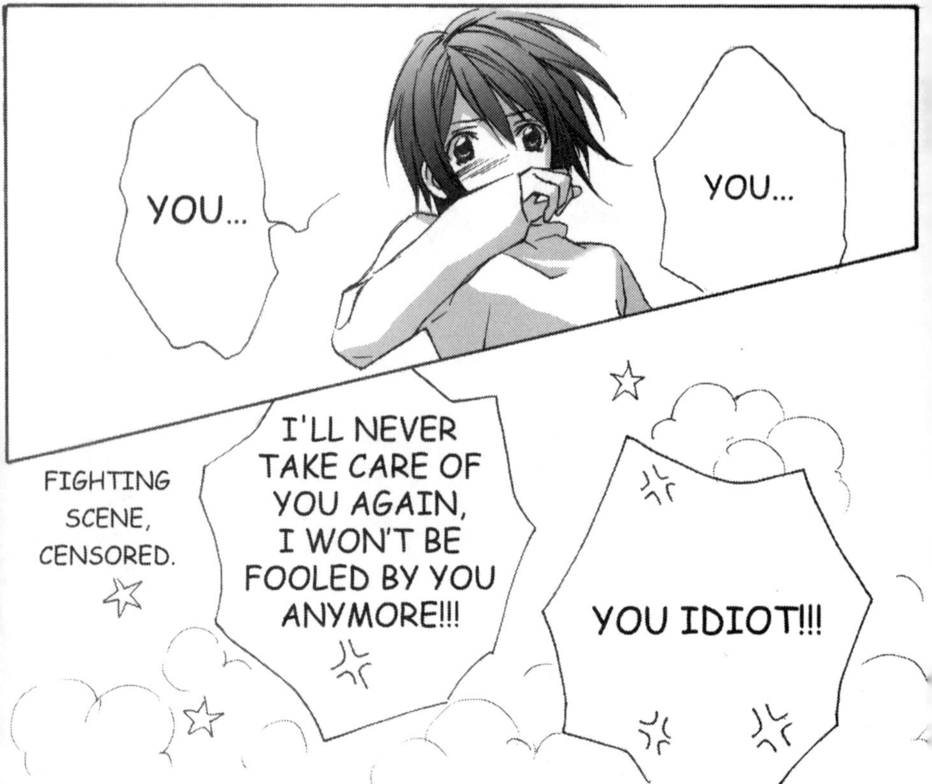
YOU...
YOU...
I'LL NEVER TAKE CARE OF YOU AGAIN, I WON'T BE FOOLED BY YOU ANYMORE!!!
YOU IDIOT!!!
FIGHTING SCENE, CENSORED.

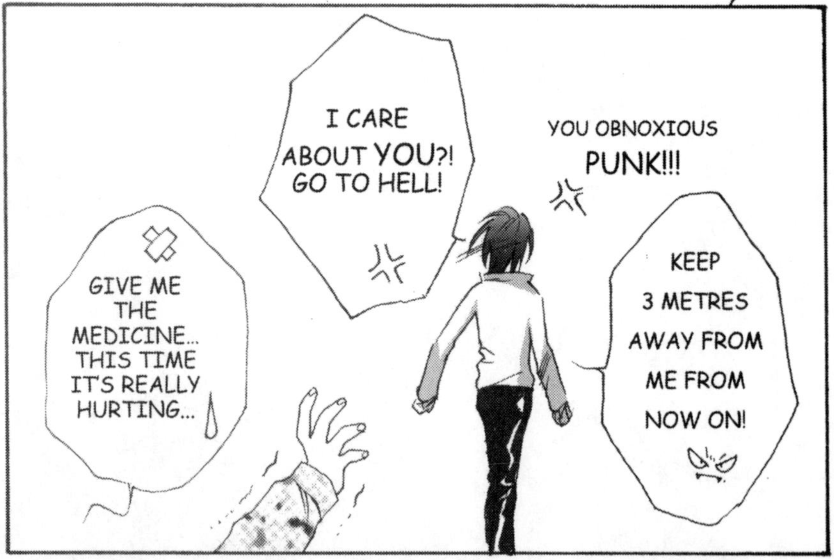
YOU OBNOXIOUS PUNK!!!
I CARE ABOUT YOU?! GO TO HELL!
KEEP 3 METRES AWAY FROM ME FROM NOW ON!
GIVE ME THE MEDICINE... THIS TIME IT'S REALLY HURTING...

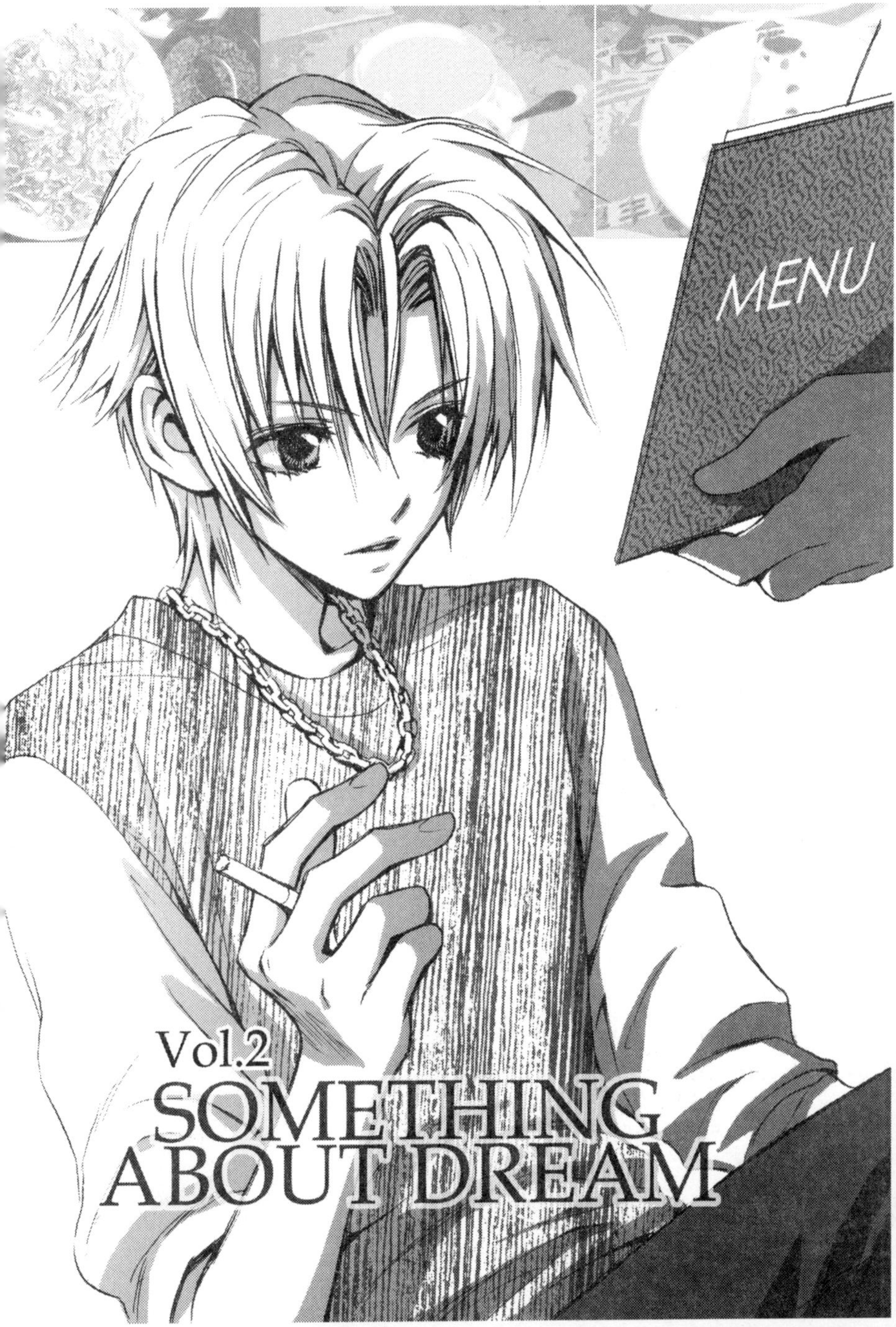
MENU
Vol.2
SOMETHING
ABOUT DREAM

FARMERS WEEDING AT NOON,
SWEAT DOWN THE FIELD SOON.
WHO KNOWS FOOD ON A TRAY
DUE TO THEIR TOILING DAY?
---LI SHEN TANG DYNASTY

GOOD, THIS ANCIENT POEM
TELLS US,THE FARMERS WORK
HARD ON CROPS,
SO WE SHOULD NOT WASTE THE
FOOD.REMEMBER THIS!
XIAO QIU.

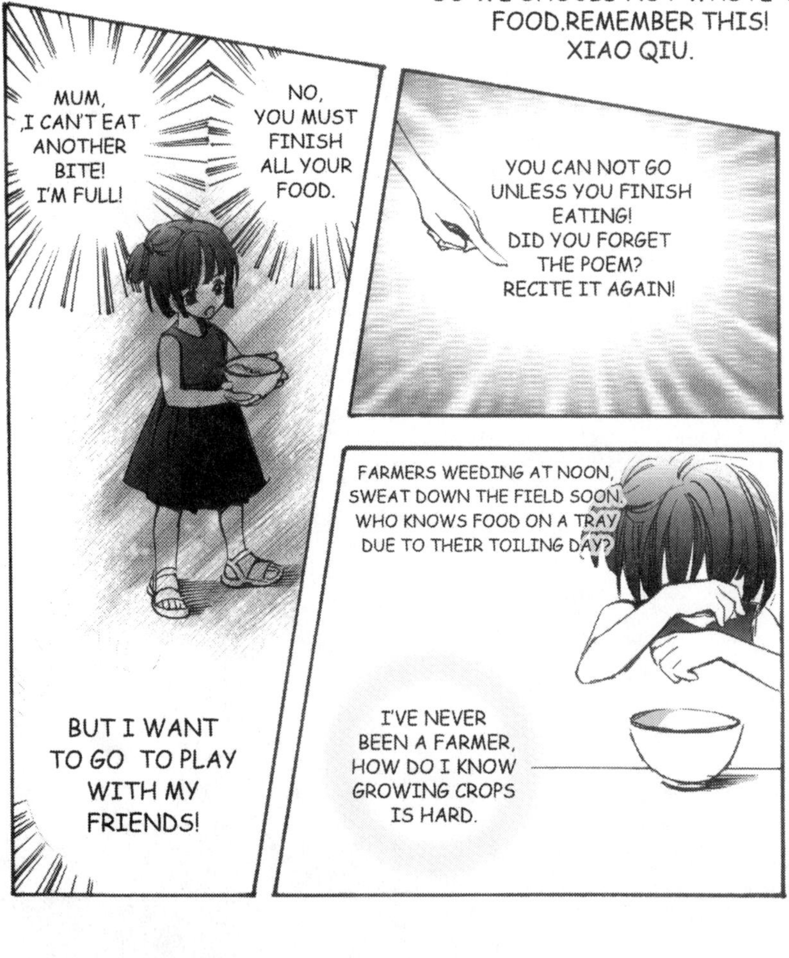
NO, YOU MUST FINISH ALL YOUR FOOD.
MUM, I CAN'T EAT ANOTHER BITE! I'M FULL!
BUT I WANT TO GO TO PLAY WITH MY FRIENDS!
YOU CAN NOT GO UNLESS YOU FINISH EATING! DID YOU FORGET THE POEM? RECITE IT AGAIN!
FARMERS WEEDING AT NOON, SWEAT DOWN THE FIELD SOON. WHO KNOWS FOOD ON A TRAY DUE TO THEIR TOILING DAY?
I'VE NEVER BEEN A FARMER, HOW DO I KNOW GROWING CROPS IS HARD.

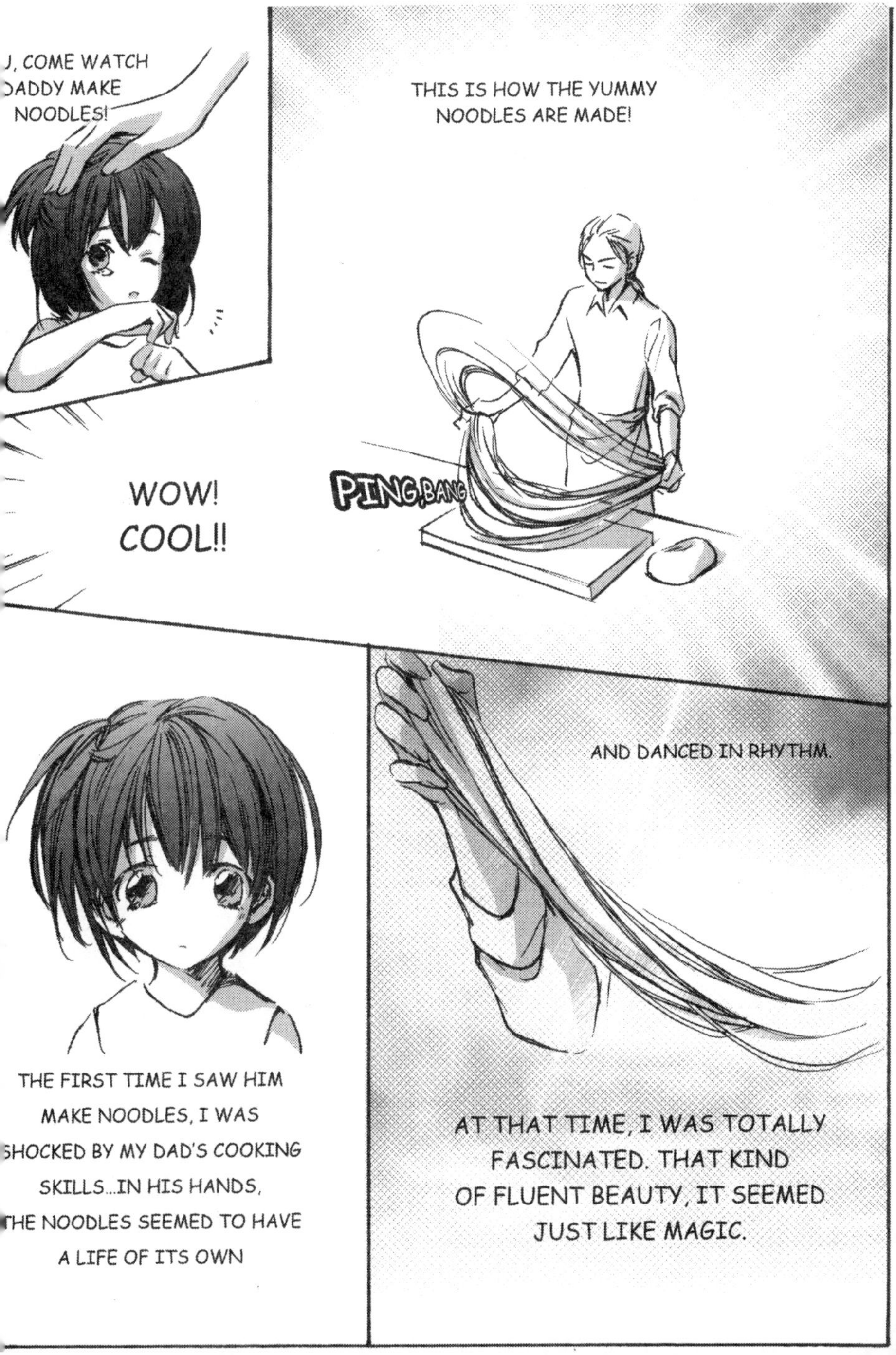
J, COME WATCH DADDY MAKE NOODLES!
THIS IS HOW THE YUMMY NOODLES ARE MADE!
WOW! COOL!!
PING, BANG
THE FIRST TIME I SAW HIM MAKE NOODLES, I WAS SHOCKED BY MY DAD'S COOKING SKILLS...IN HIS HANDS, THE NOODLES SEEMED TO HAVE A LIFE OF ITS OWN
AND DANCED IN RHYTHM.
AT THAT TIME, I WAS TOTALLY FASCINATED. THAT KIND OF FLUENT BEAUTY, IT SEEMED JUST LIKE MAGIC.

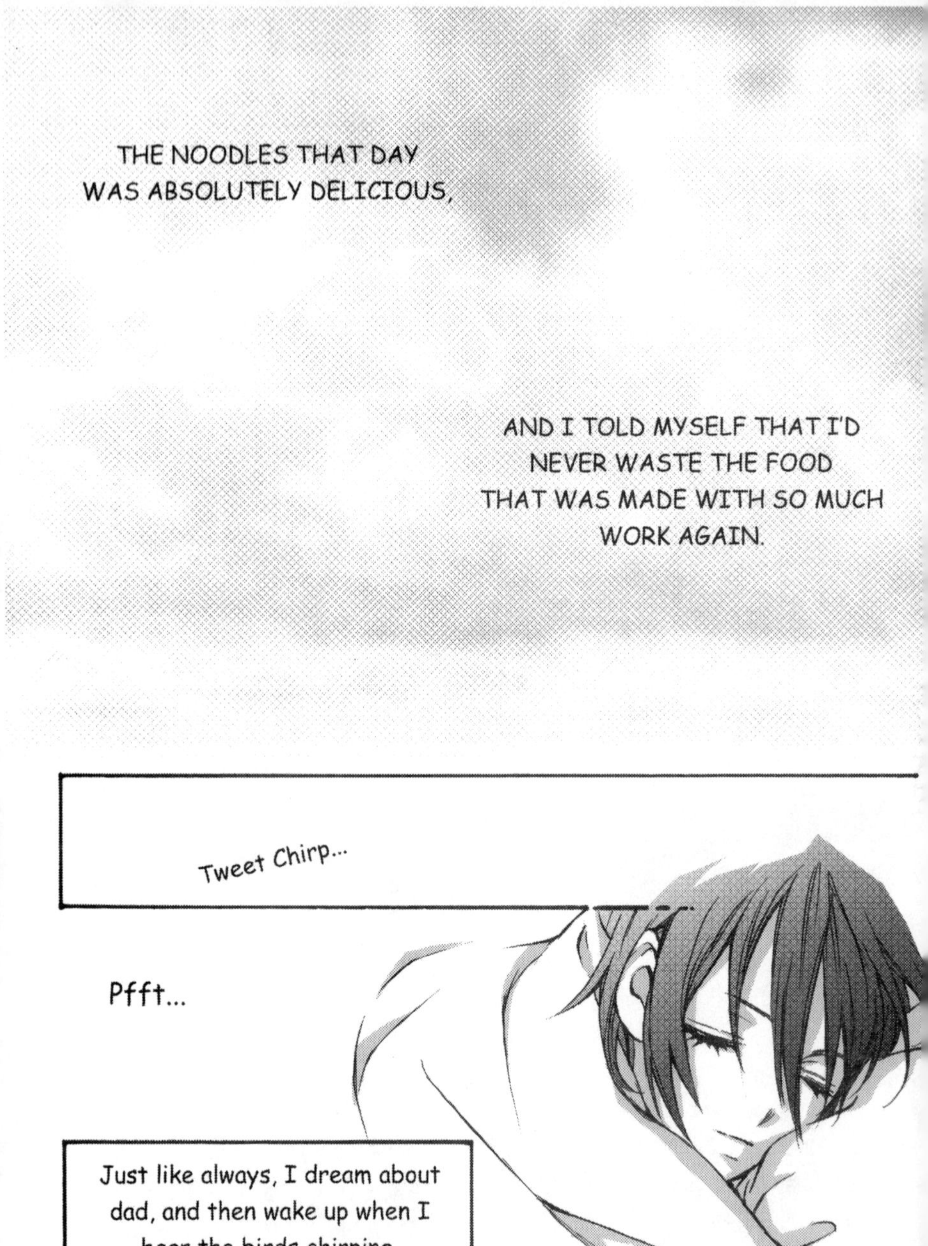
THE NOODLES THAT DAY WAS ABSOLUTELY DELICIOUS,
AND I TOLD MYSELF THAT I'D NEVER WASTE THE FOOD THAT WAS MADE WITH SO MUCH WORK AGAIN.
Tweet Chirp...
Pfft...
Just like always, I dream about dad, and then wake up when I hear the birds chirping.

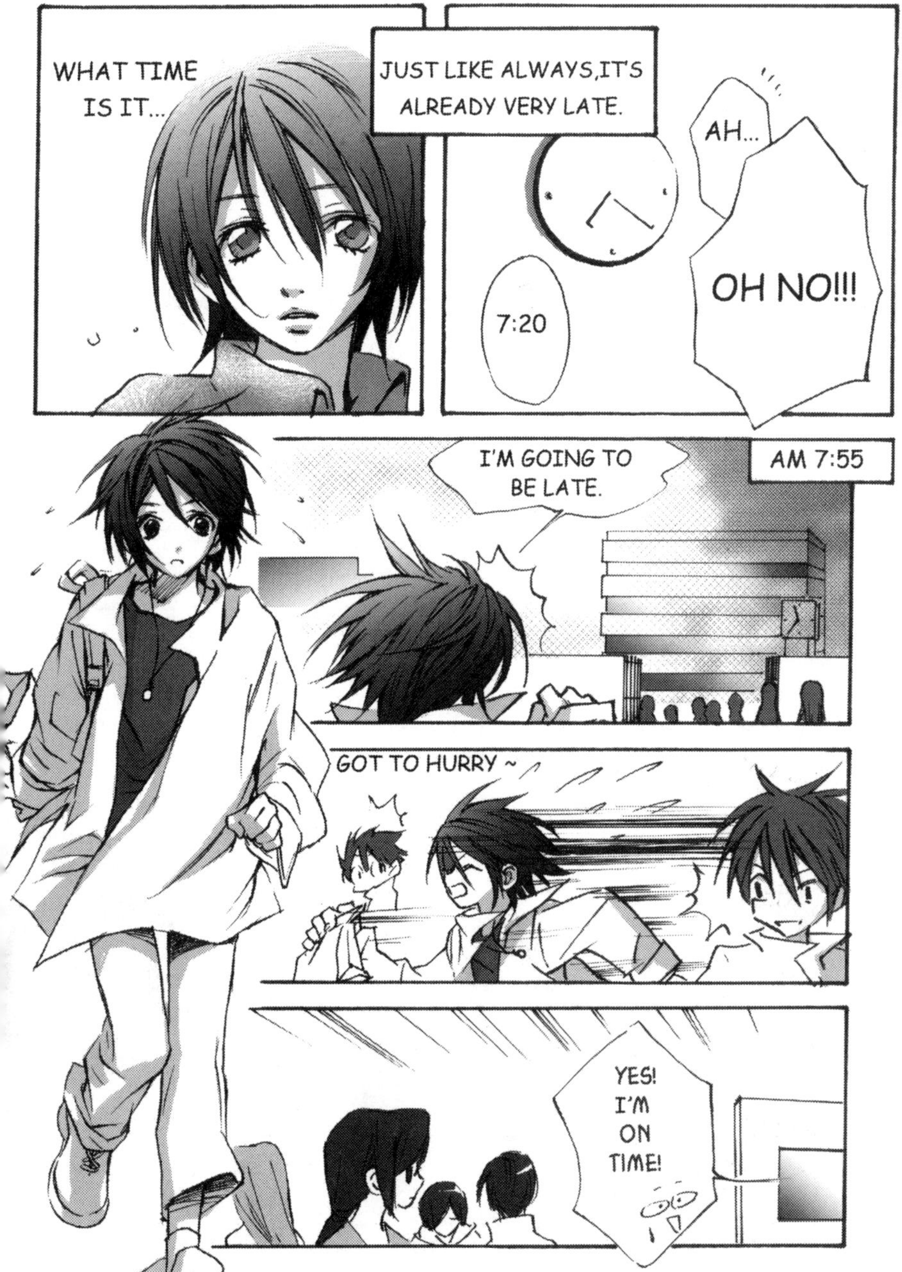
WHAT TIME IS IT...
JUST LIKE ALWAYS,IT'S ALREADY VERY LATE.
AH...
7:20
OH NO!!!
AM 7:55
I'M GOING TO BE LATE.
GOT TO HURRY ~
YES! I'M ON TIME!

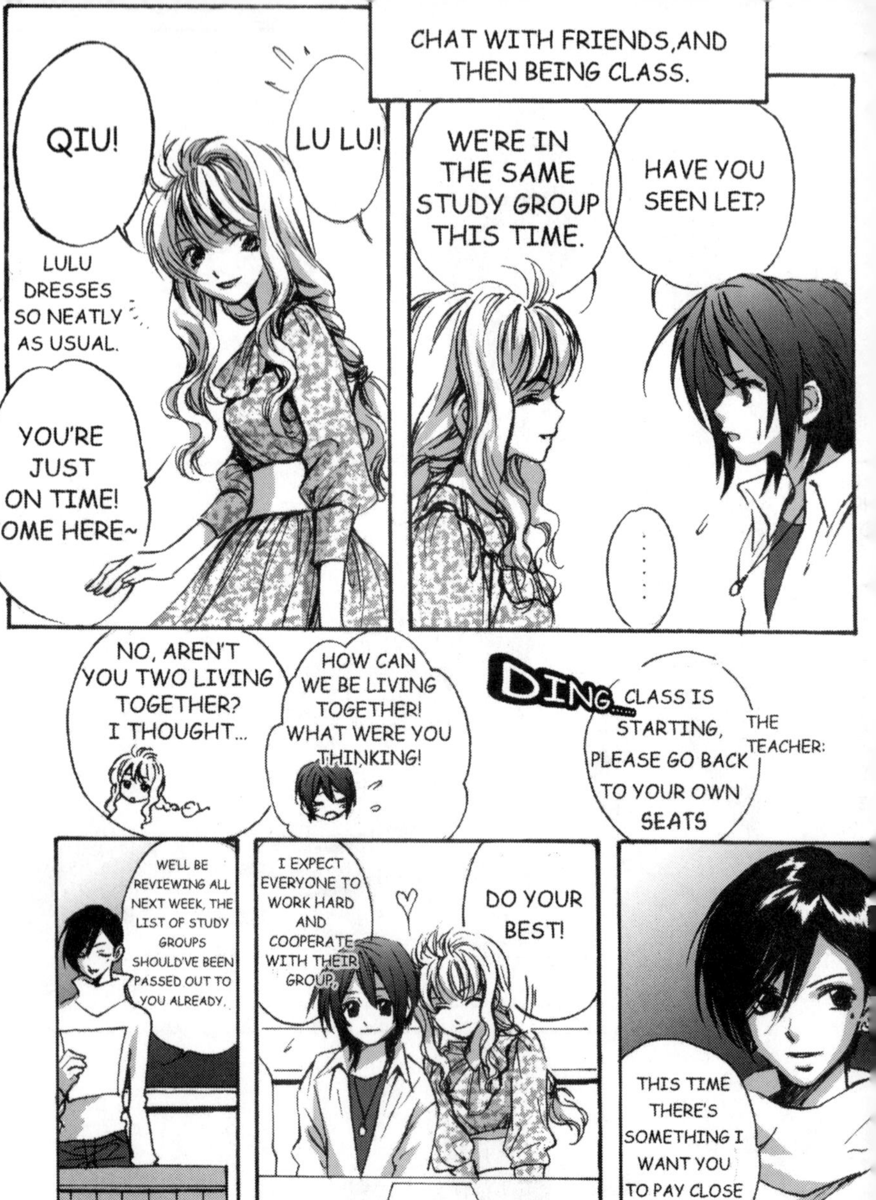

CHAT WITH FRIENDS,AND THEN BEING CLASS.
QIU!
LU LU!
LULU DRESSES SO NEATLY AS USUAL.
YOU'RE JUST ON TIME! COME HERE~
WE'RE IN THE SAME STUDY GROUP THIS TIME.
HAVE YOU SEEN LEI?
......
NO, AREN'T YOU TWO LIVING TOGETHER? I THOUGHT...
HOW CAN WE BE LIVING TOGETHER! WHAT WERE YOU THINKING!
DING.....
THE TEACHER:
CLASS IS STARTING, PLEASE GO BACK TO YOUR OWN SEATS
WE'LL BE REVIEWING ALL NEXT WEEK, THE LIST OF STUDY GROUPS SHOULD'VE BEEN PASSED OUT TO YOU ALREADY.
I EXPECT EVERYONE TO WORK HARD AND COOPERATE WITH THEIR GROUP.
DO YOUR BEST!
THIS TIME THERE'S SOMETHING I WANT YOU TO PAY CLOSE ATTENTION TO.

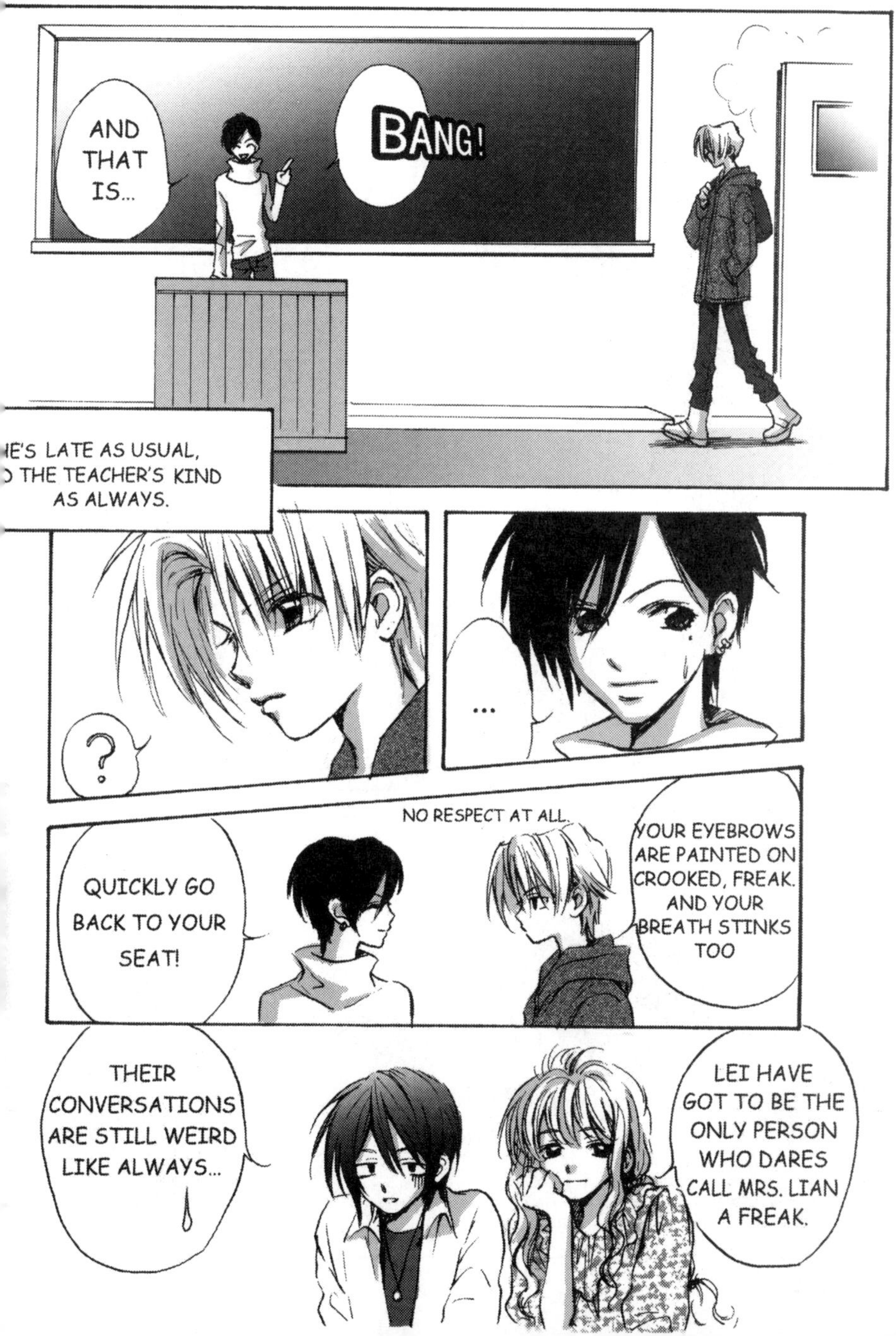
AND THAT IS...
BANG!
E'S LATE AS USUAL, THE TEACHER'S KIND AS ALWAYS.
?
...
QUICKLY GO BACK TO YOUR SEAT!
NO RESPECT AT ALL.
YOUR EYEBROWS ARE PAINTED ON CROOKED, FREAK. AND YOUR BREATH STINKS TOO
THEIR CONVERSATIONS ARE STILL WEIRD LIKE ALWAYS...
LEI HAVE GOT TO BE THE ONLY PERSON WHO DARES CALL MRS. LIAN A FREAK.

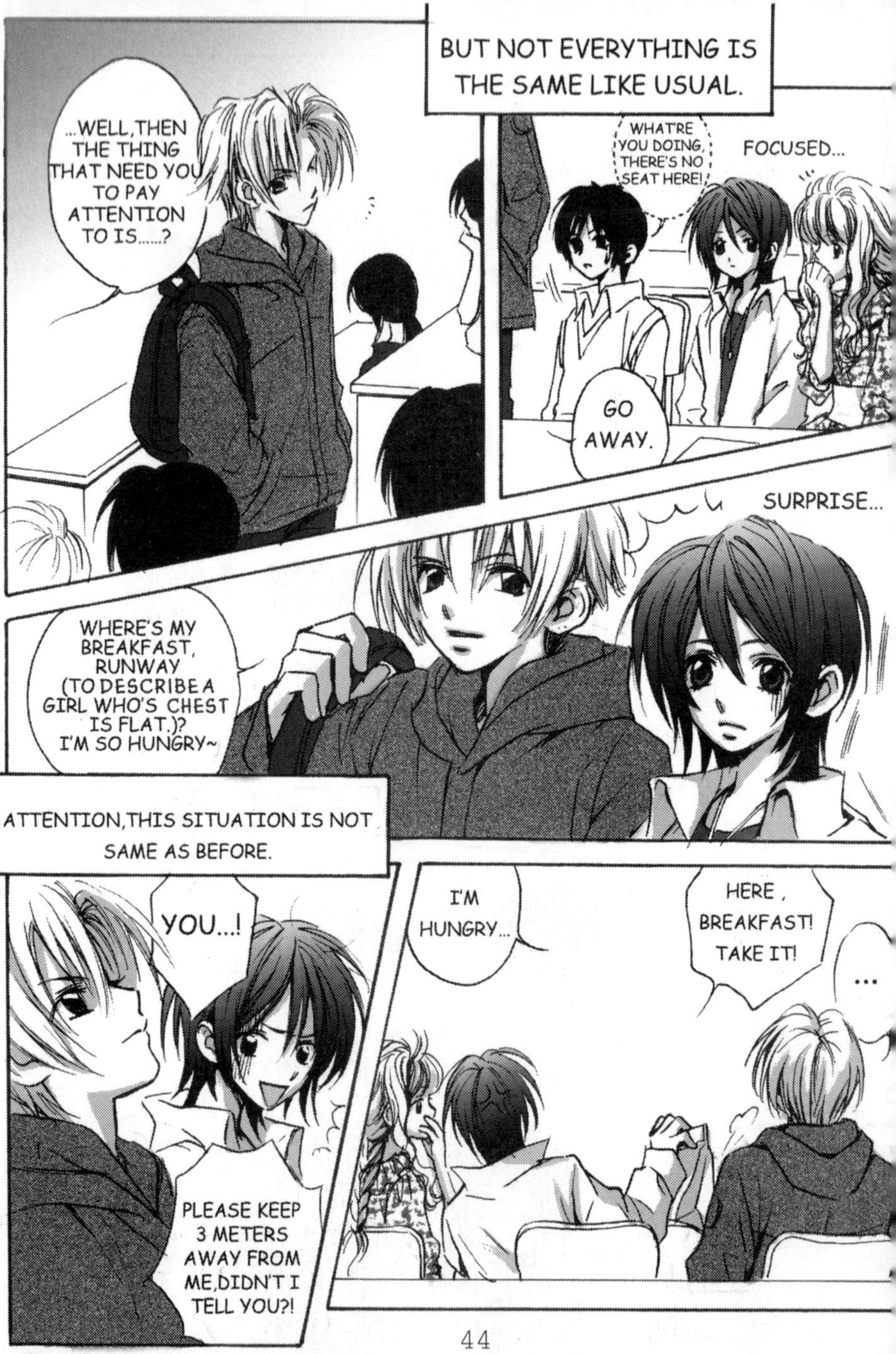
BUT NOT EVERYTHING IS THE SAME LIKE USUAL.
...WELL,THEN THE THING THAT NEED YOU TO PAY ATTENTION TO IS......?
WHAT'RE YOU DOING, THERE'S NO SEAT HERE!
FOCUSED...
GO AWAY.
SURPRISE...
WHERE'S MY BREAKFAST, RUNWAY (TO DESCRIBE A GIRL WHO'S CHEST IS FLAT.)? I'M SO HUNGRY~
ATTENTION,THIS SITUATION IS NOT SAME AS BEFORE.
YOU...!
PLEASE KEEP 3 METERS AWAY FROM ME,DIDN'T I TELL YOU?!
I'M HUNGRY...
HERE , BREAKFAST! TAKE IT!
...

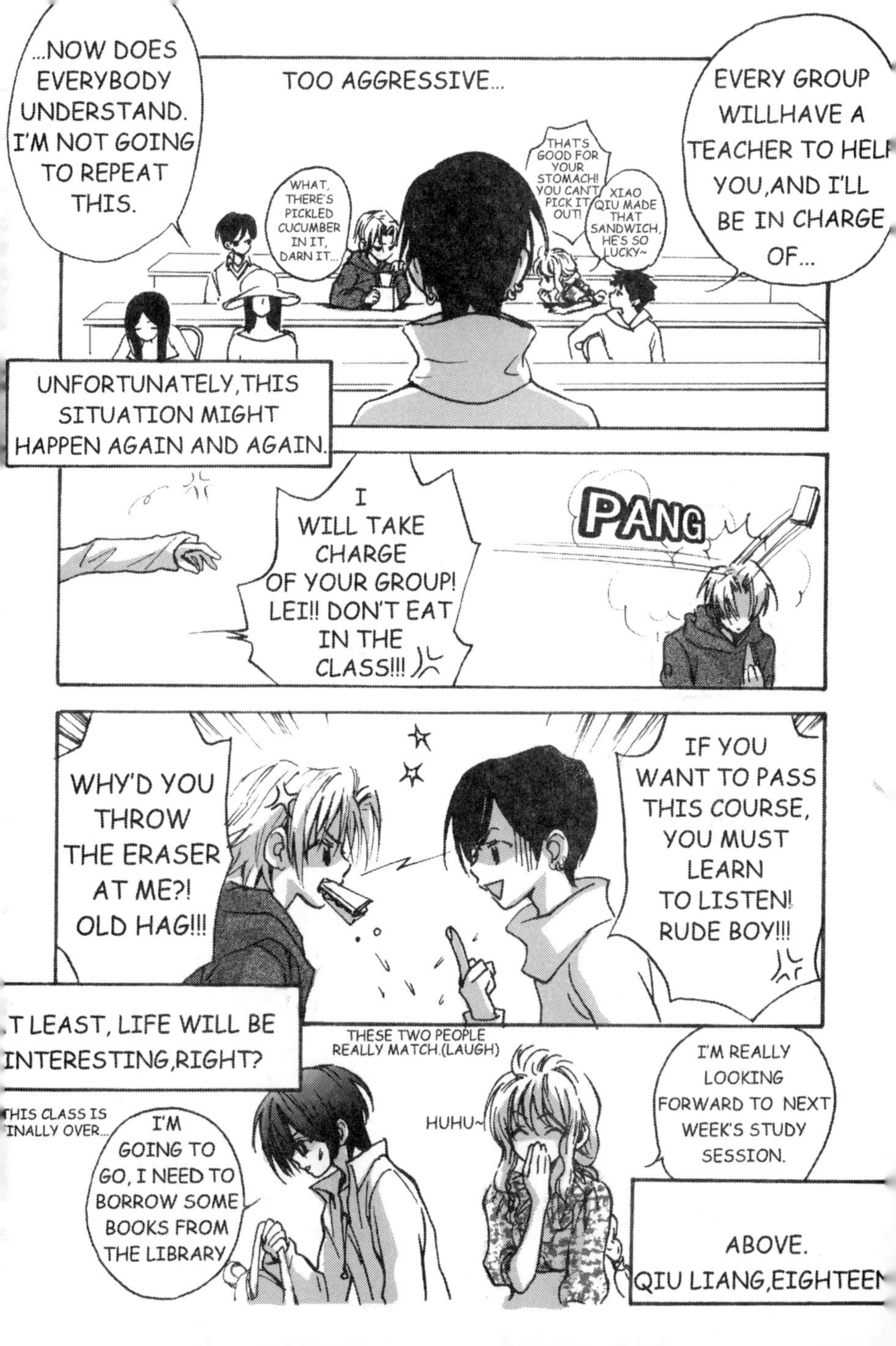
...NOW DOES EVERYBODY UNDERSTAND. I'M NOT GOING TO REPEAT THIS.
TOO AGGRESSIVE...
WHAT, THERE'S PICKLED CUCUMBER IN IT, DARN IT...
THAT'S GOOD FOR YOUR STOMACH! YOU CAN'T PICK IT OUT!
XIAO QIU MADE THAT SANDWICH, HE'S SO LUCKY~
EVERY GROUP WILLHAVE A TEACHER TO HEL YOU,AND I'LL BE IN CHARGE OF...
UNFORTUNATELY,THIS SITUATION MIGHT HAPPEN AGAIN AND AGAIN.
I WILL TAKE CHARGE OF YOUR GROUP! LEI!! DON'T EAT IN THE CLASS!!!
PANG
WHY'D YOU THROW THE ERASER AT ME?! OLD HAG!!!
IF YOU WANT TO PASS THIS COURSE, YOU MUST LEARN TO LISTEN! RUDE BOY!!!
T LEAST, LIFE WILL BE INTERESTING,RIGHT?
THESE TWO PEOPLE REALLY MATCH.(LAUGH)
THIS CLASS IS INALLY OVER...
I'M GOING TO GO, I NEED TO BORROW SOME BOOKS FROM THE LIBRARY
HUHU~
I'M REALLY LOOKING FORWARD TO NEXT WEEK'S STUDY SESSION.
ABOVE. QIU LIANG,EIGHTEE

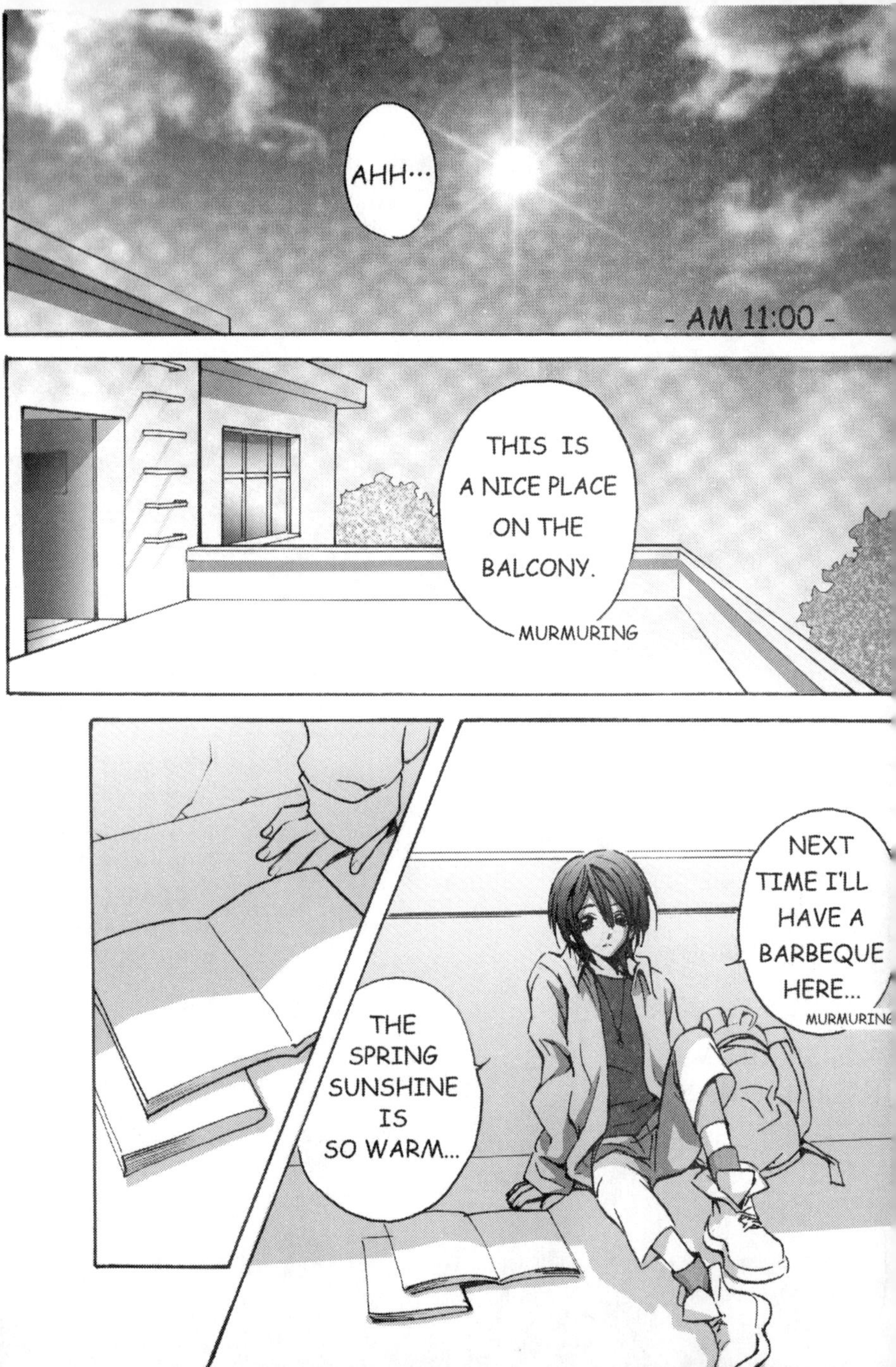
AHH…
- AM 11:00 -
THIS IS A NICE PLACE ON THE BALCONY.
MURMURING
NEXT TIME I'LL HAVE A BARBEQUE HERE...
MURMURING
THE SPRING SUNSHINE IS SO WARM...

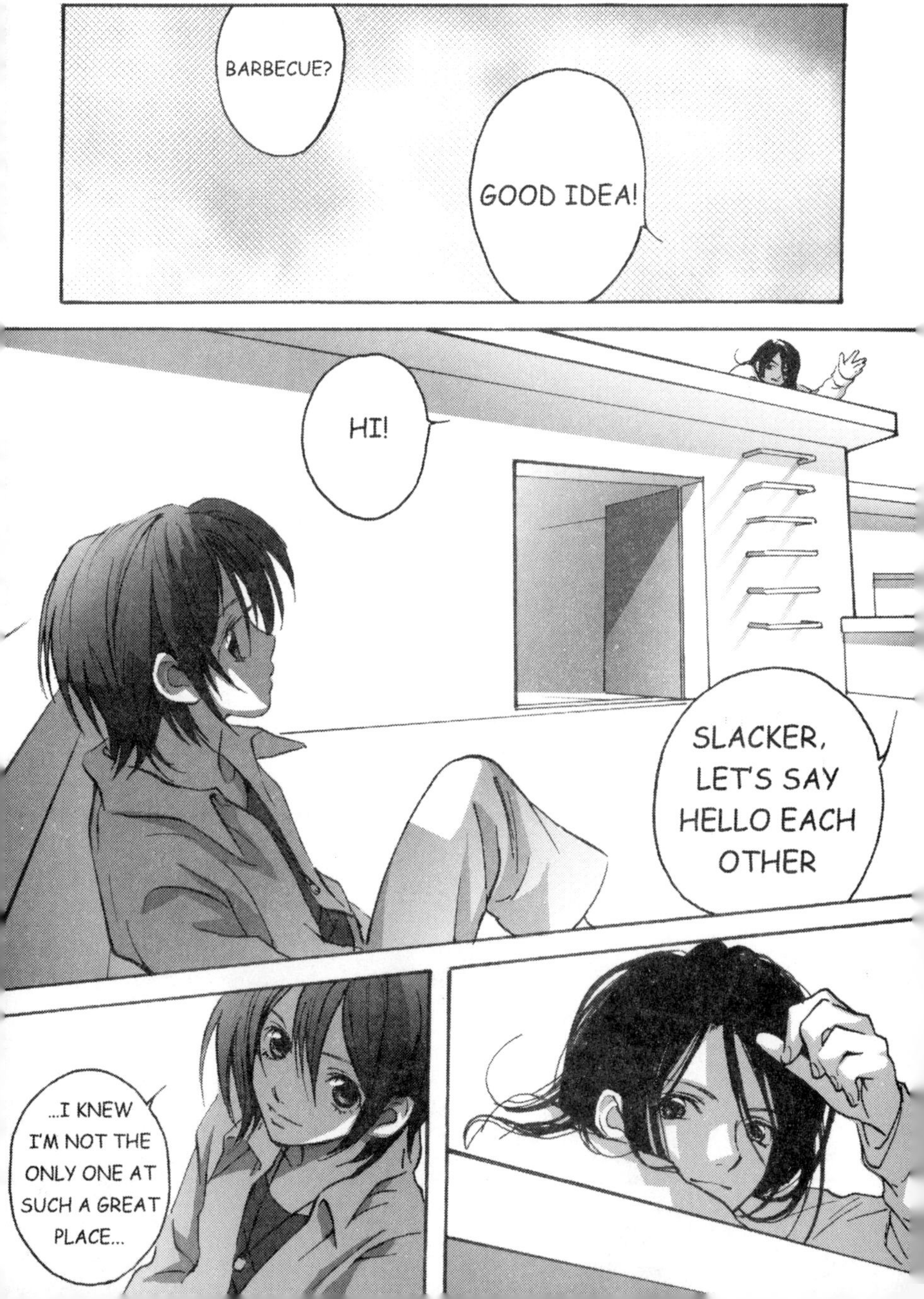
BARBECUE?
GOOD IDEA!
HI!
SLACKER, LET'S SAY HELLO EACH OTHER
...I KNEW I'M NOT THE ONLY ONE AT SUCH A GREAT PLACE...

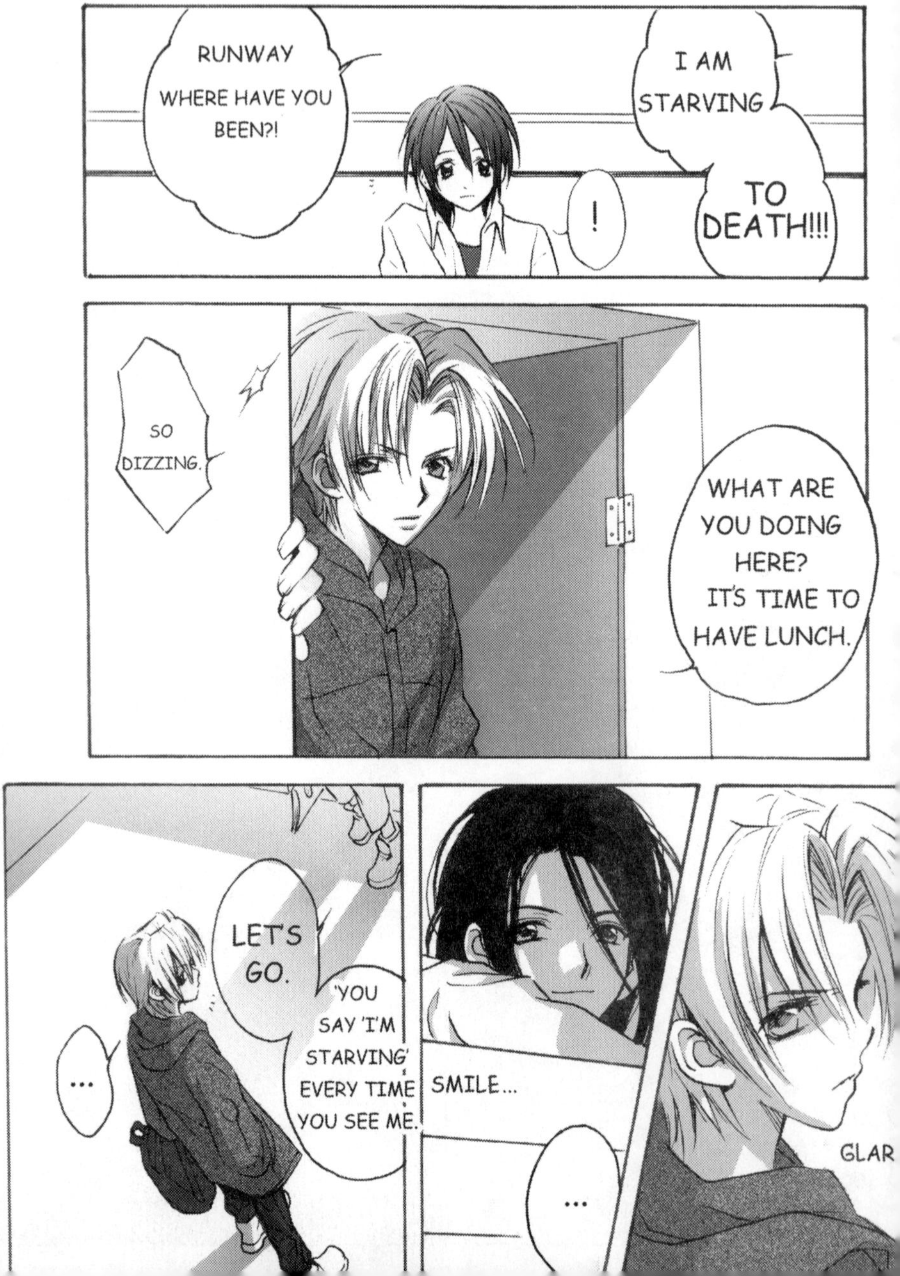
I AM STARVING TO DEATH!!!
RUNWAY WHERE HAVE YOU BEEN?!
!
WHAT ARE YOU DOING HERE? IT'S TIME TO HAVE LUNCH.
SO DIZZING.
GLAR
...
SMILE...
LET'S GO.
'YOU SAY 'I'M STARVING' EVERY TIME YOU SEE ME.
...

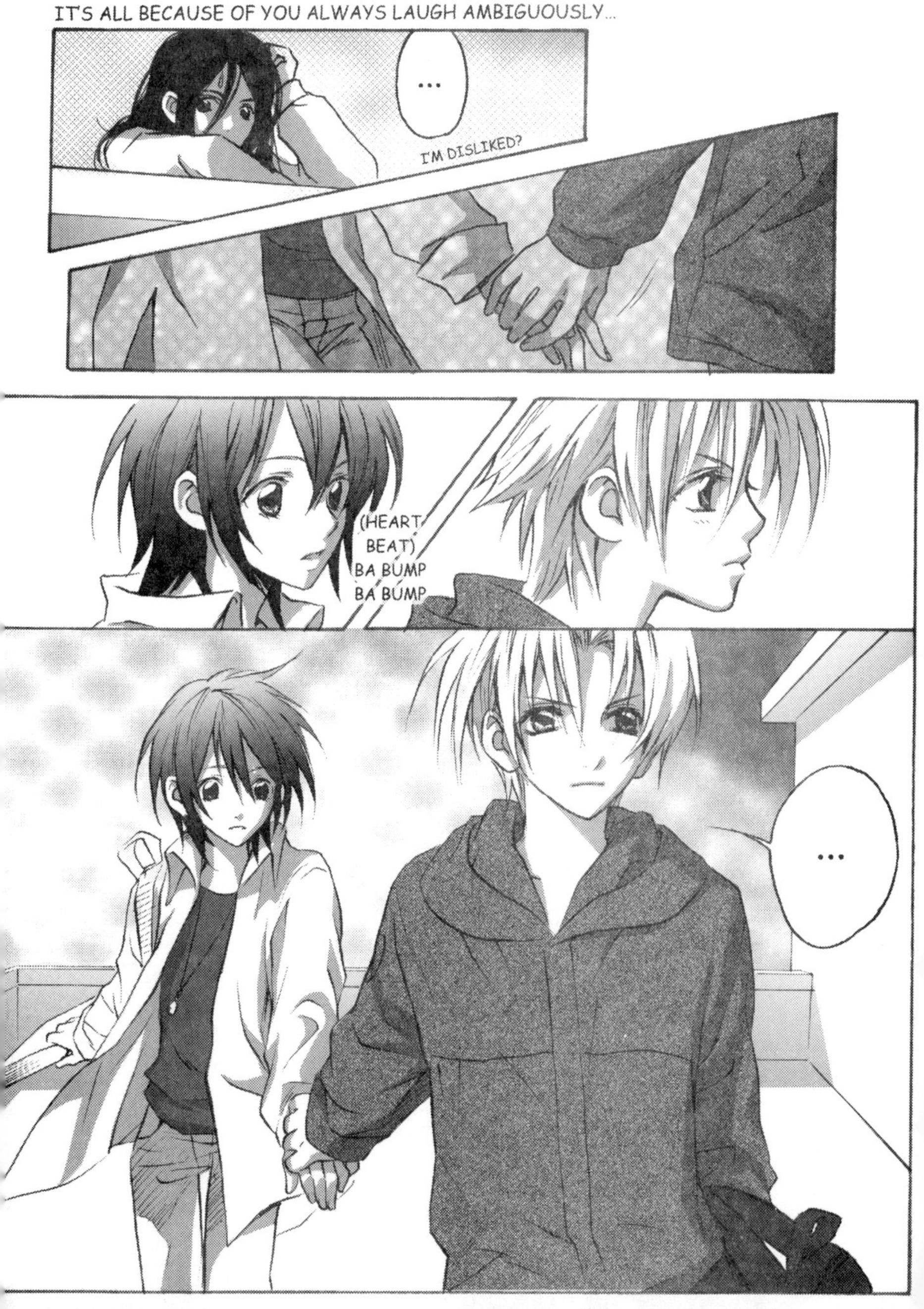
IT'S ALL BECAUSE OF YOU ALWAYS LAUGH AMBIGUOUSLY...
...
I'M DISLIKED?
(HEART BEAT)
BA BUMP
BA BUMP
...

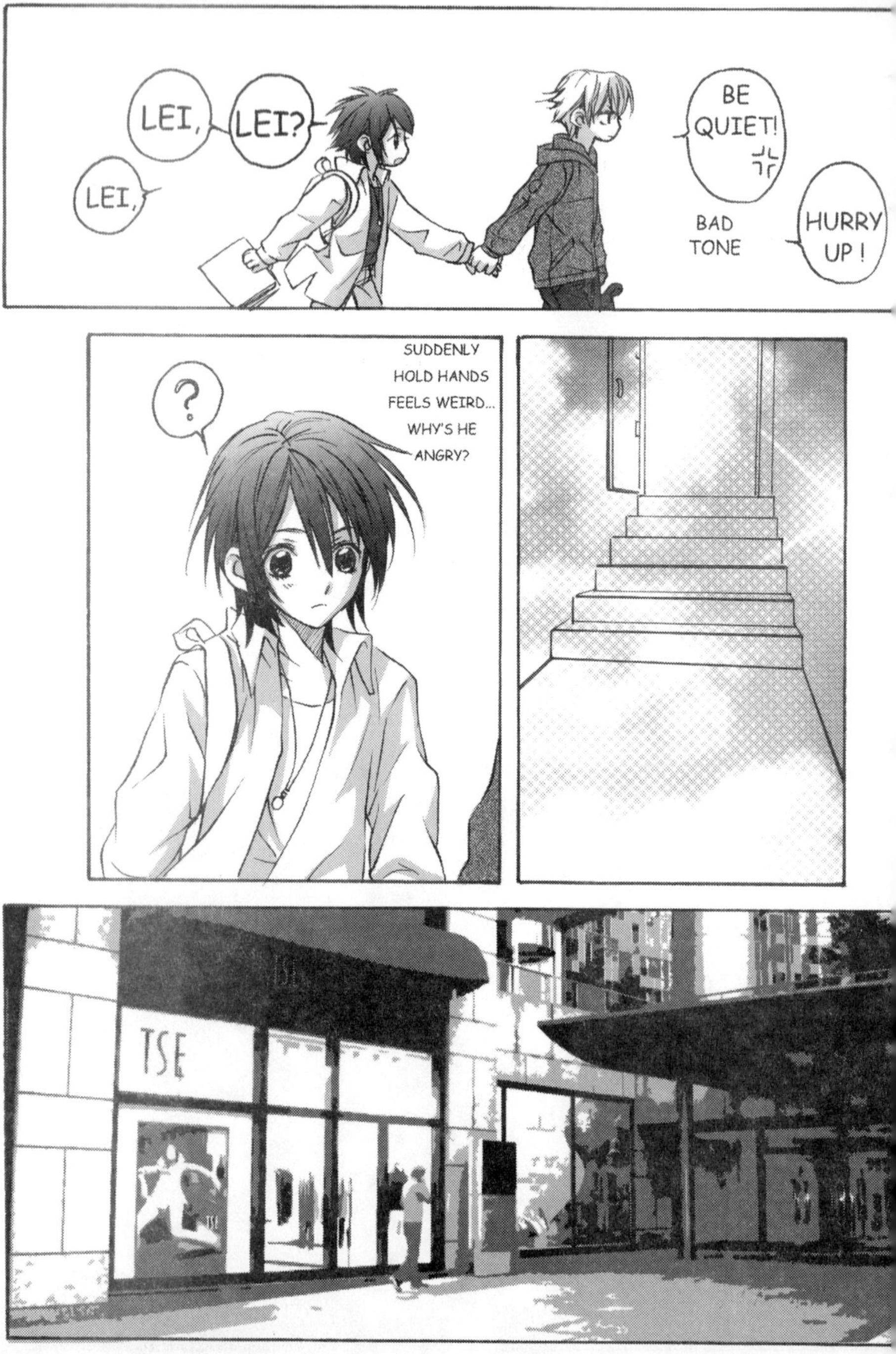

LEI,
LEI,
LEI?
BE QUIET!
HURRY UP !
BAD TONE
?
SUDDENLY HOLD HANDS FEELS WEIRD... WHY'S HE ANGRY?
TSE

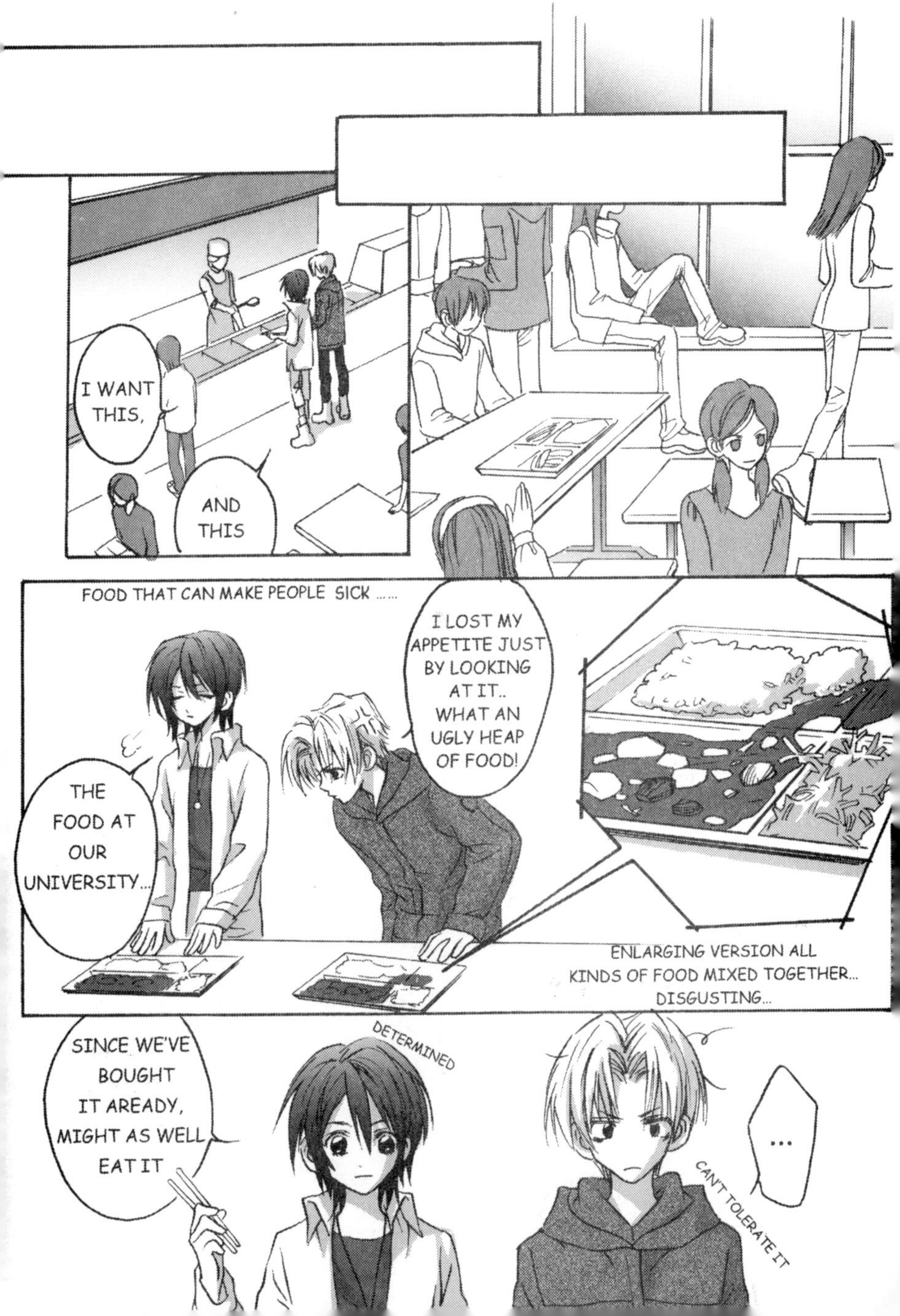

I WANT THIS,
AND THIS
FOOD THAT CAN MAKE PEOPLE SICK ......
I LOST MY APPETITE JUST BY LOOKING AT IT.. WHAT AN UGLY HEAP OF FOOD!
THE FOOD AT OUR UNIVERSITY...
ENLARGING VERSION ALL KINDS OF FOOD MIXED TOGETHER... DISGUSTING...
SINCE WE'VE BOUGHT IT AREADY, MIGHT AS WELL EAT IT
DETERMINED
...
CAN'T TOLERATE IT

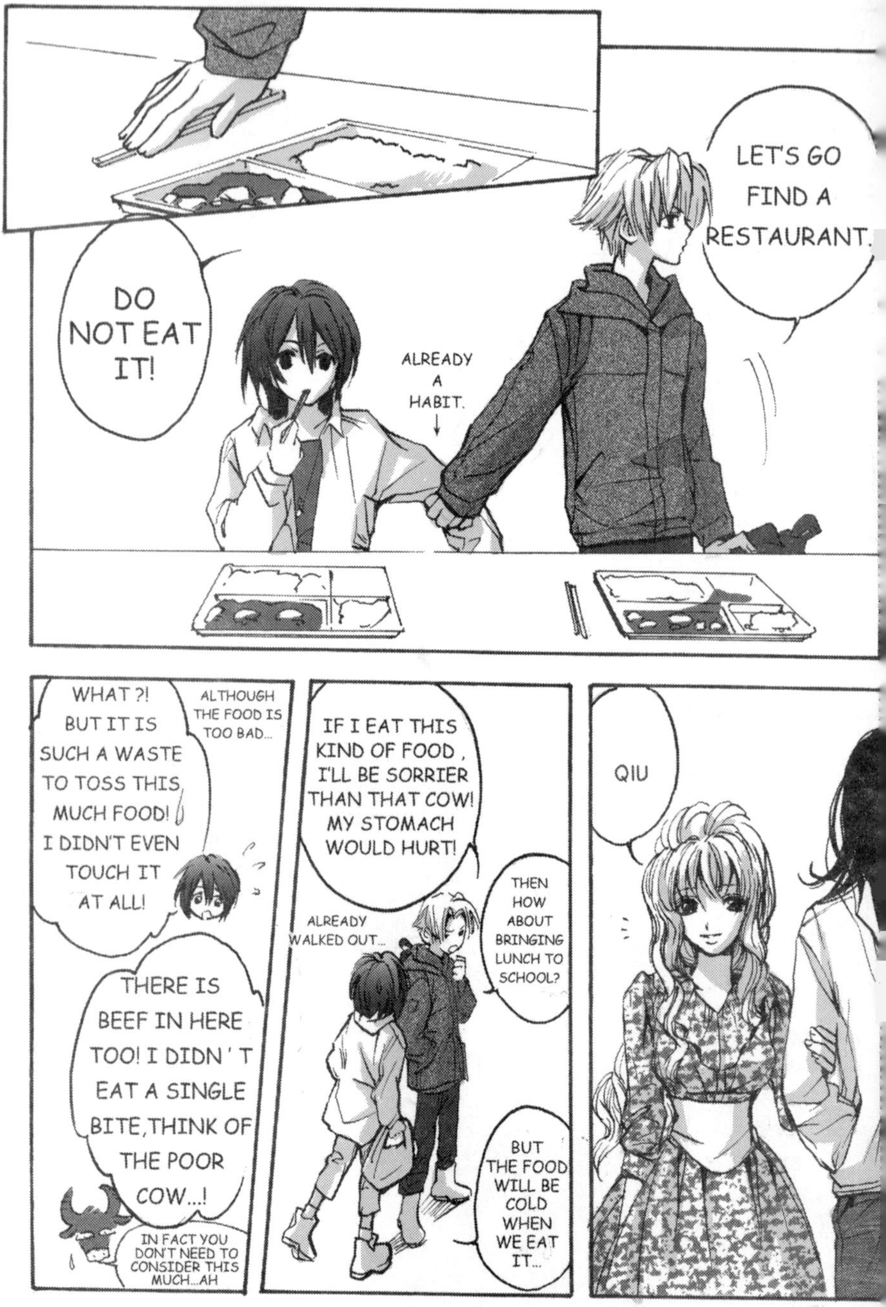
LET'S GO FIND A RESTAURANT.
DO NOT EAT IT!
ALREADY A HABIT.
WHAT ?! BUT IT IS SUCH A WASTE TO TOSS THIS MUCH FOOD! I DIDN'T EVEN TOUCH IT AT ALL!
ALTHOUGH THE FOOD IS TOO BAD...
THERE IS BEEF IN HERE TOO! I DIDN'T EAT A SINGLE BITE,THINK OF THE POOR COW...!
IN FACT YOU DON'T NEED TO CONSIDER THIS MUCH...AH
IF I EAT THIS KIND OF FOOD , I'LL BE SORRIER THAN THAT COW! MY STOMACH WOULD HURT!
ALREADY WALKED OUT...
THEN HOW ABOUT BRINGING LUNCH TO SCHOOL?
BUT THE FOOD WILL BE COLD WHEN WE EAT IT...
QIU

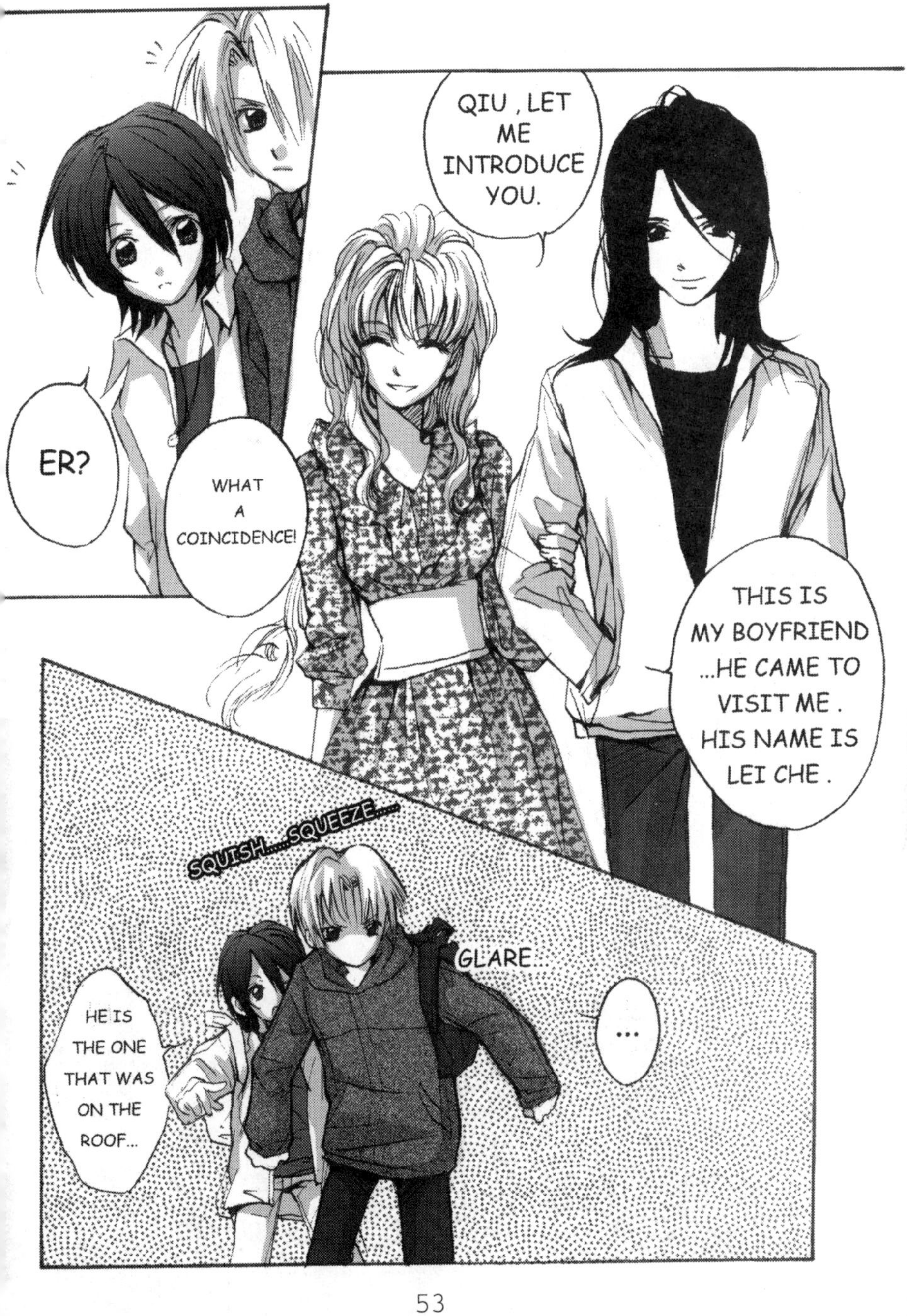
QIU , LET ME INTRODUCE YOU.
ER?
WHAT A COINCIDENCE!
THIS IS MY BOYFRIEND ...HE CAME TO VISIT ME . HIS NAME IS LEI CHE .
SQUISH.....SQUEEZE.....
GLARE..
...
HE IS THE ONE THAT WAS ON THE ROOF...

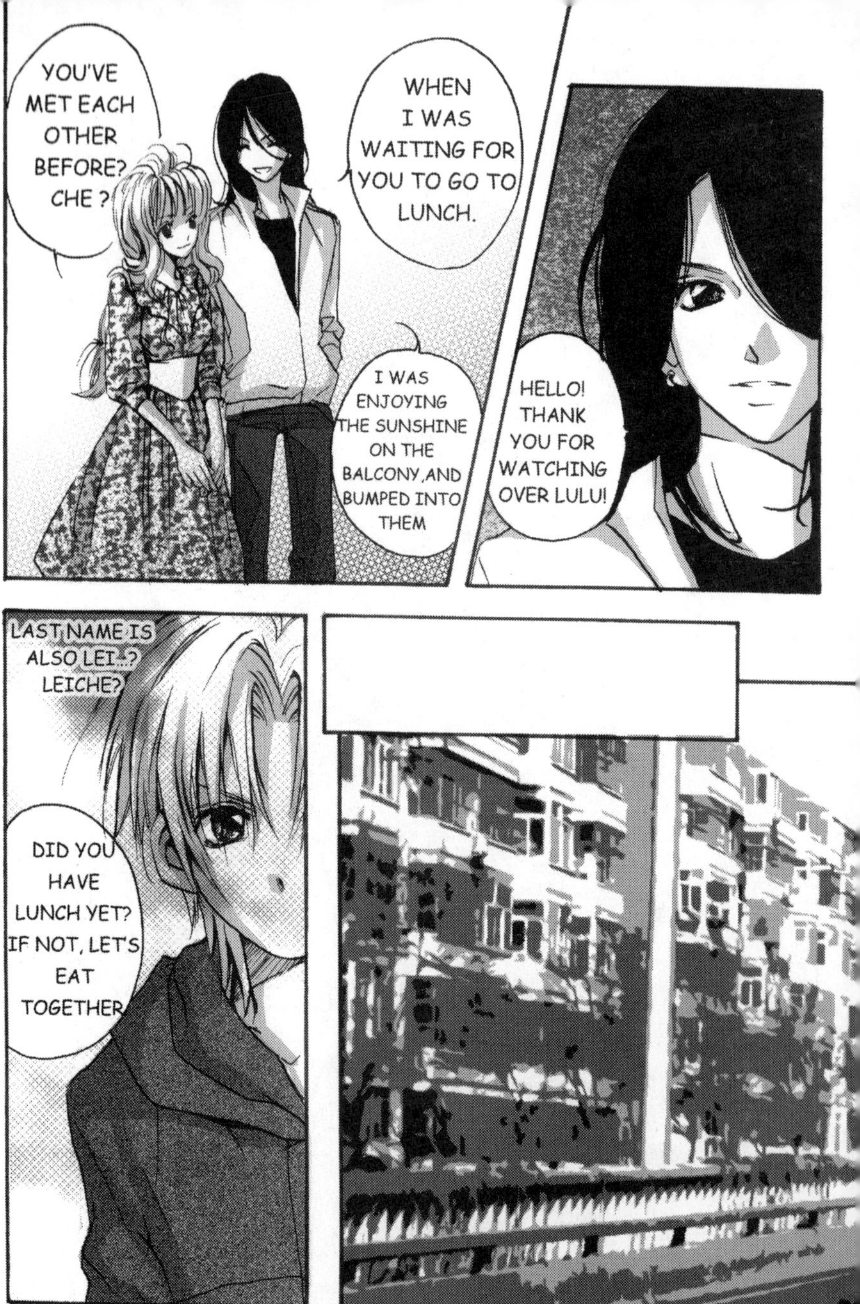
YOU'VE MET EACH OTHER BEFORE? CHE ?
WHEN I WAS WAITING FOR YOU TO GO TO LUNCH.
I WAS ENJOYING THE SUNSHINE ON THE BALCONY,AND BUMPED INTO THEM
HELLO! THANK YOU FOR WATCHING OVER LULU!
LAST NAME IS ALSO LEI...? LEICHE?
DID YOU HAVE LUNCH YET? IF NOT, LET'S EAT TOGETHER

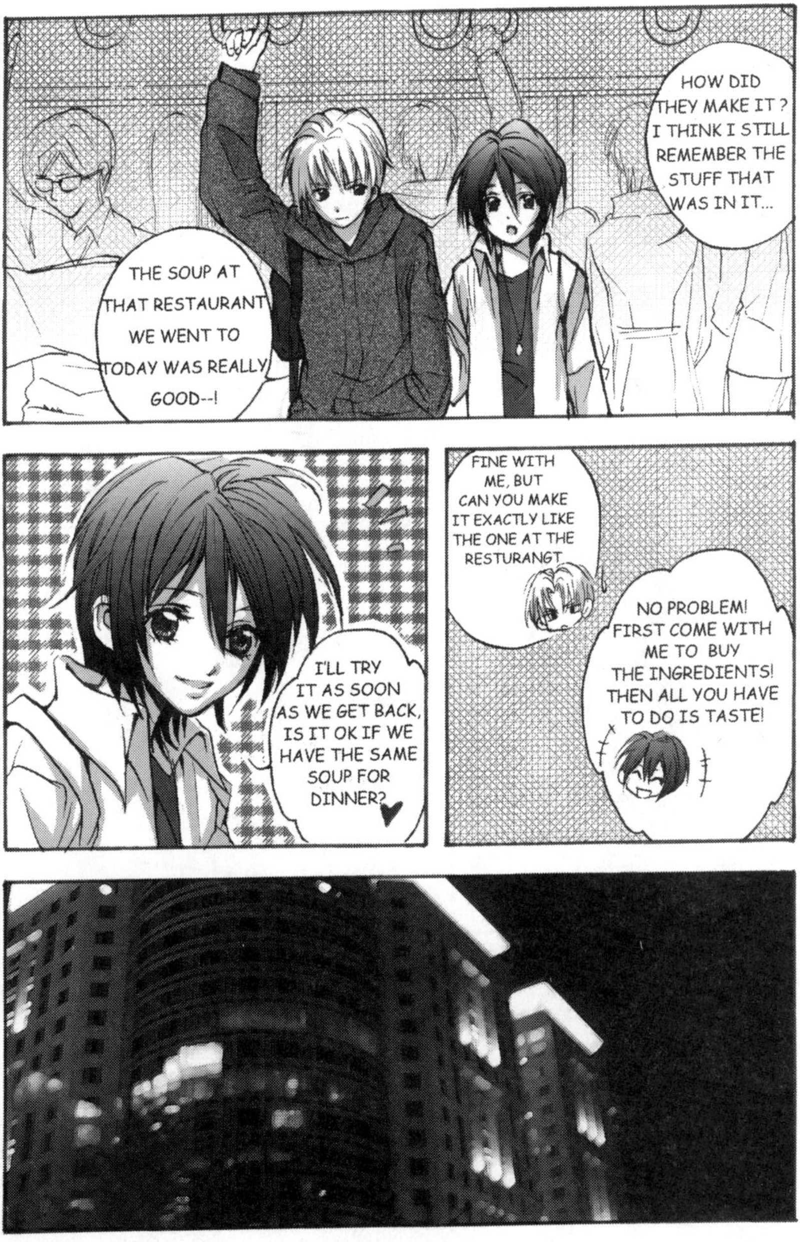
THE SOUP AT THAT RESTAURANT WE WENT TO TODAY WAS REALLY GOOD--!
HOW DID THEY MAKE IT ? I THINK I STILL REMEMBER THE STUFF THAT WAS IN IT...
I'LL TRY IT AS SOON AS WE GET BACK, IS IT OK IF WE HAVE THE SAME SOUP FOR DINNER?
FINE WITH ME, BUT CAN YOU MAKE IT EXACTLY LIKE THE ONE AT THE RESTURANGT
NO PROBLEM! FIRST COME WITH ME TO BUY THE INGREDIENTS! THEN ALL YOU HAVE TO DO IS TASTE!

- PM 5:00 - XIAO QIU'S PREPARATION TIME

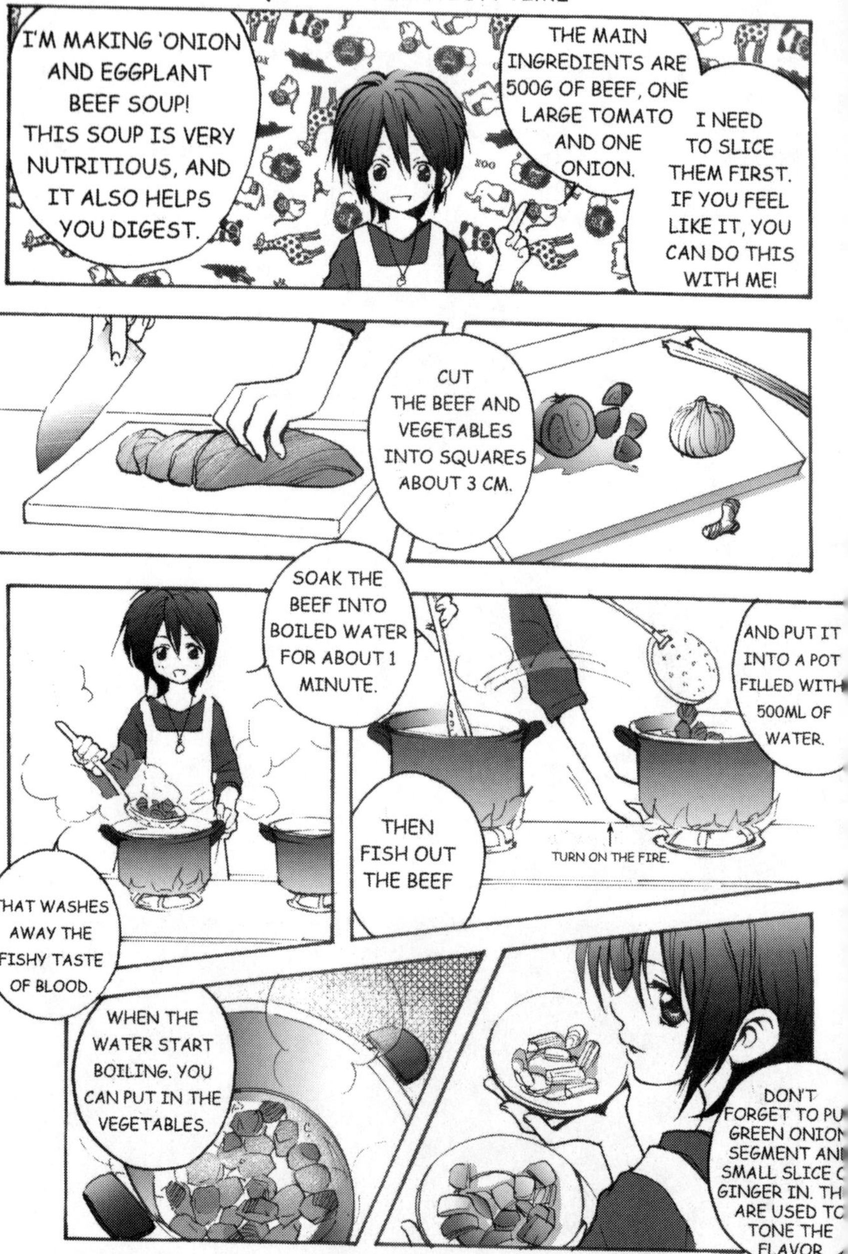
I'M MAKING 'ONION AND EGGPLANT BEEF SOUP! THIS SOUP IS VERY NUTRITIOUS, AND IT ALSO HELPS YOU DIGEST.
THE MAIN INGREDIENTS ARE 500G OF BEEF, ONE LARGE TOMATO AND ONE ONION.
I NEED TO SLICE THEM FIRST. IF YOU FEEL LIKE IT, YOU CAN DO THIS WITH ME!
CUT THE BEEF AND VEGETABLES INTO SQUARES ABOUT 3 CM.
SOAK THE BEEF INTO BOILED WATER FOR ABOUT 1 MINUTE.
AND PUT IT INTO A POT FILLED WITH 500ML OF WATER.
THEN FISH OUT THE BEEF
TURN ON THE FIRE.
THAT WASHES AWAY THE FISHY TASTE OF BLOOD.
WHEN THE WATER START BOILING. YOU CAN PUT IN THE VEGETABLES.
DON'T FORGET TO PU GREEN ONION SEGMENT AN SMALL SLICE GINGER IN. TH ARE USED TO TONE THE FLAVOR

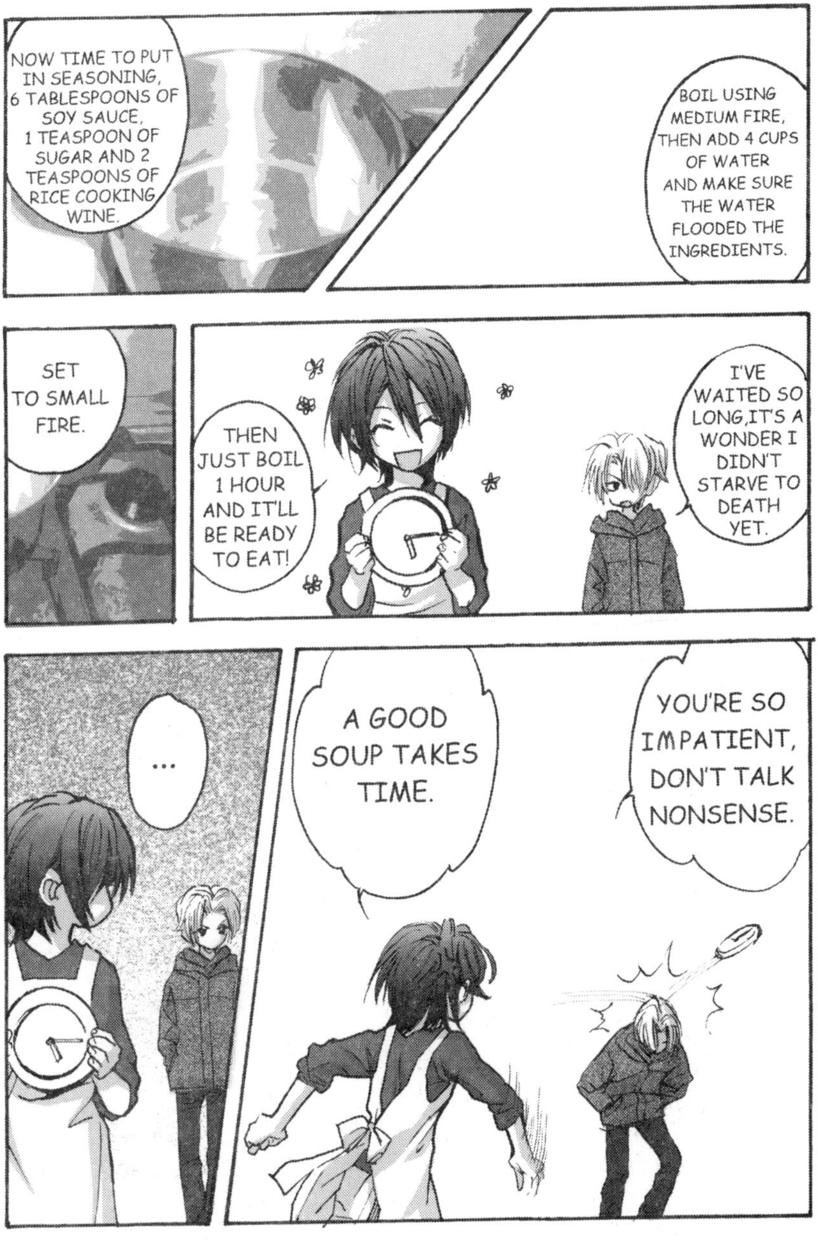

NOW TIME TO PUT IN SEASONING, 6 TABLESPOONS OF SOY SAUCE, 1 TEASPOON OF SUGAR AND 2 TEASPOONS OF RICE COOKING WINE.
BOIL USING MEDIUM FIRE, THEN ADD 4 CUPS OF WATER AND MAKE SURE THE WATER FLOODED THE INGREDIENTS.
SET TO SMALL FIRE.
THEN JUST BOIL 1 HOUR AND IT'LL BE READY TO EAT!
I'VE WAITED SO LONG,IT'S A WONDER I DIDN'T STARVE TO DEATH YET.
...
A GOOD SOUP TAKES TIME.
YOU'RE SO IMPATIENT, DON'T TALK NONSENSE.

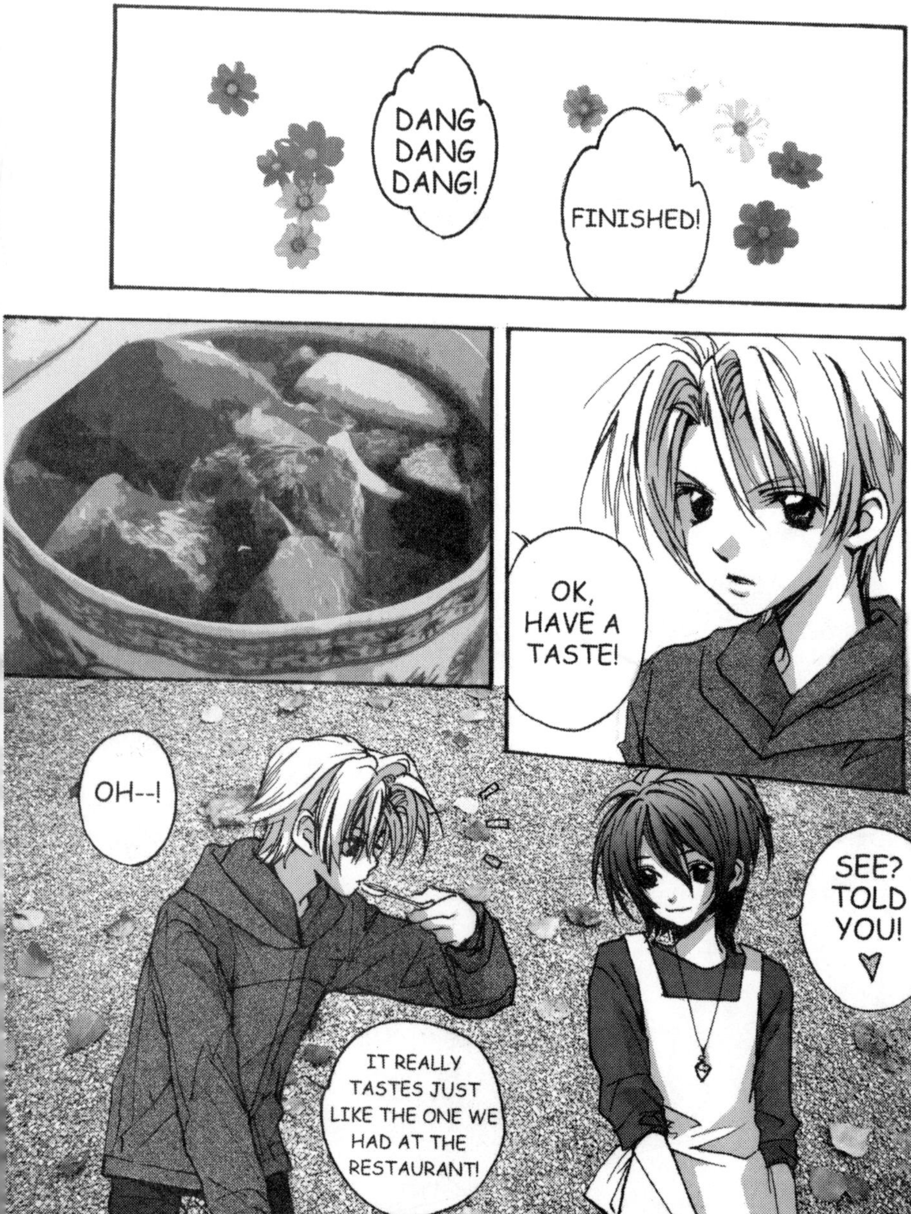
FINISHED!
DANG DANG DANG!
OK, HAVE A TASTE!
SEE? TOLD YOU! ♥
OH--!
IT REALLY TASTES JUST LIKE THE ONE WE HAD AT THE RESTAURANT!

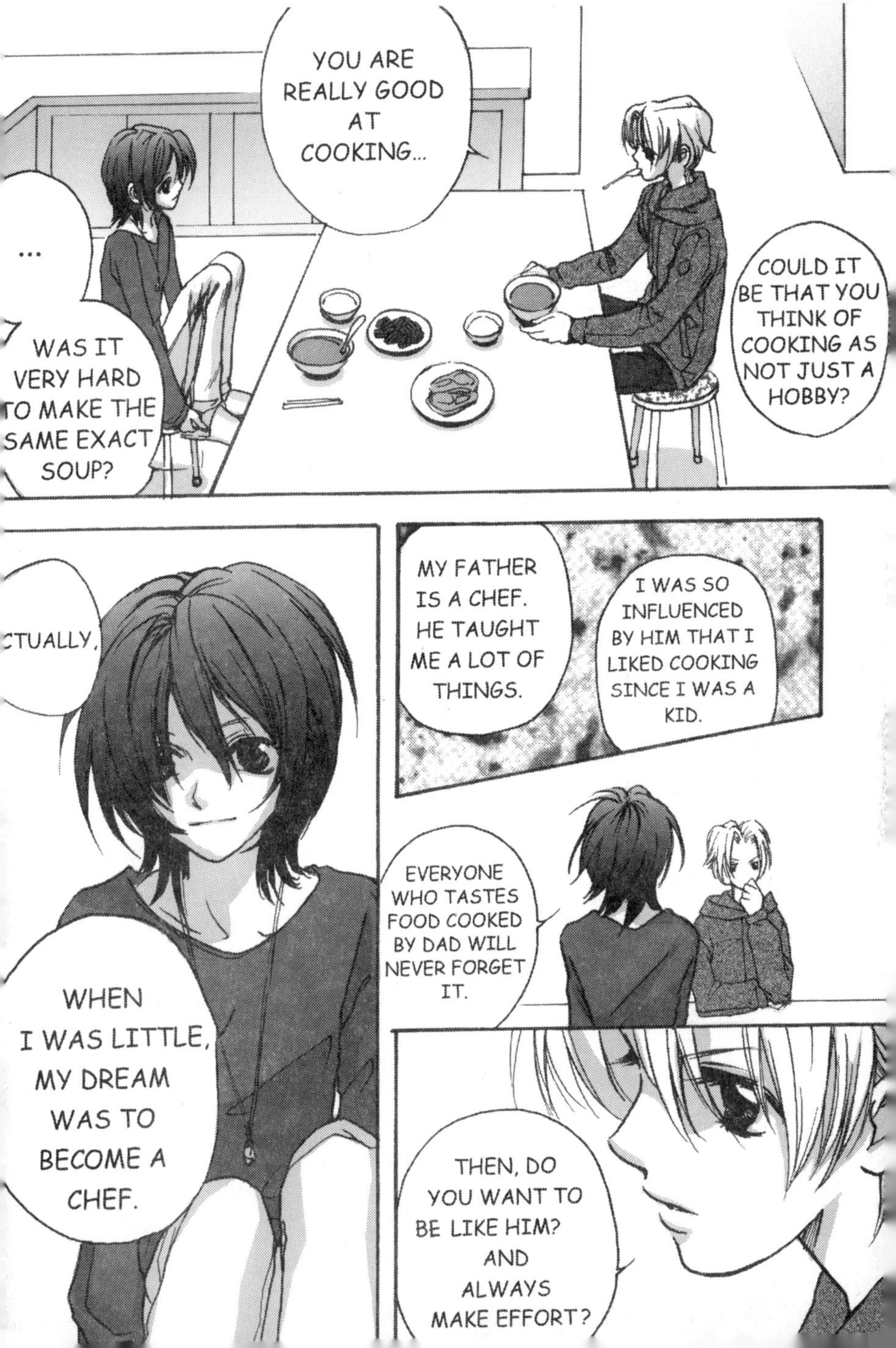

YOU ARE REALLY GOOD AT COOKING...
...
WAS IT VERY HARD TO MAKE THE SAME EXACT SOUP?
COULD IT BE THAT YOU THINK OF COOKING AS NOT JUST A HOBBY?
CTUALLY,
WHEN I WAS LITTLE, MY DREAM WAS TO BECOME A CHEF.
MY FATHER IS A CHEF. HE TAUGHT ME A LOT OF THINGS.
I WAS SO INFLUENCED BY HIM THAT I LIKED COOKING SINCE I WAS A KID.
EVERYONE WHO TASTES FOOD COOKED BY DAD WILL NEVER FORGET IT.
THEN, DO YOU WANT TO BE LIKE HIM? AND ALWAYS MAKE EFFORT?

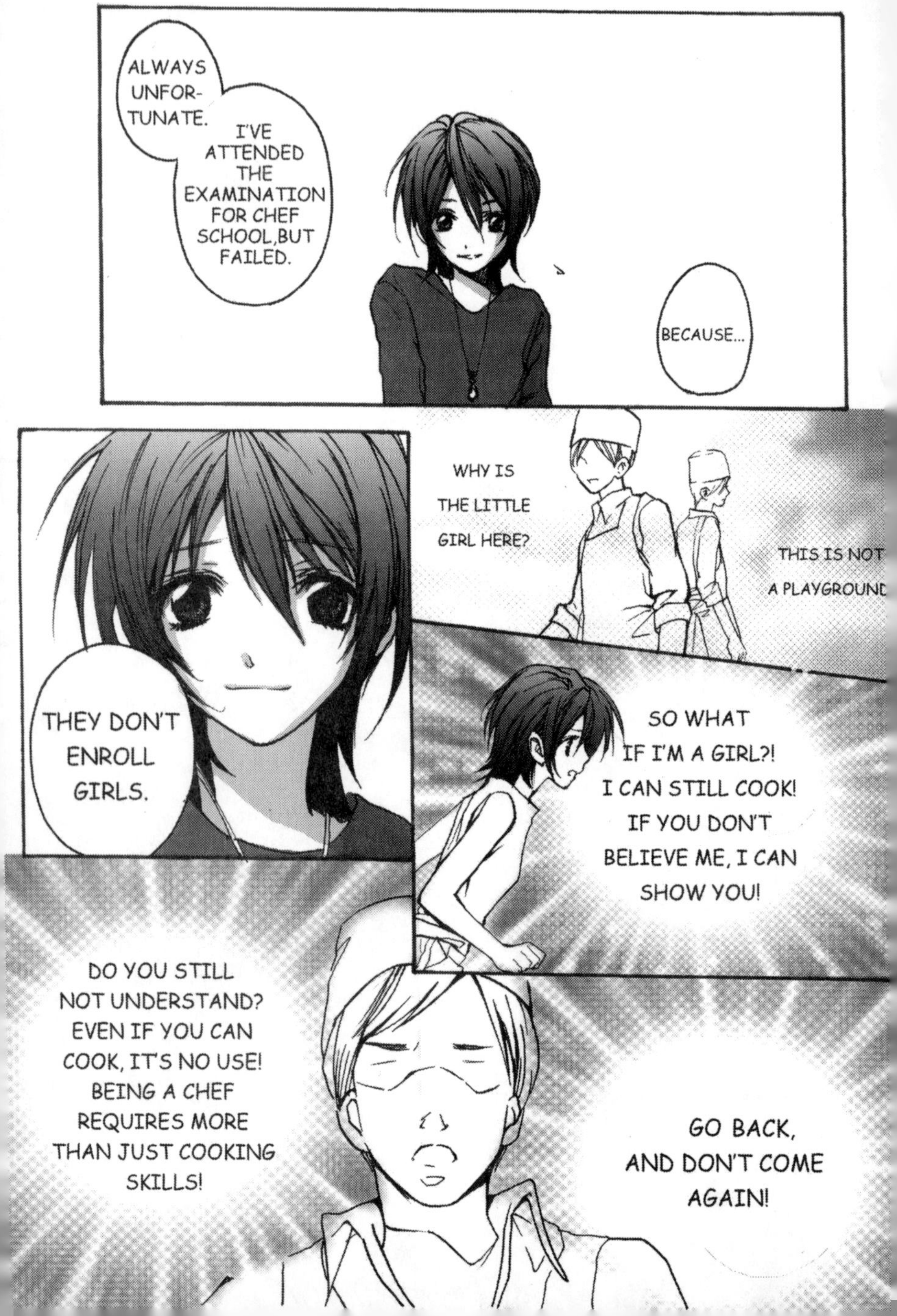
ALWAYS UNFOR-TUNATE.
I'VE ATTENDED THE EXAMINATION FOR CHEF SCHOOL,BUT FAILED.
BECAUSE...
THEY DON'T ENROLL GIRLS.
WHY IS THE LITTLE GIRL HERE?
THIS IS NOT A PLAYGROUND
SO WHAT IF I'M A GIRL?! I CAN STILL COOK! IF YOU DON'T BELIEVE ME, I CAN SHOW YOU!
DO YOU STILL NOT UNDERSTAND? EVEN IF YOU CAN COOK, IT'S NO USE! BEING A CHEF REQUIRES MORE THAN JUST COOKING SKILLS!
GO BACK, AND DON'T COME AGAIN!

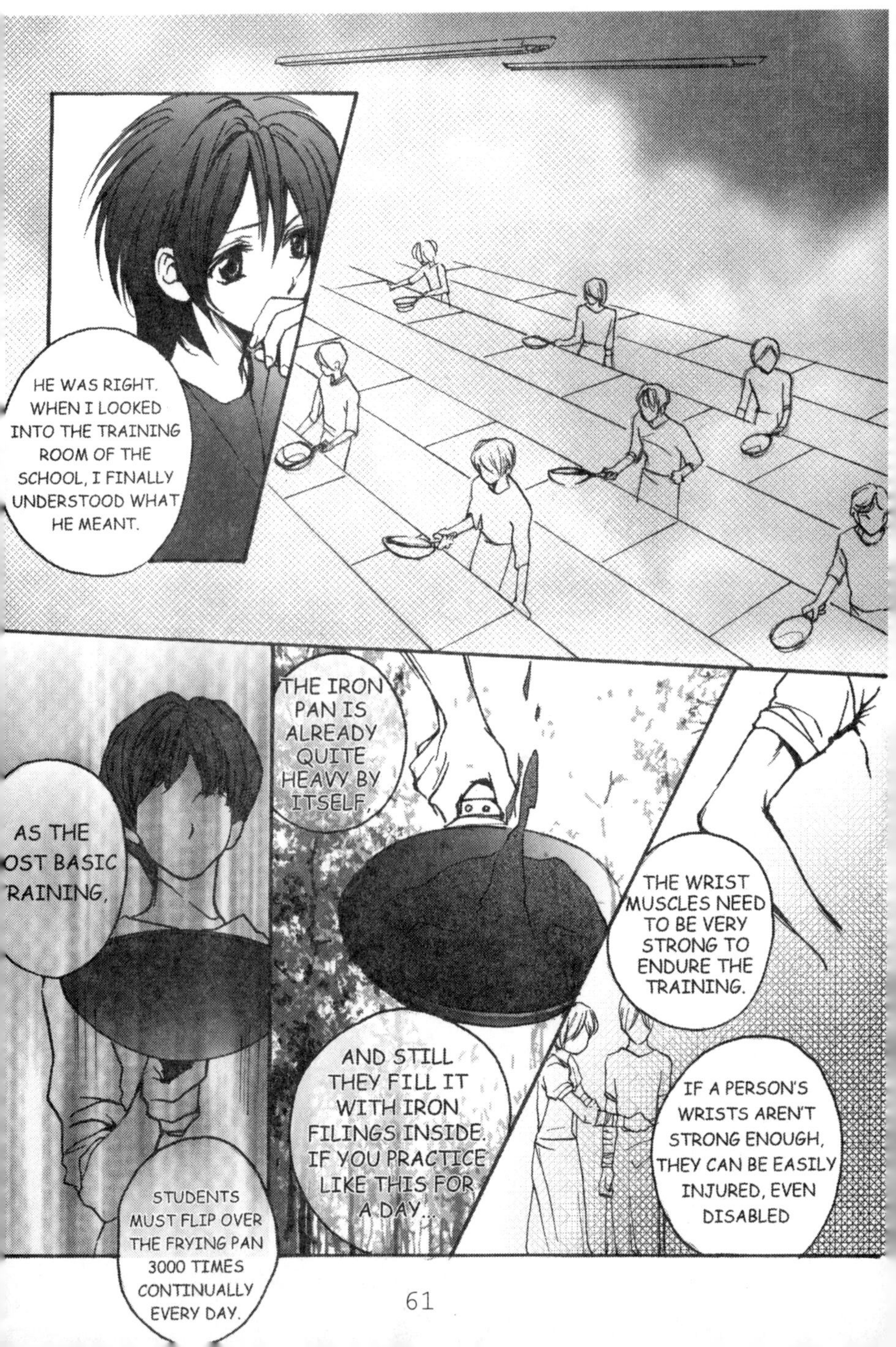
HE WAS RIGHT. WHEN I LOOKED INTO THE TRAINING ROOM OF THE SCHOOL, I FINALLY UNDERSTOOD WHAT HE MEANT.
AS THE OST BASIC RAINING,
STUDENTS MUST FLIP OVER THE FRYING PAN 3000 TIMES CONTINUALLY EVERY DAY.
THE IRON PAN IS ALREADY QUITE HEAVY BY ITSELF,
AND STILL THEY FILL IT WITH IRON FILINGS INSIDE. IF YOU PRACTICE LIKE THIS FOR A DAY...
THE WRIST MUSCLES NEED TO BE VERY STRONG TO ENDURE THE TRAINING.
IF A PERSON'S WRISTS AREN'T STRONG ENOUGH, THEY CAN BE EASILY INJURED, EVEN DISABLED

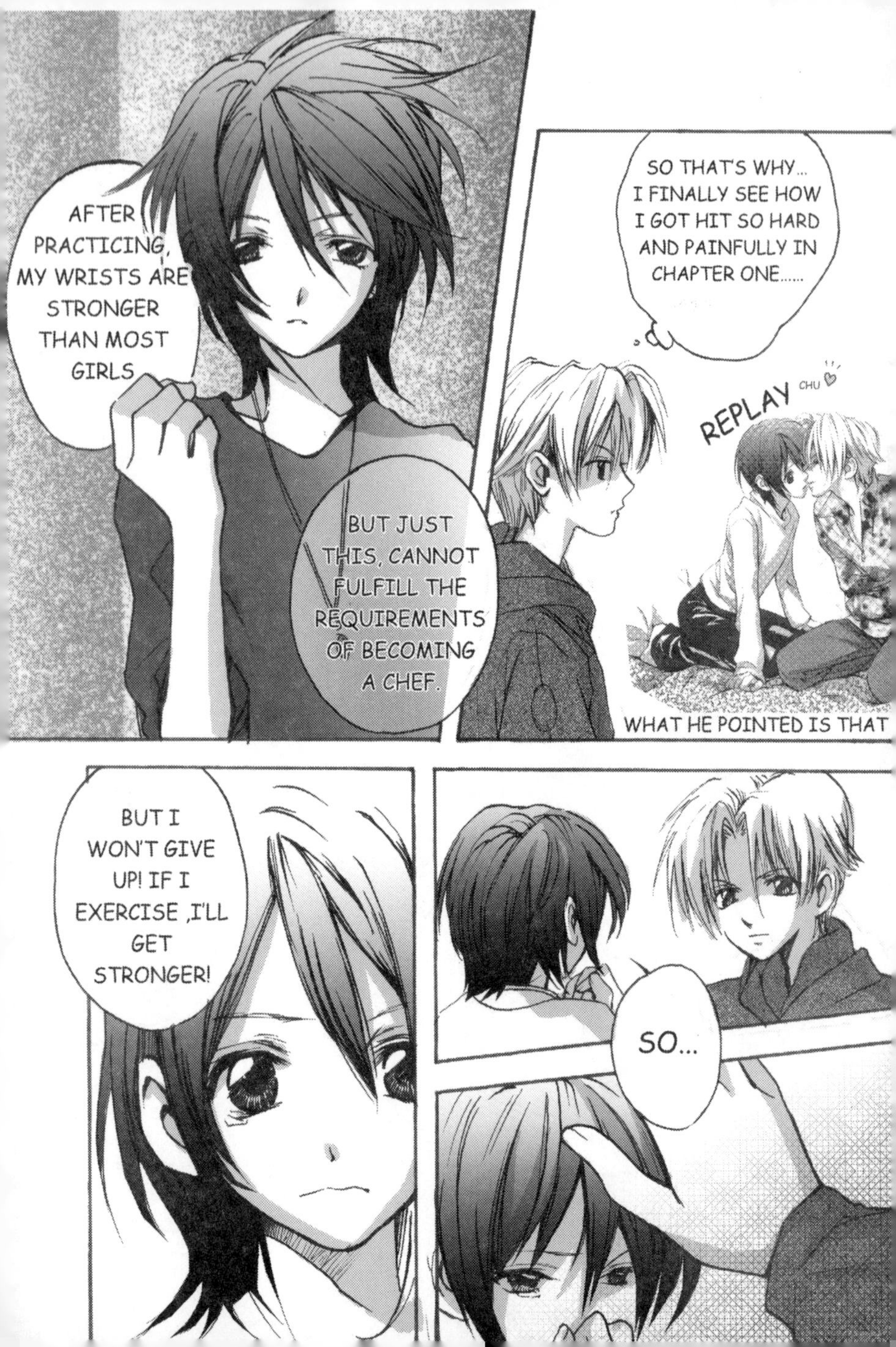
AFTER PRACTICING, MY WRISTS ARE STRONGER THAN MOST GIRLS
BUT JUST THIS, CANNOT FULFILL THE REQUIREMENTS OF BECOMING A CHEF.
SO THAT'S WHY... I FINALLY SEE HOW I GOT HIT SO HARD AND PAINFULLY IN CHAPTER ONE......
REPLAY
CHU
WHAT HE POINTED IS THAT
BUT I WON'T GIVE UP! IF I EXERCISE ,I'LL GET STRONGER!
SO...

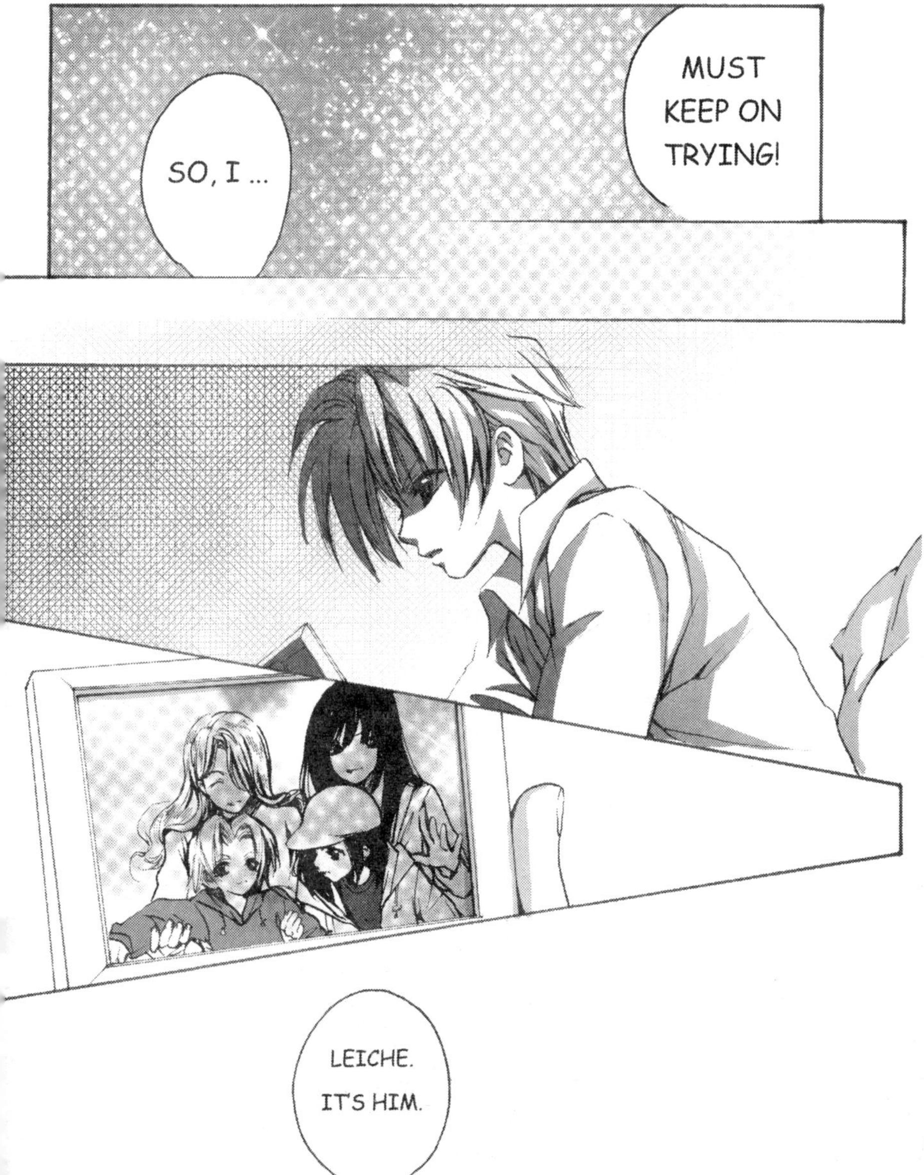
MUST KEEP ON TRYING!
SO, I ...
LEICHE. IT'S HIM.

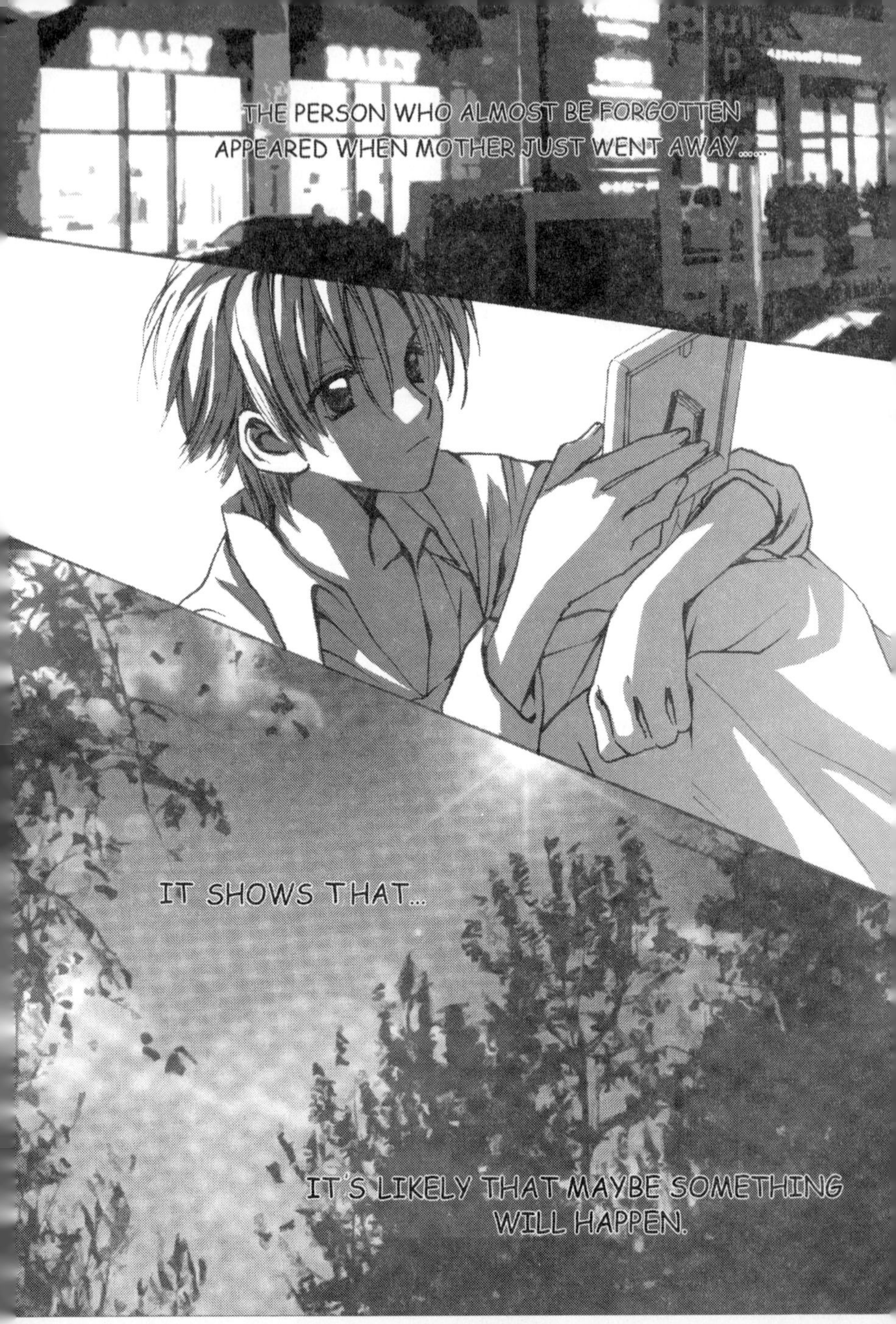

BALLY
BALLY
THE PERSON WHO ALMOST BE FORGOTTEN
APPEARED WHEN MOTHER JUST WENT AWAY......
IT SHOWS THAT...
IT'S LIKELY THAT MAYBE SOMETHING
WILL HAPPEN.

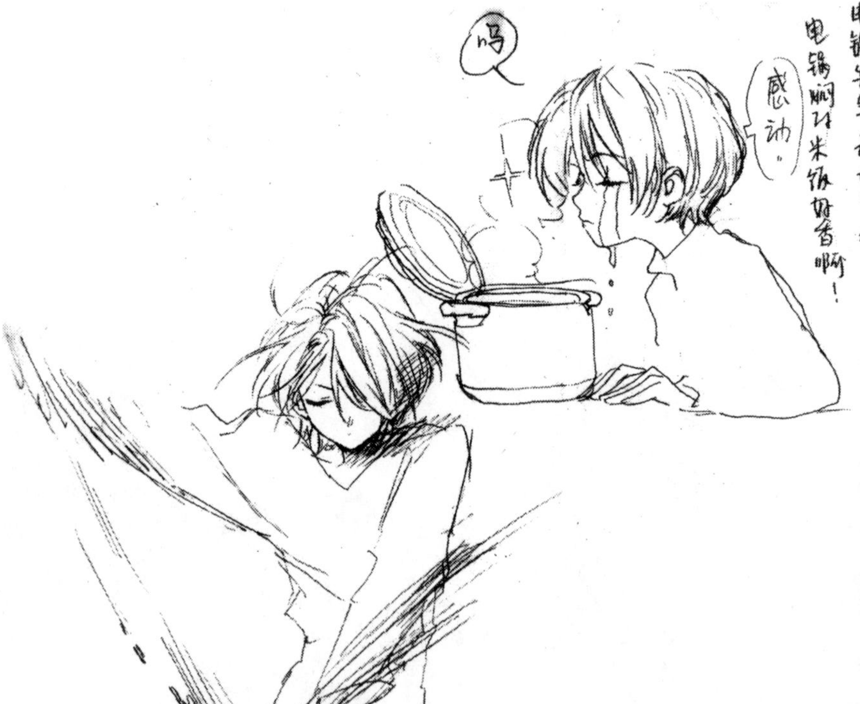
电锅先生，我好崇拜
电锅啊！！米饭好香啊！
感动。
呜

BIRTHDAY

Vol.3

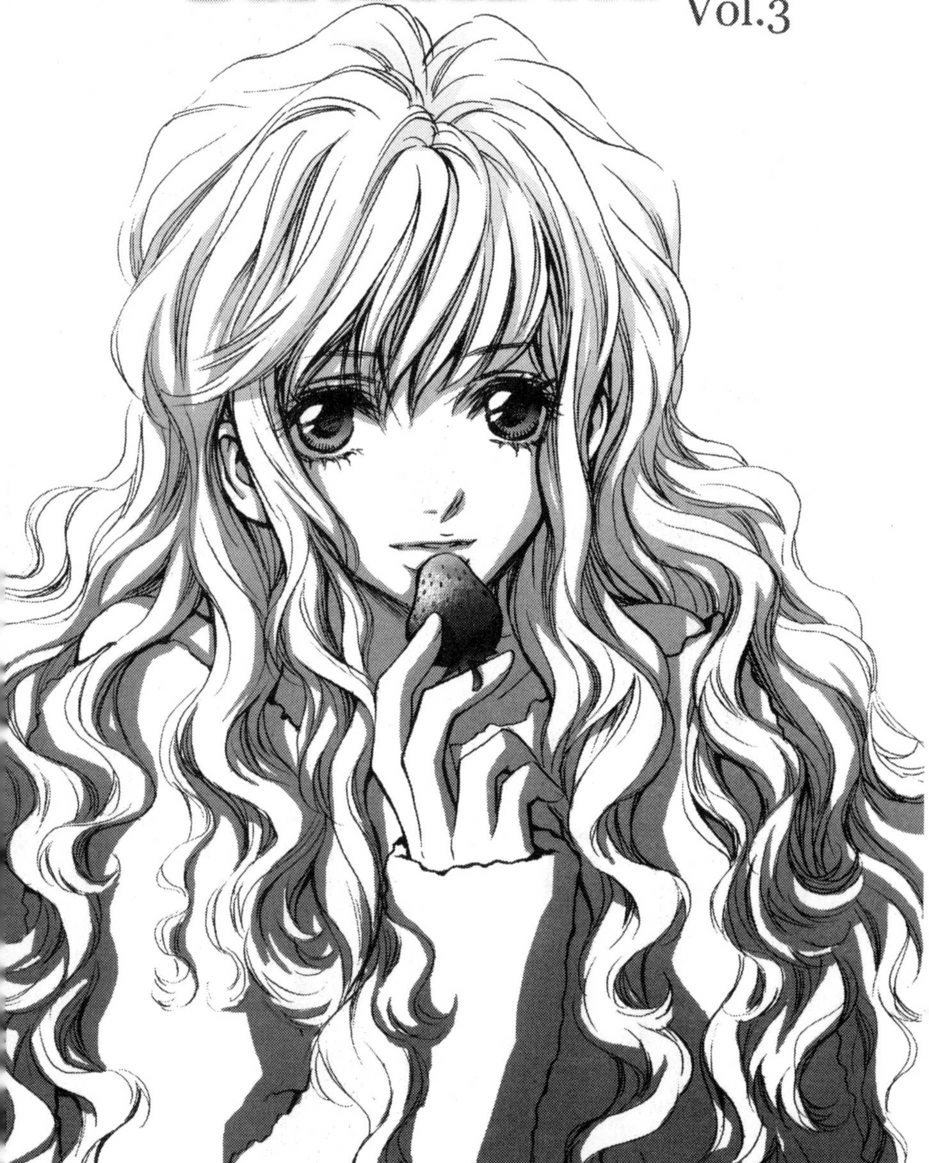

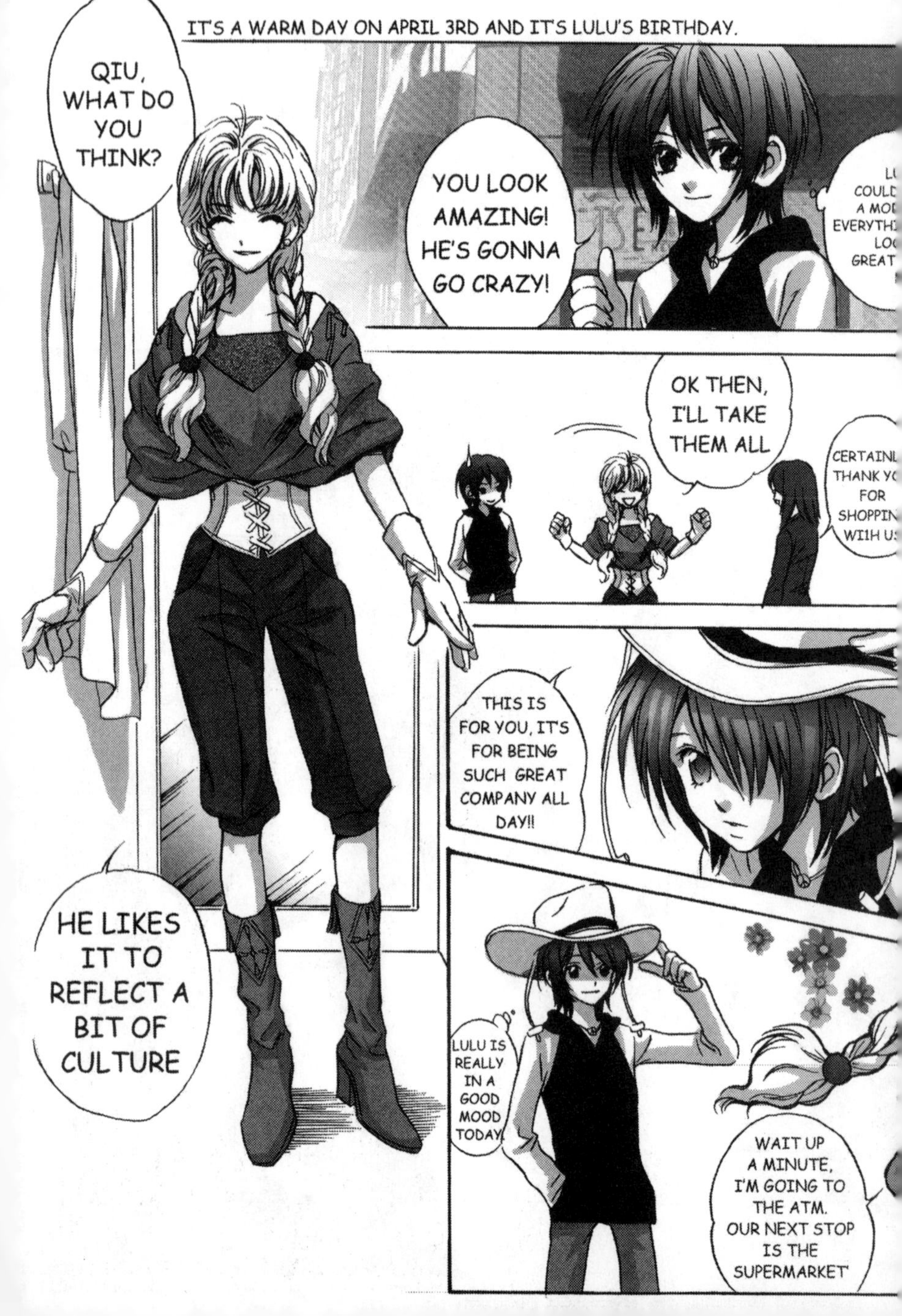

IT'S A WARM DAY ON APRIL 3RD AND IT'S LULU'S BIRTHDAY.
QIU, WHAT DO YOU THINK?
HE LIKES IT TO REFLECT A BIT OF CULTURE
YOU LOOK AMAZING! HE'S GONNA GO CRAZY!
LU COULD A MOD EVERYTHI LO GREAT
OK THEN, I'LL TAKE THEM ALL
CERTAINL THANK YO FOR SHOPPIN WI1H U
THIS IS FOR YOU, IT'S FOR BEING SUCH GREAT COMPANY ALL DAY!!
LULU IS REALLY IN A GOOD MOOD TODAY
WAIT UP A MINUTE, I'M GOING TO THE ATM. OUR NEXT STOP IS THE SUPERMARKET'

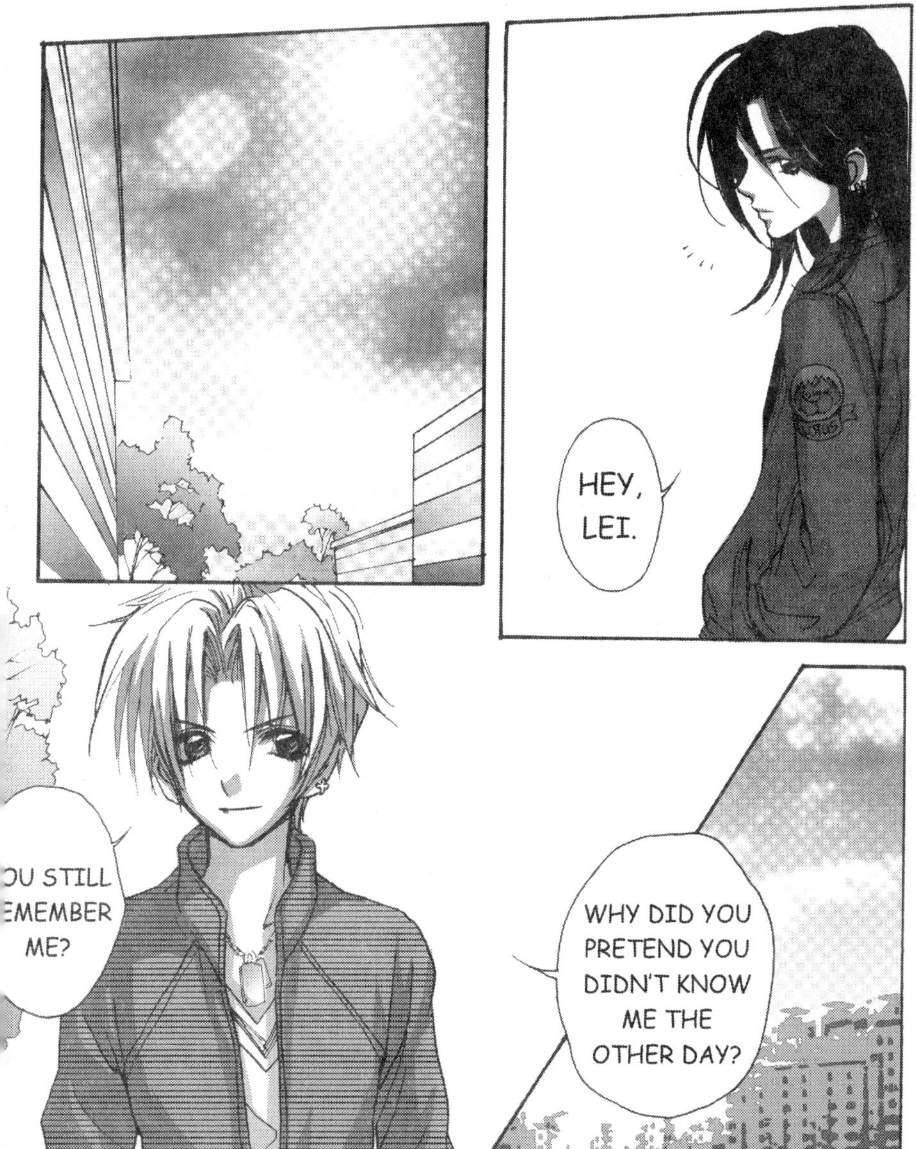
HEY, LEI.
OU STILL EMEMBER ME?
WHY DID YOU PRETEND YOU DIDN'T KNOW ME THE OTHER DAY?

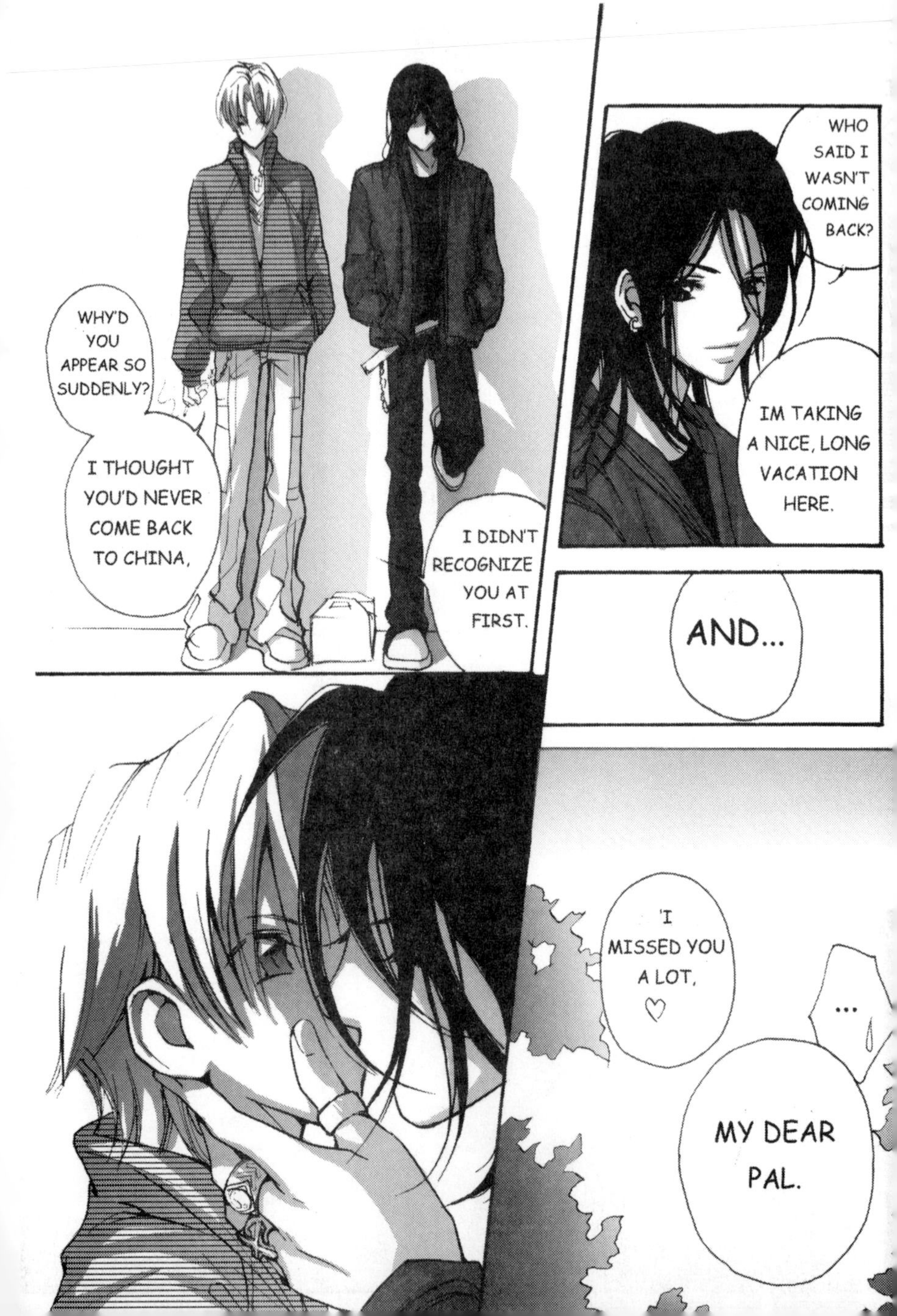
WHY'D YOU APPEAR SO SUDDENLY?
I THOUGHT YOU'D NEVER COME BACK TO CHINA,
I DIDN'T RECOGNIZE YOU AT FIRST.
WHO SAID I WASN'T COMING BACK?
IM TAKING A NICE, LONG VACATION HERE.
AND...
'I MISSED YOU A LOT, ♡
...
MY DEAR PAL.

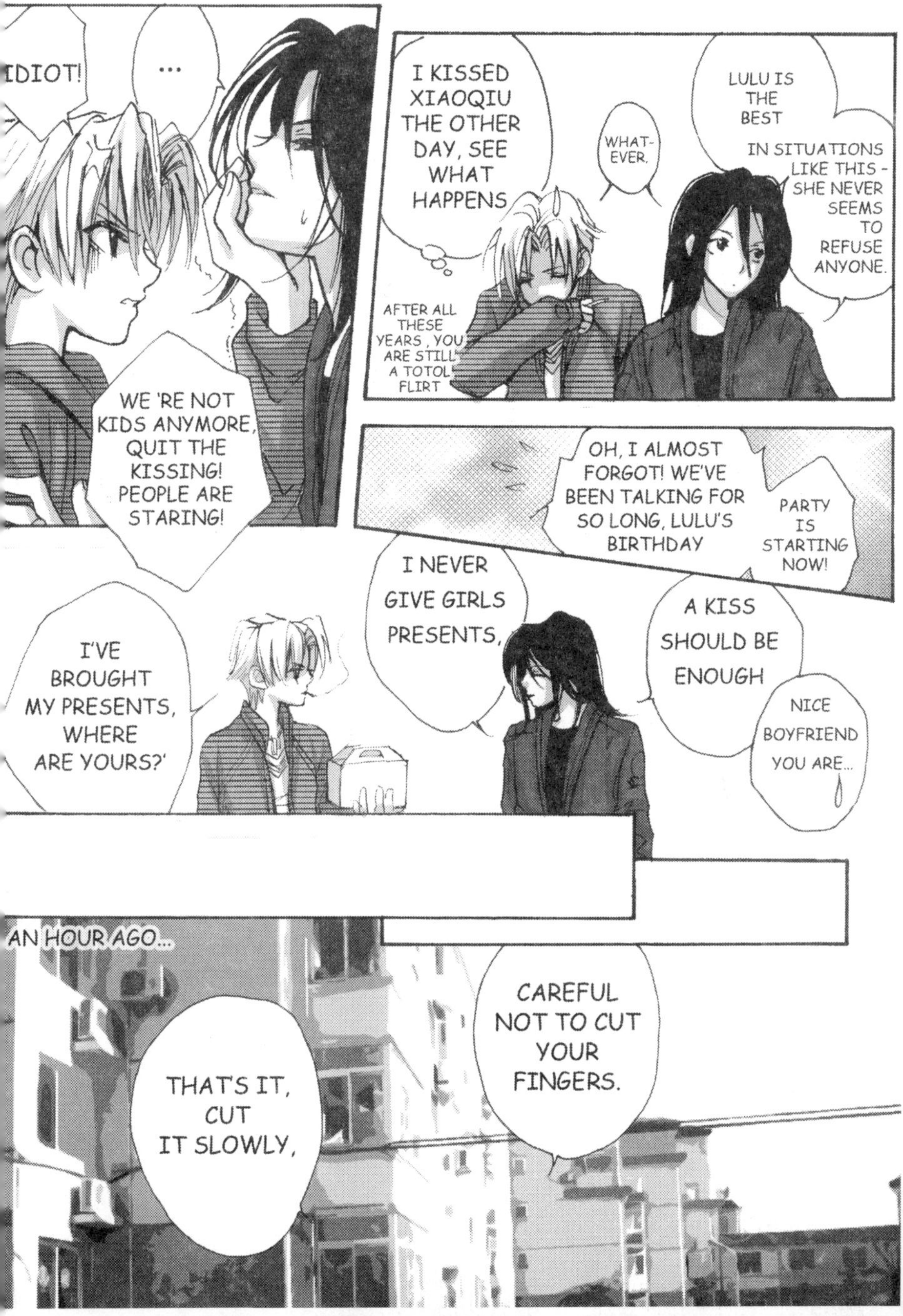
IDIOT!
...
WE 'RE NOT KIDS ANYMORE, QUIT THE KISSING! PEOPLE ARE STARING!
I KISSED XIAOQIU THE OTHER DAY, SEE WHAT HAPPENS
WHAT-EVER.
LULU IS THE BEST
IN SITUATIONS LIKE THIS - SHE NEVER SEEMS TO REFUSE ANYONE.
AFTER ALL THESE YEARS , YOU ARE STILL A TOTOL FLIRT
OH, I ALMOST FORGOT! WE'VE BEEN TALKING FOR SO LONG, LULU'S BIRTHDAY
PARTY IS STARTING NOW!
I'VE BROUGHT MY PRESENTS, WHERE ARE YOURS?'
I NEVER GIVE GIRLS PRESENTS,
A KISS SHOULD BE ENOUGH
NICE BOYFRIEND YOU ARE...
AN HOUR AGO...
CAREFUL NOT TO CUT YOUR FINGERS.
THAT'S IT, CUT IT SLOWLY,

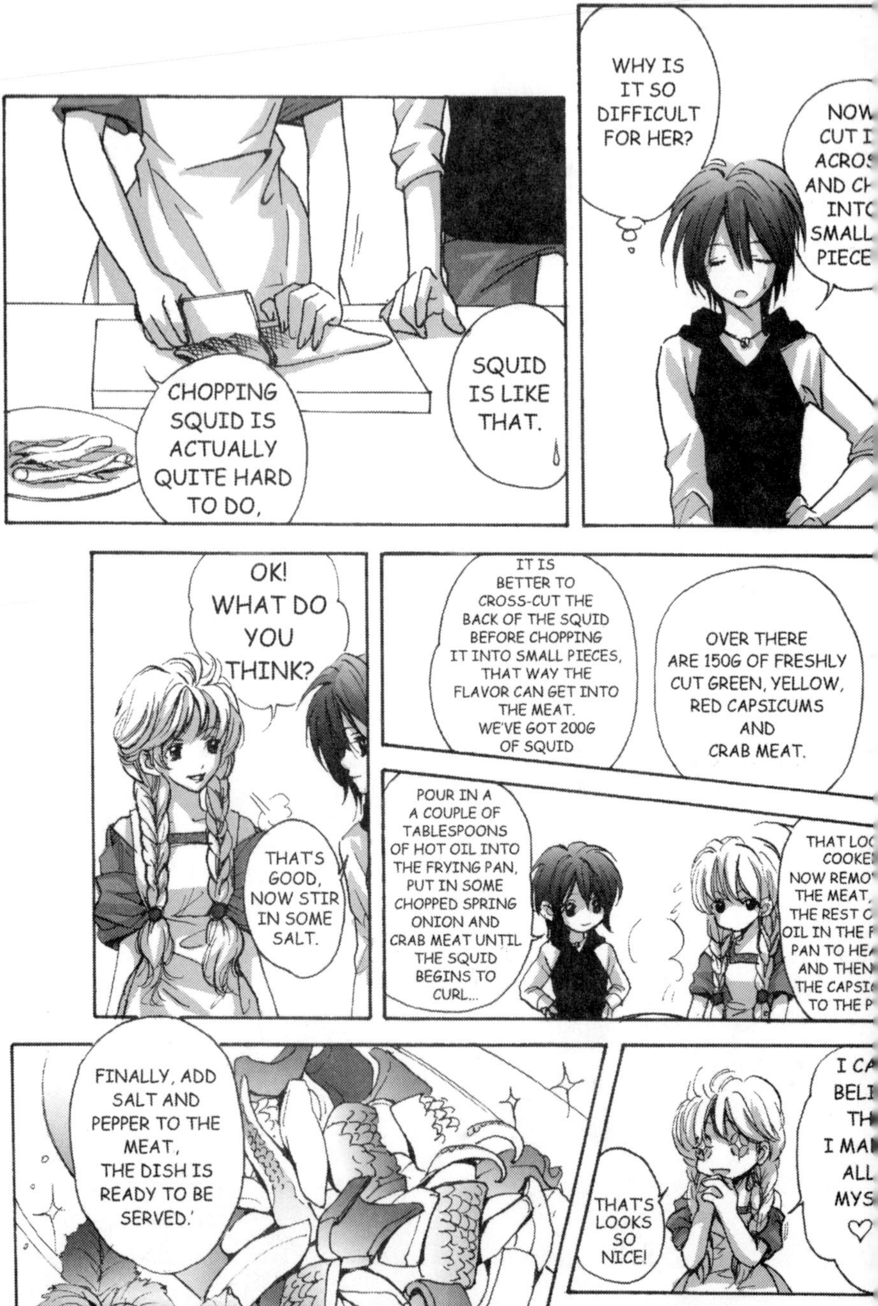

NOW CUT I ACROS AND CH INTO SMALL PIECE
WHY IS IT SO DIFFICULT FOR HER?
CHOPPING SQUID IS ACTUALLY QUITE HARD TO DO,
SQUID IS LIKE THAT.
IT IS BETTER TO CROSS-CUT THE BACK OF THE SQUID BEFORE CHOPPING IT INTO SMALL PIECES, THAT WAY THE FLAVOR CAN GET INTO THE MEAT. WE'VE GOT 200G OF SQUID
OVER THERE ARE 150G OF FRESHLY CUT GREEN, YELLOW, RED CAPSICUMS AND CRAB MEAT.
POUR IN A A COUPLE OF TABLESPOONS OF HOT OIL INTO THE FRYING PAN, PUT IN SOME CHOPPED SPRING ONION AND CRAB MEAT UNTIL THE SQUID BEGINS TO CURL...
THAT LOO COOKE NOW REMO THE MEAT, THE REST O OIL IN THE F PAN TO HEA AND THEN THE CAPSI TO THE P
OK! WHAT DO YOU THINK?
THAT'S GOOD, NOW STIR IN SOME SALT.
I CA BELI TH I MA ALL MYS ♡
THAT'S LOOKS SO NICE!
FINALLY, ADD SALT AND PEPPER TO THE MEAT., THE DISH IS READY TO BE SERVED.'

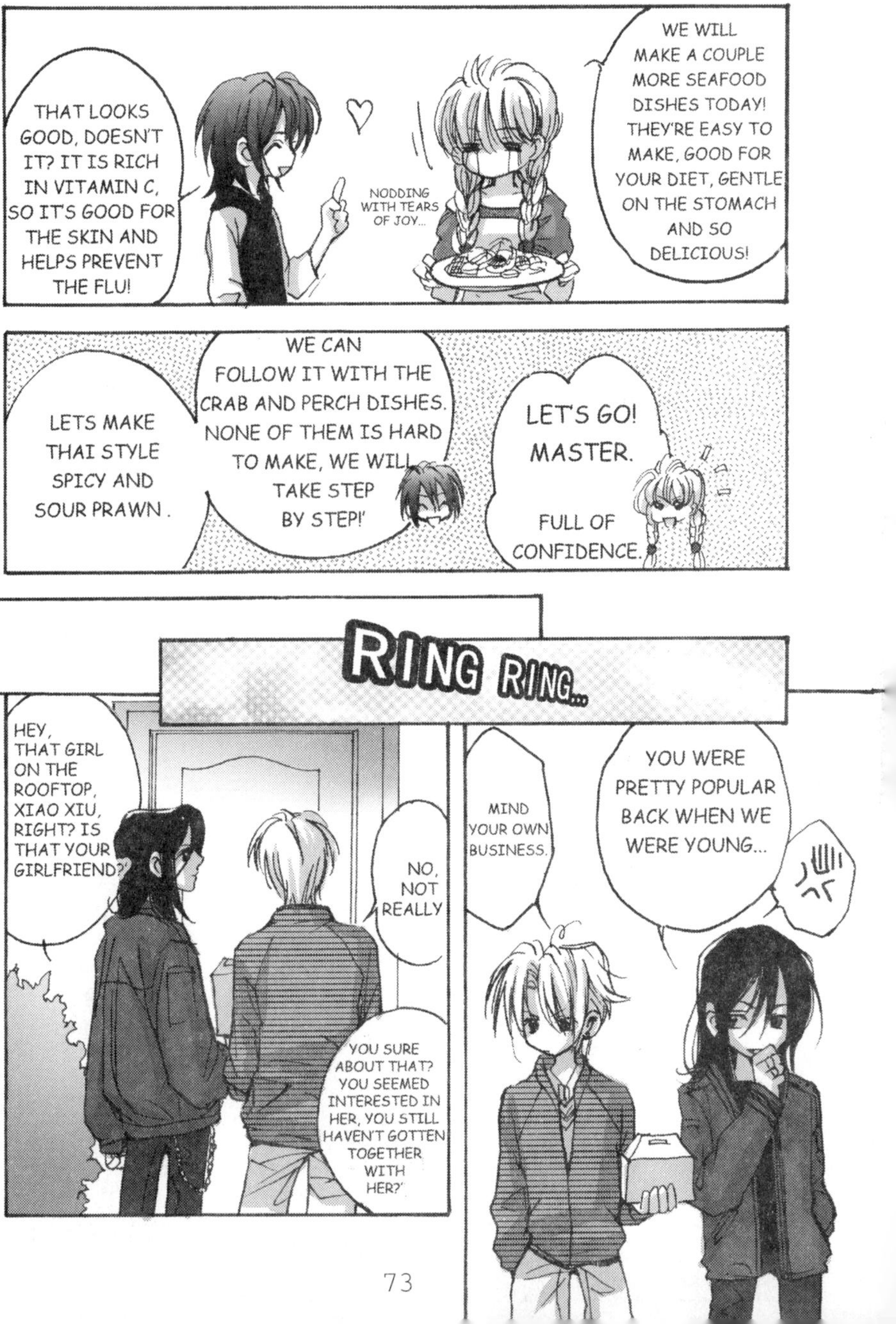
THAT LOOKS GOOD, DOESN'T IT? IT IS RICH IN VITAMIN C, SO IT'S GOOD FOR THE SKIN AND HELPS PREVENT THE FLU!
NODDING WITH TEARS OF JOY...
WE WILL MAKE A COUPLE MORE SEAFOOD DISHES TODAY! THEY'RE EASY TO MAKE, GOOD FOR YOUR DIET, GENTLE ON THE STOMACH AND SO DELICIOUS!
LETS MAKE THAI STYLE SPICY AND SOUR PRAWN .
WE CAN FOLLOW IT WITH THE CRAB AND PERCH DISHES. NONE OF THEM IS HARD TO MAKE, WE WILL TAKE STEP BY STEP!'
LET'S GO! MASTER.
FULL OF CONFIDENCE.
RING RING...
HEY, THAT GIRL ON THE ROOFTOP, XIAO XIU, RIGHT? IS THAT YOUR GIRLFRIEND?'
NO, NOT REALLY
YOU SURE ABOUT THAT? YOU SEEMED INTERESTED IN HER, YOU STILL HAVEN'T GOTTEN TOGETHER WITH HER?'
MIND YOUR OWN BUSINESS.
YOU WERE PRETTY POPULAR BACK WHEN WE WERE YOUNG...

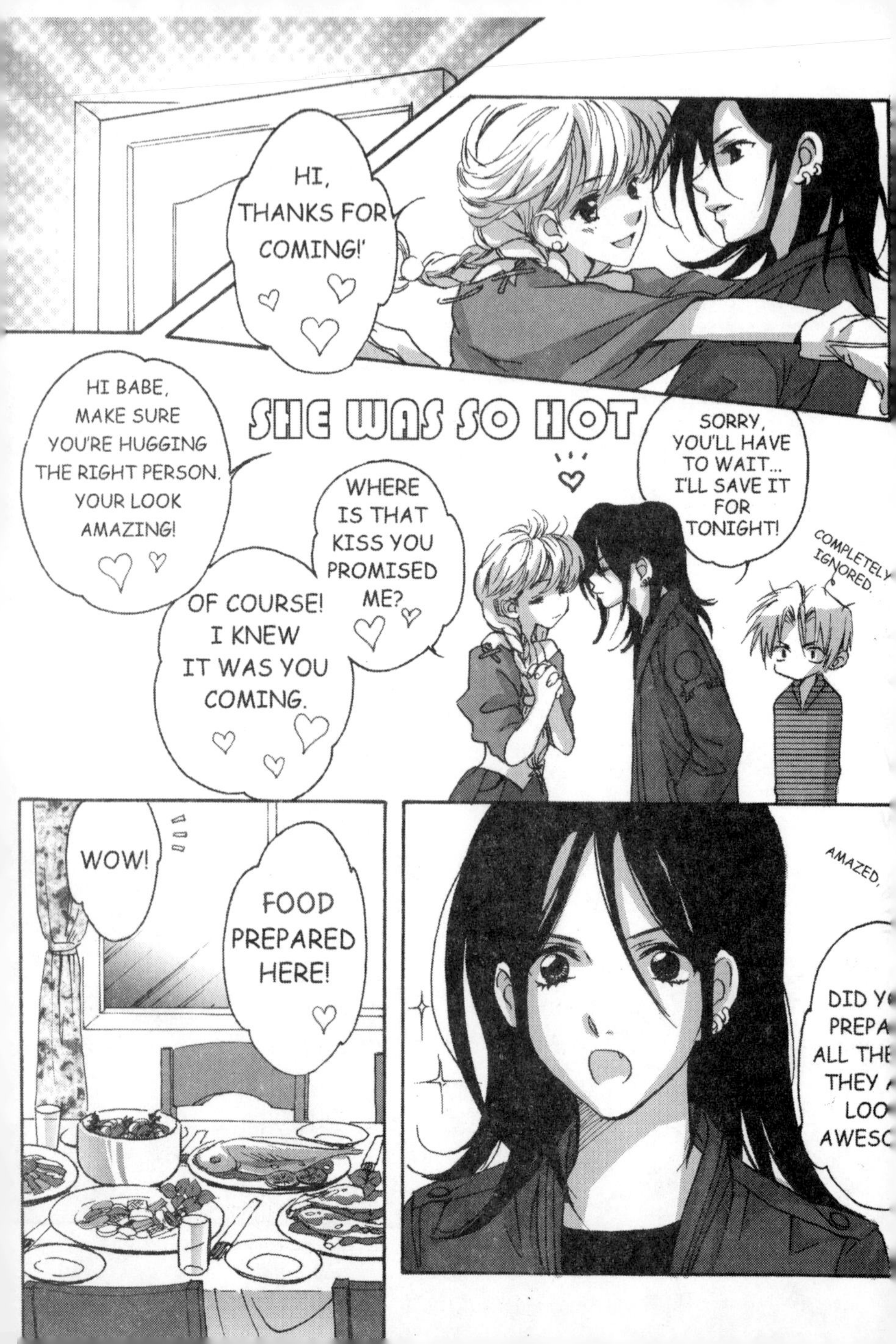
HI, THANKS FOR COMING!'
HI BABE, MAKE SURE YOU'RE HUGGING THE RIGHT PERSON. YOUR LOOK AMAZING!
SHE WAS SO HOT
SORRY, YOU'LL HAVE TO WAIT... I'LL SAVE IT FOR TONIGHT!
WHERE IS THAT KISS YOU PROMISED ME?
OF COURSE! I KNEW IT WAS YOU COMING.
COMPLETELY IGNORED.
WOW!
FOOD PREPARED HERE!
AMAZED,

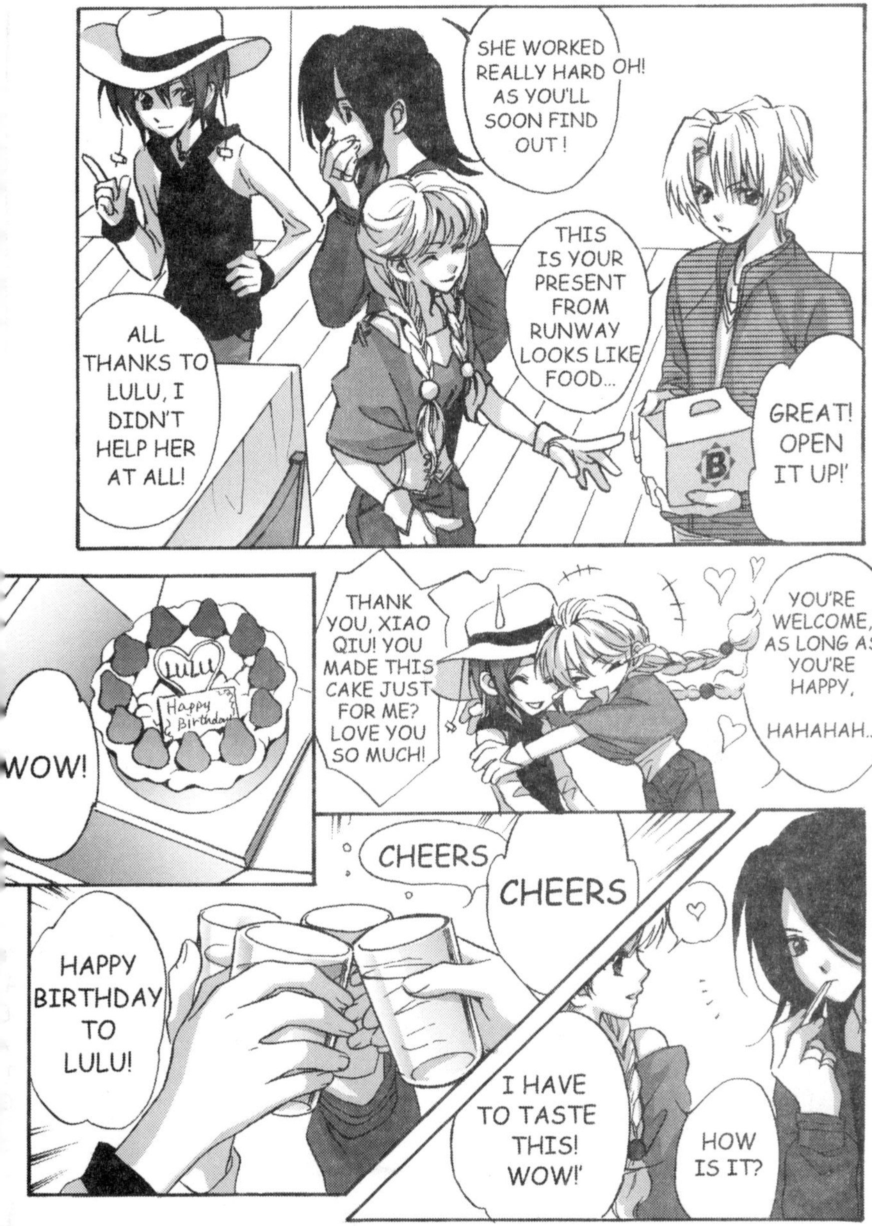
SHE WORKED REALLY HARD AS YOU'LL SOON FIND OUT !
OH!
THIS IS YOUR PRESENT FROM RUNWAY LOOKS LIKE FOOD...
ALL THANKS TO LULU, I DIDN'T HELP HER AT ALL!
GREAT! OPEN IT UP!'
LULU
Happy Birthday
WOW!
THANK YOU, XIAO QIU! YOU MADE THIS CAKE JUST FOR ME? LOVE YOU SO MUCH!
YOU'RE WELCOME, AS LONG AS YOU'RE HAPPY,
HAHAHAH...
CHEERS
CHEERS
HAPPY BIRTHDAY TO LULU!
I HAVE TO TASTE THIS! WOW!'
HOW IS IT?

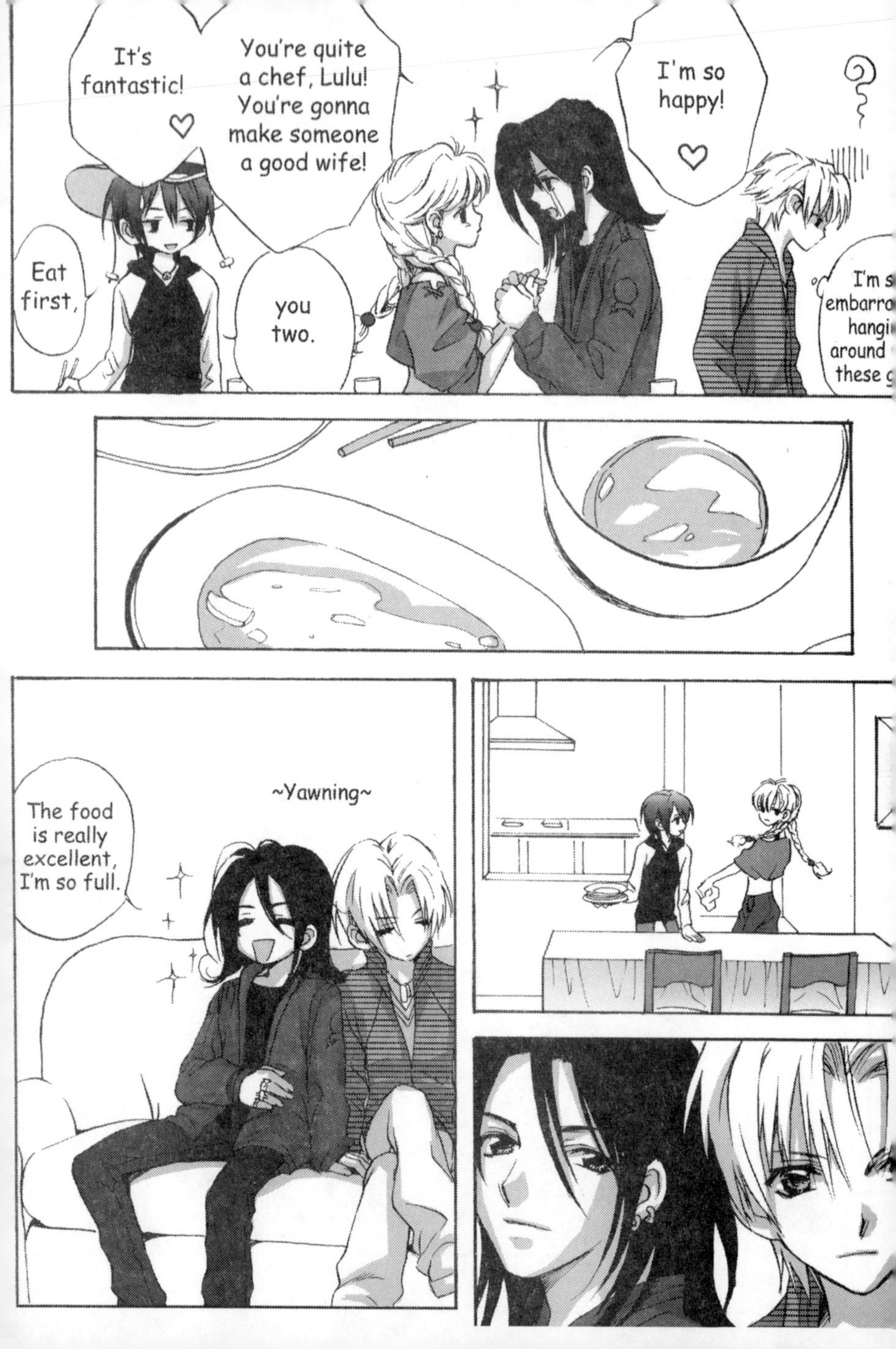

It's fantastic! ♡
You're quite a chef, Lulu! You're gonna make someone a good wife!
I'm so happy! ♡
Eat first,
you two.
I'm s embarra hangi around these g
~Yawning~
The food is really excellent, I'm so full.

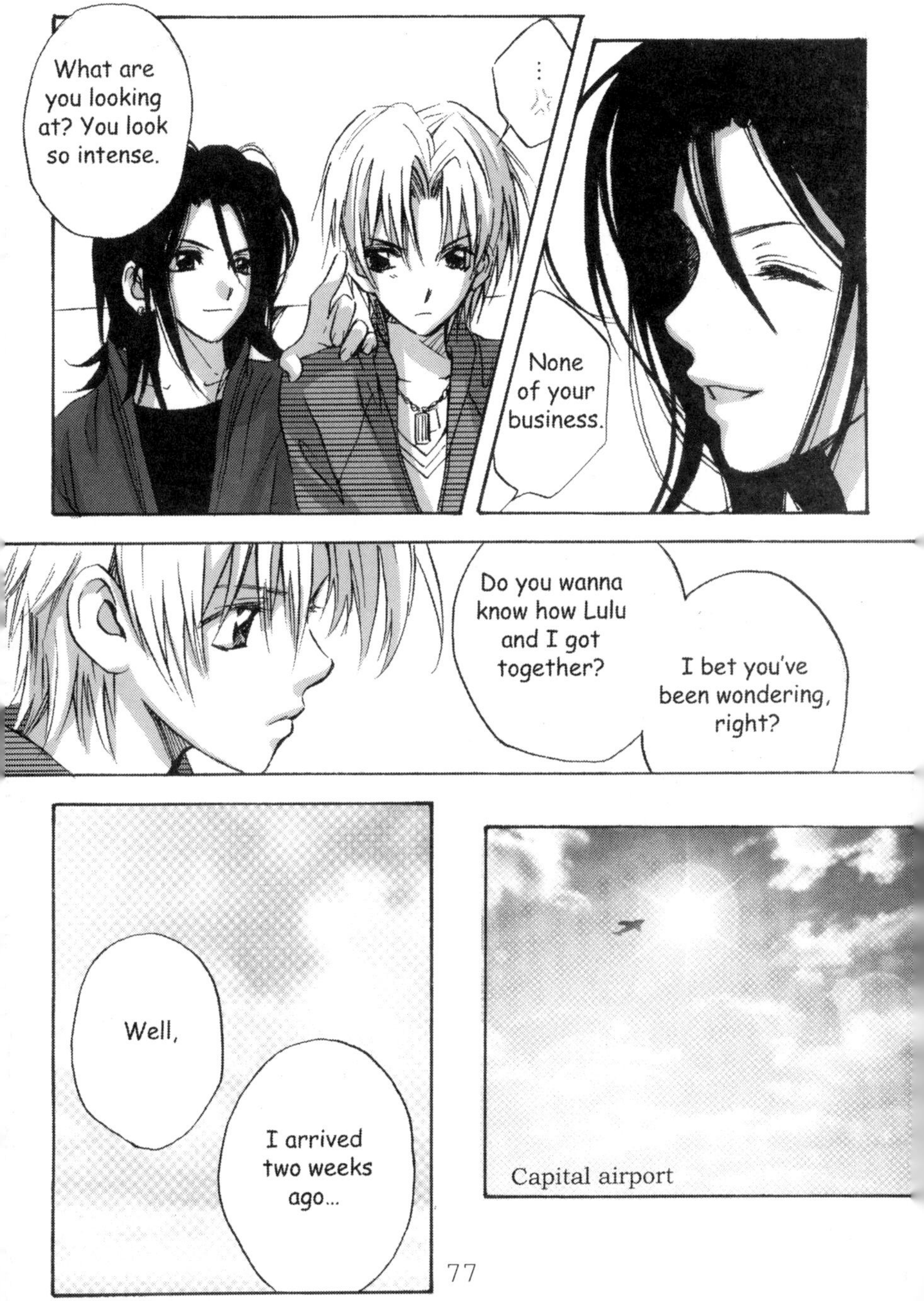
What are you looking at? You look so intense.
…
None of your business.
Do you wanna know how Lulu and I got together?
I bet you've been wondering, right?
Well,
I arrived two weeks ago...
Capital airport

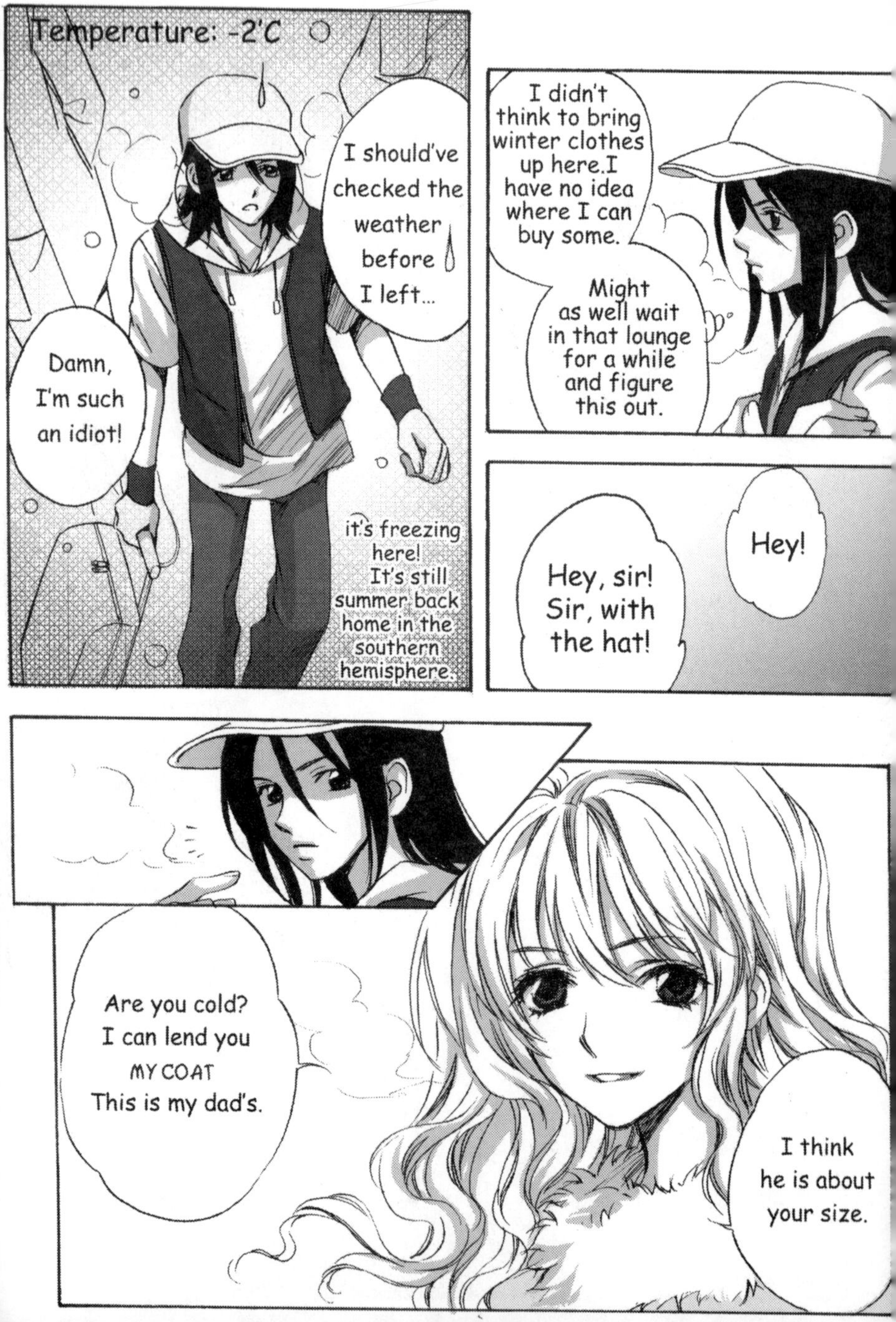
Temperature: -2'C
I should've checked the weather before I left...
Damn, I'm such an idiot!
it's freezing here! It's still summer back home in the southern hemisphere.
I didn't think to bring winter clothes up here.I have no idea where I can buy some.
Might as well wait in that lounge for a while and figure this out.
Hey!
Hey, sir! Sir, with the hat!
Are you cold? I can lend you MY COAT This is my dad's.
I think he is about your size.

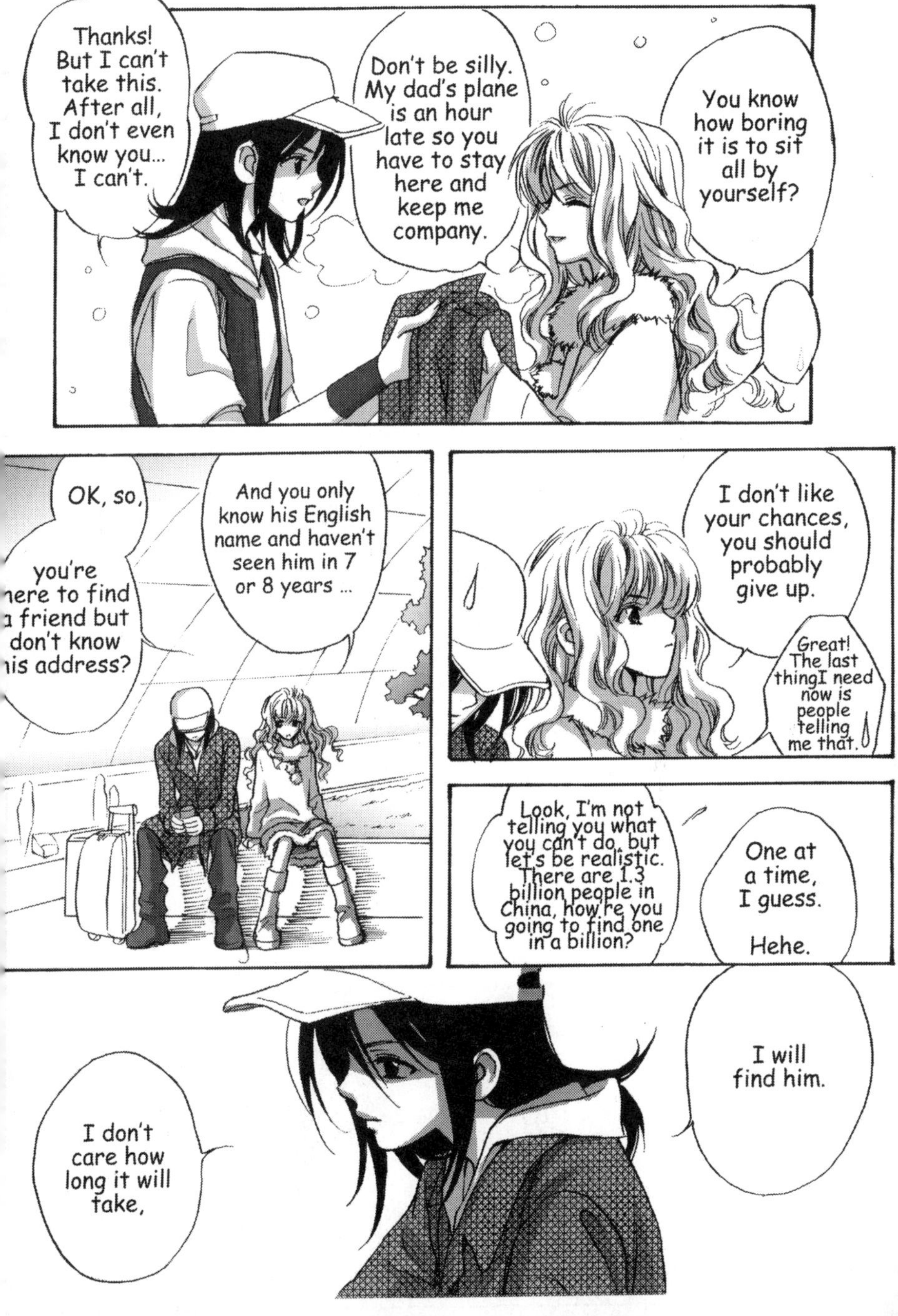

Thanks! But I can't take this. After all, I don't even know you... I can't.
Don't be silly. My dad's plane is an hour late so you have to stay here and keep me company.
You know how boring it is to sit all by yourself?
OK, so,
you're here to find a friend but don't know his address?
And you only know his English name and haven't seen him in 7 or 8 years ...
I don't like your chances, you should probably give up.
Great! The last thingI need now is people telling me that.
Look, I'm not telling you what you can't do, but let's be realistic. There are 1.3 billion people in China, how're you going to find one in a billion?
One at a time, I guess.
Hehe.
I don't care how long it will take,
I will find him.

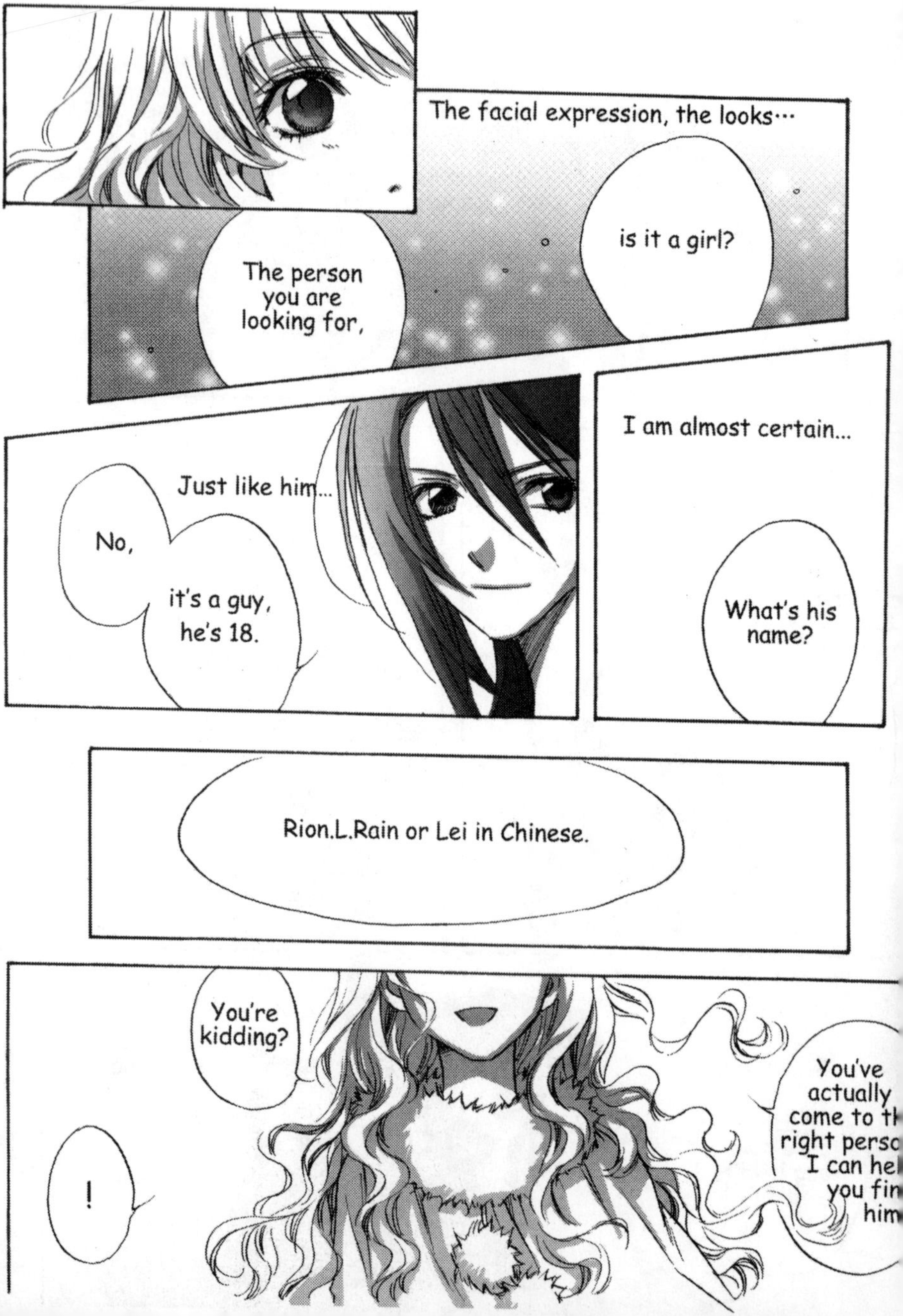
The facial expression, the looks···
The person you are looking for,
is it a girl?
No,
it's a guy, he's 18.
Just like him...
I am almost certain...
What's his name?
Rion.L.Rain or Lei in Chinese.
You're kidding?
!
You've actually come to th right perso I can hel you fin him

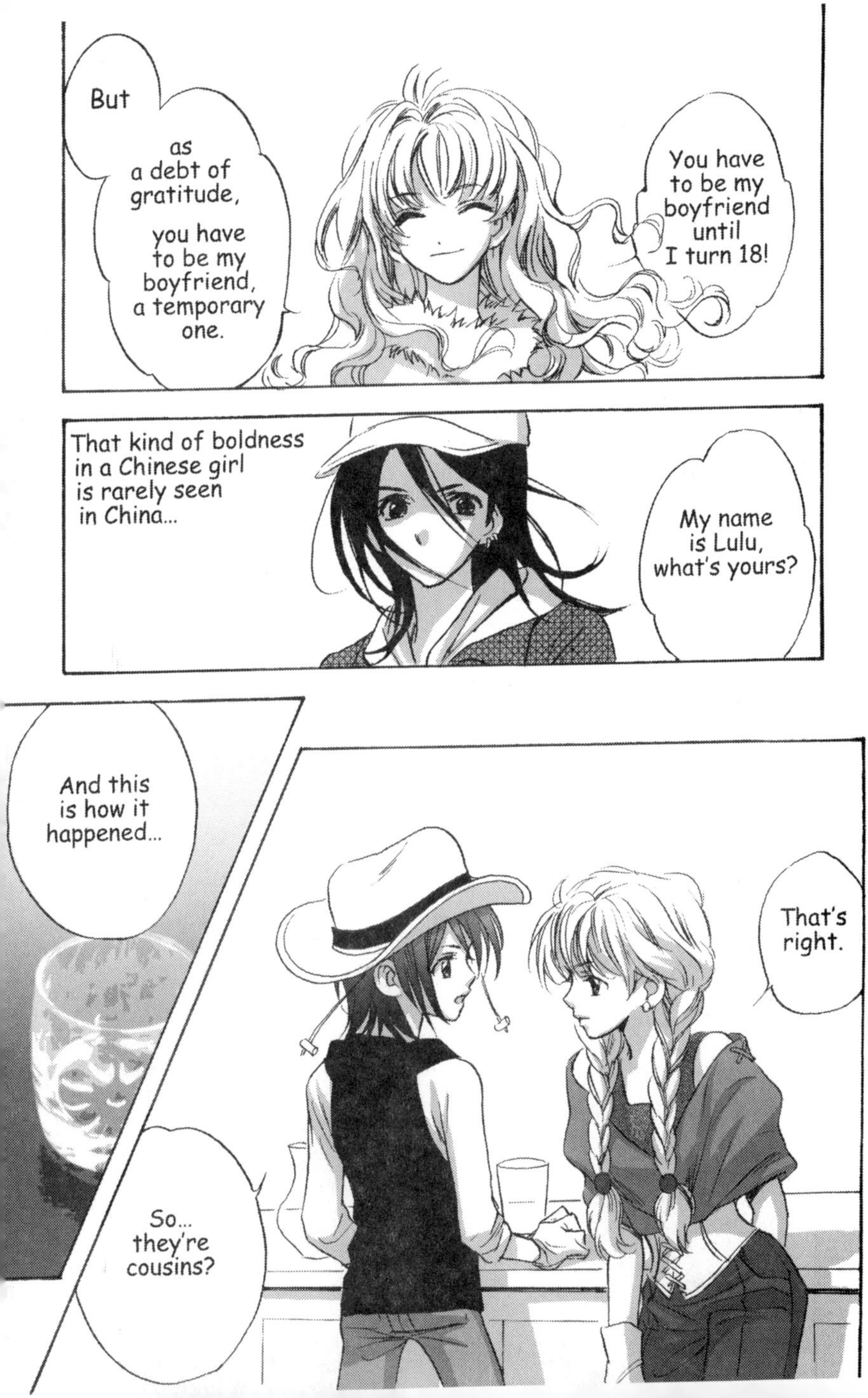
But
as a debt of gratitude,
you have to be my boyfriend, a temporary one.
You have to be my boyfriend until I turn 18!
That kind of boldness in a Chinese girl is rarely seen in China...
My name is Lulu, what's yours?
And this is how it happened...
That's right.
So... they're cousins?

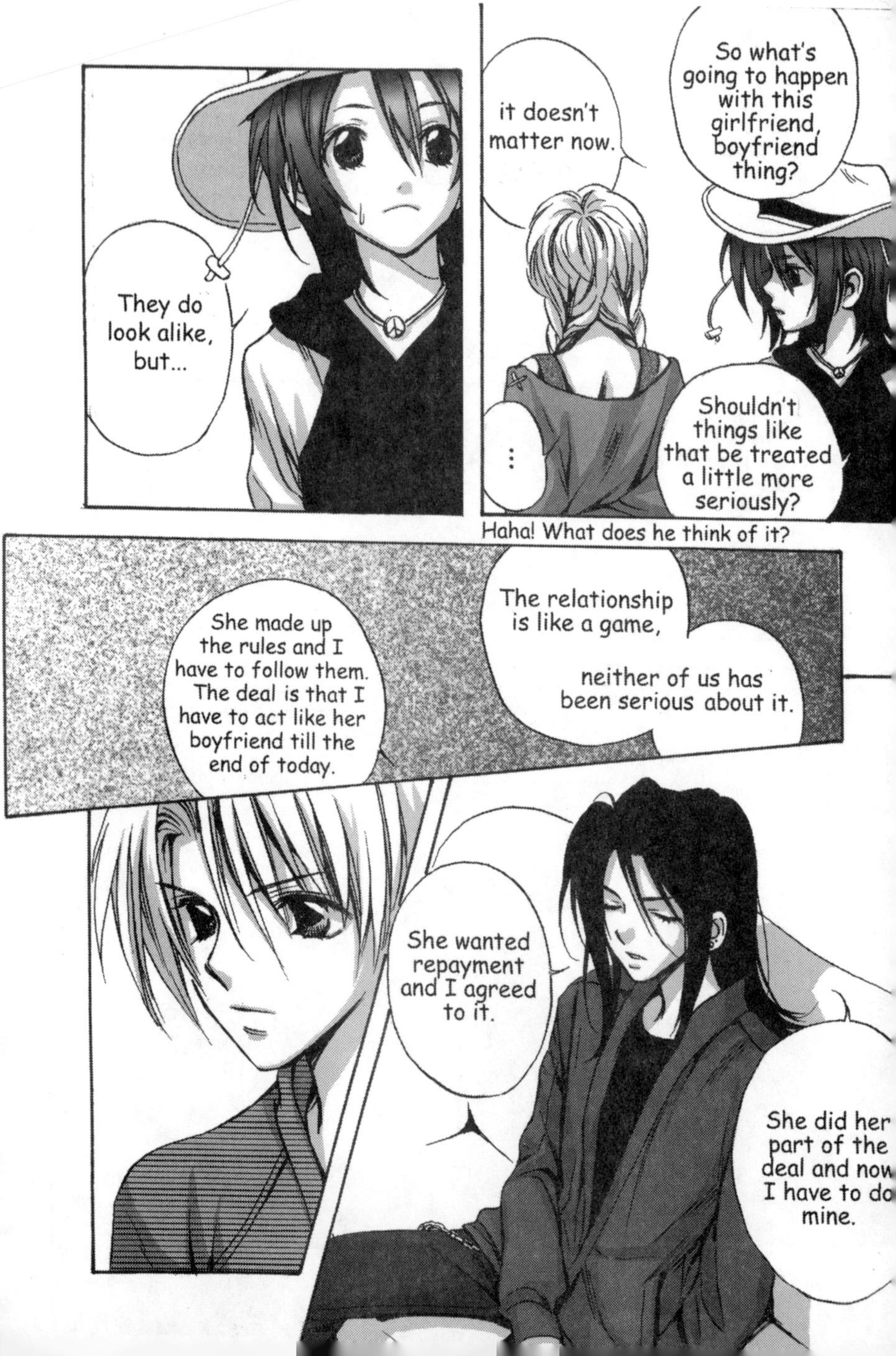

They do look alike, but...
it doesn't matter now.
So what's going to happen with this girlfriend, boyfriend thing?
...
Shouldn't things like that be treated a little more seriously?
Haha! What does he think of it?
The relationship is like a game,
neither of us has been serious about it.
She made up the rules and I have to follow them. The deal is that I have to act like her boyfriend till the end of today.
She wanted repayment and I agreed to it.
She did her part of the deal and now I have to do mine.

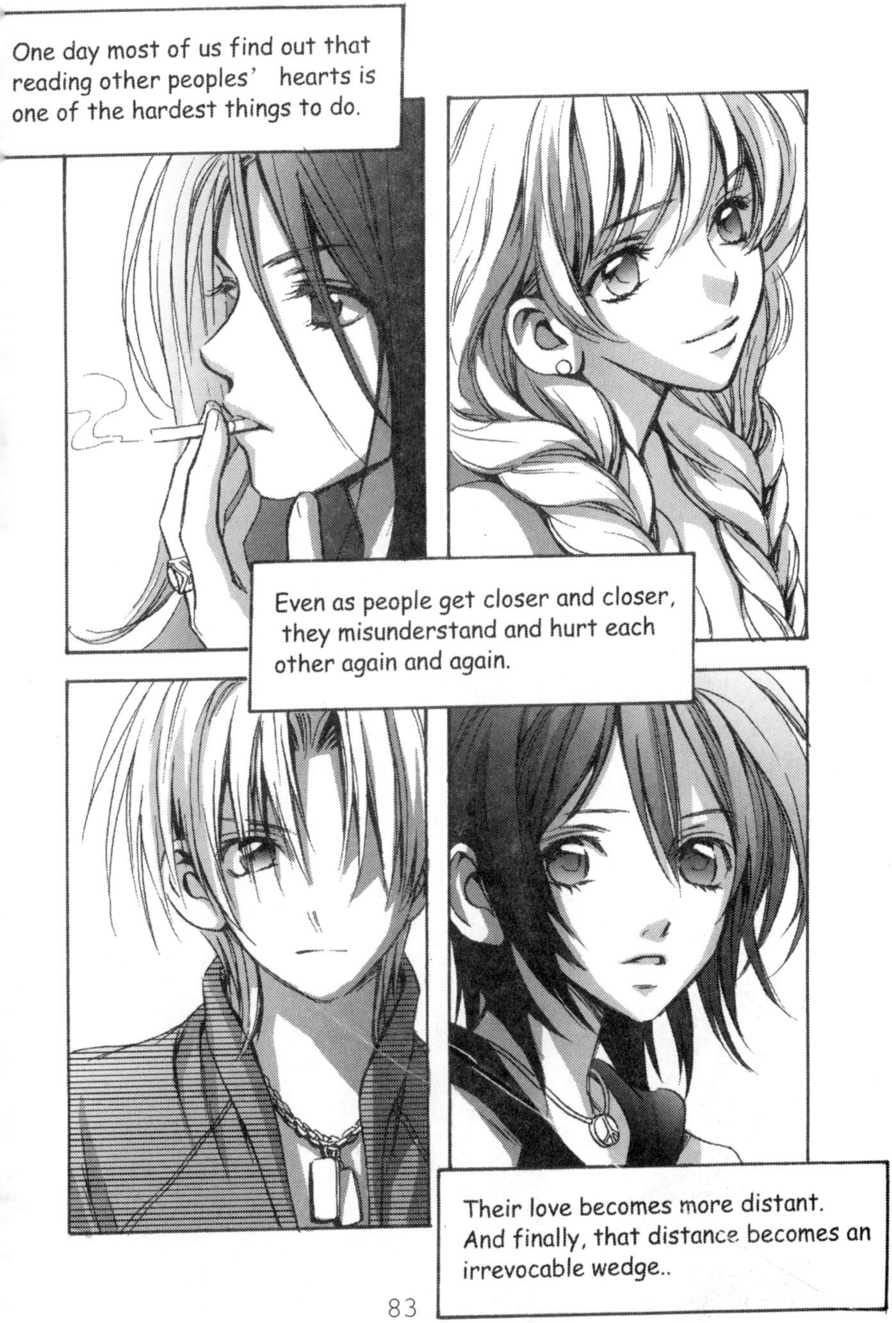
One day most of us find out that reading other peoples' hearts is one of the hardest things to do.
Even as people get closer and closer, they misunderstand and hurt each other again and again.
Their love becomes more distant. And finally, that distance becomes an irrevocable wedge..

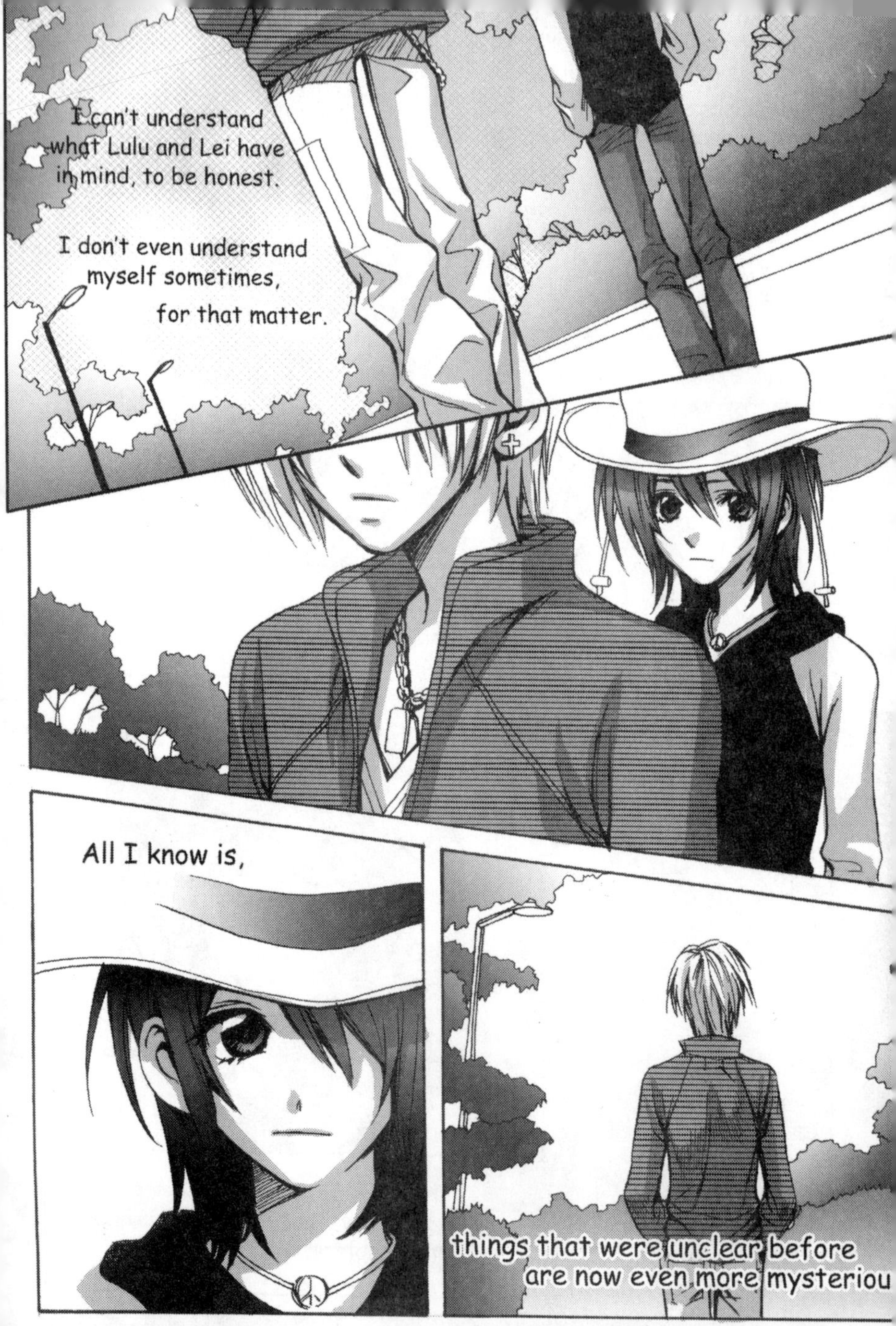
I can't understand what Lulu and Lei have in mind, to be honest.
I don't even understand myself sometimes,
for that matter.
All I know is,
things that were unclear before are now even more mysteriou

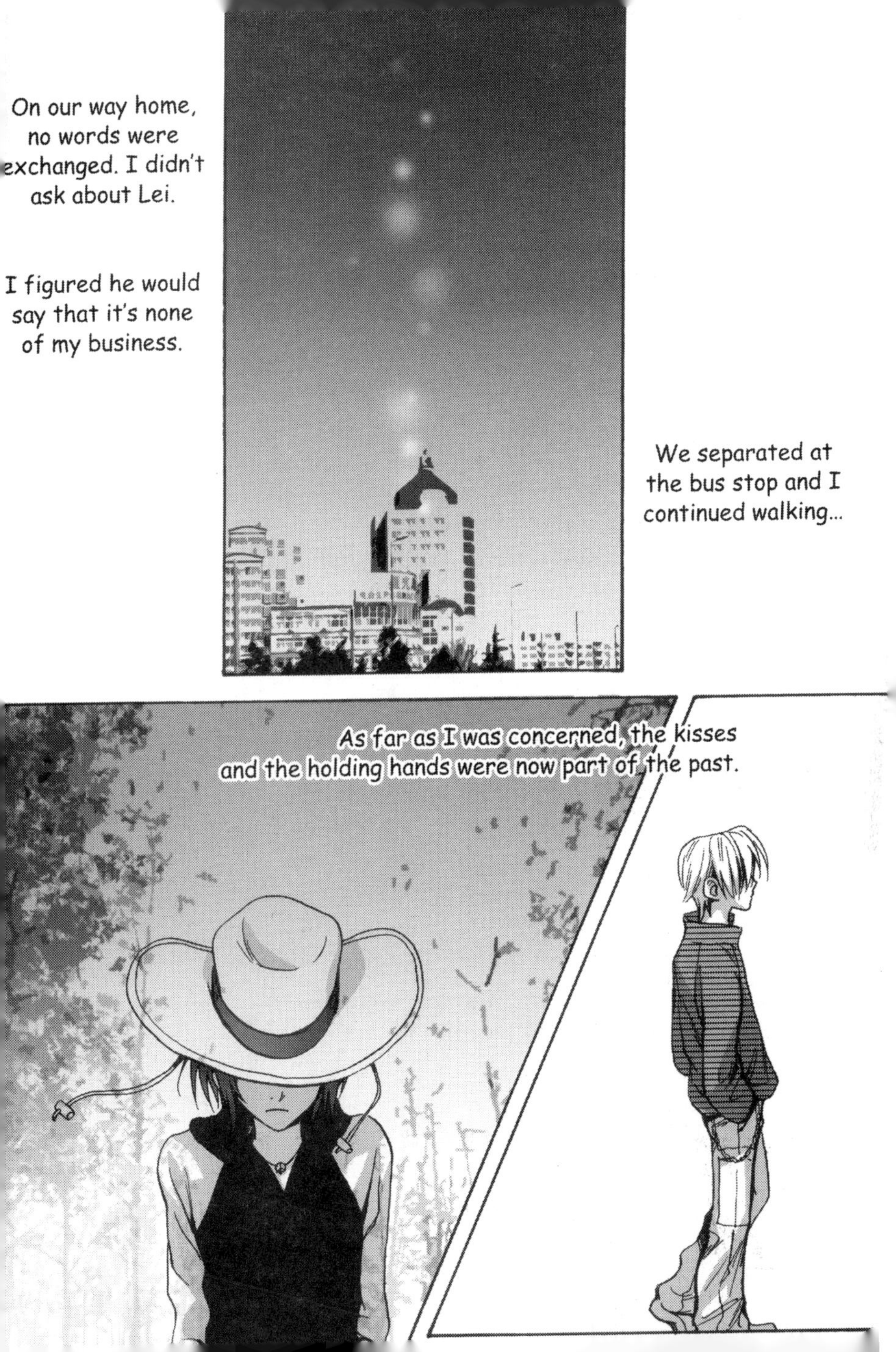
On our way home, no words were exchanged. I didn't ask about Lei.
I figured he would say that it's none of my business.
We separated at the bus stop and I continued walking...
As far as I was concerned, the kisses and the holding hands were now part of the past.

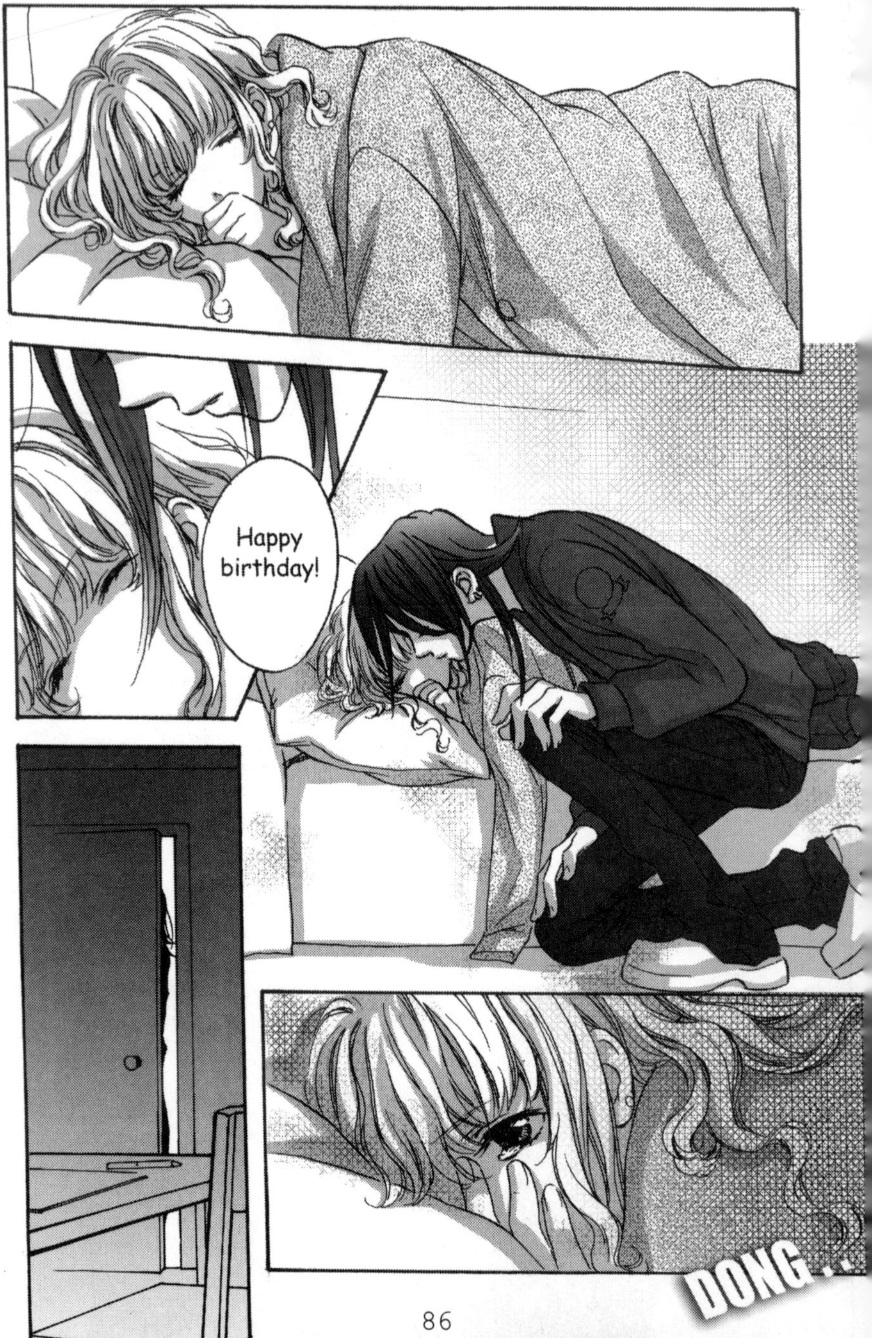
Happy birthday!
DONG . .

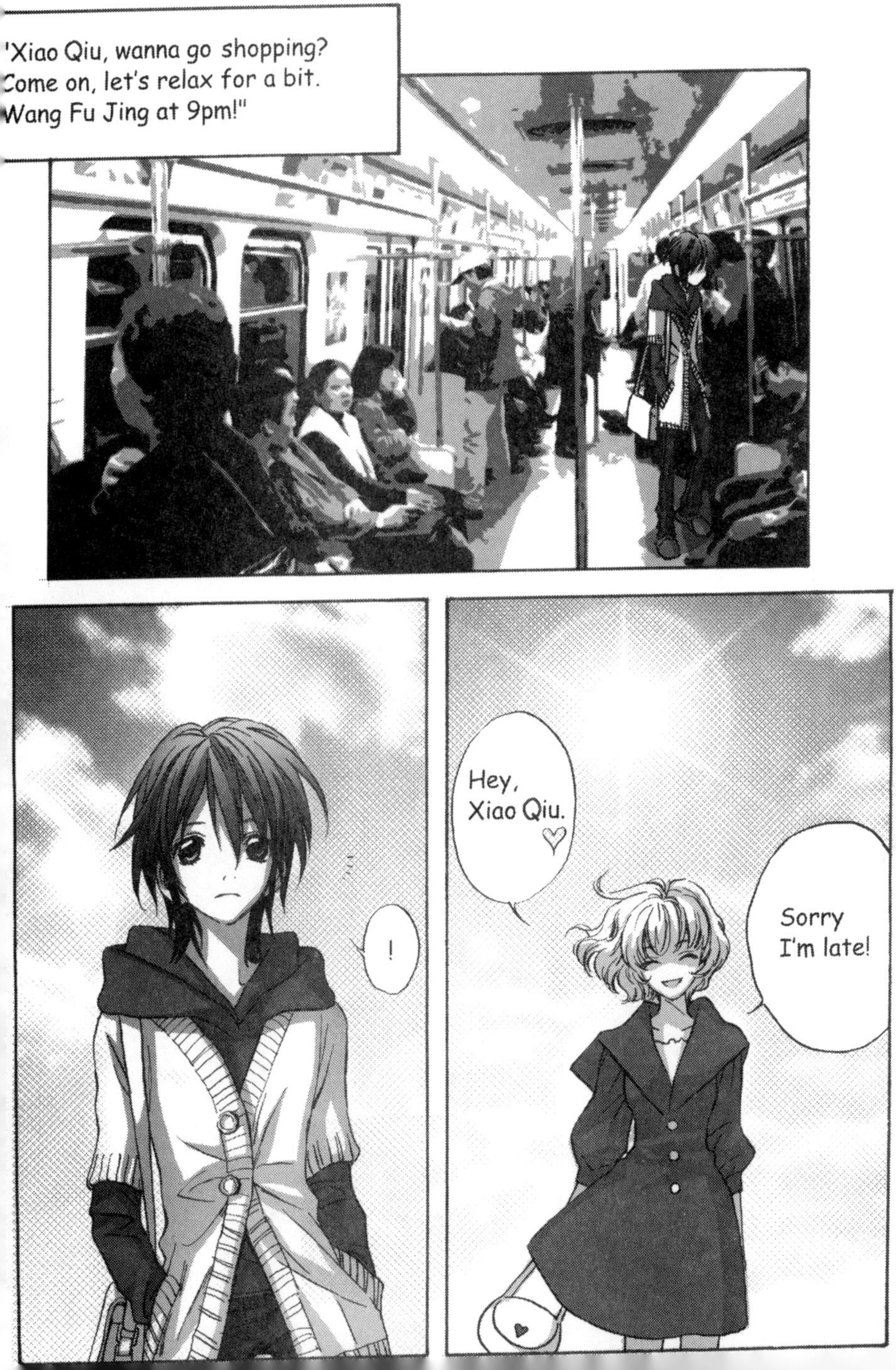
"Xiao Qiu, wanna go shopping? Come on, let's relax for a bit. Wang Fu Jing at 9pm!"
!
Hey, Xiao Qiu. ♡
Sorry I'm late!

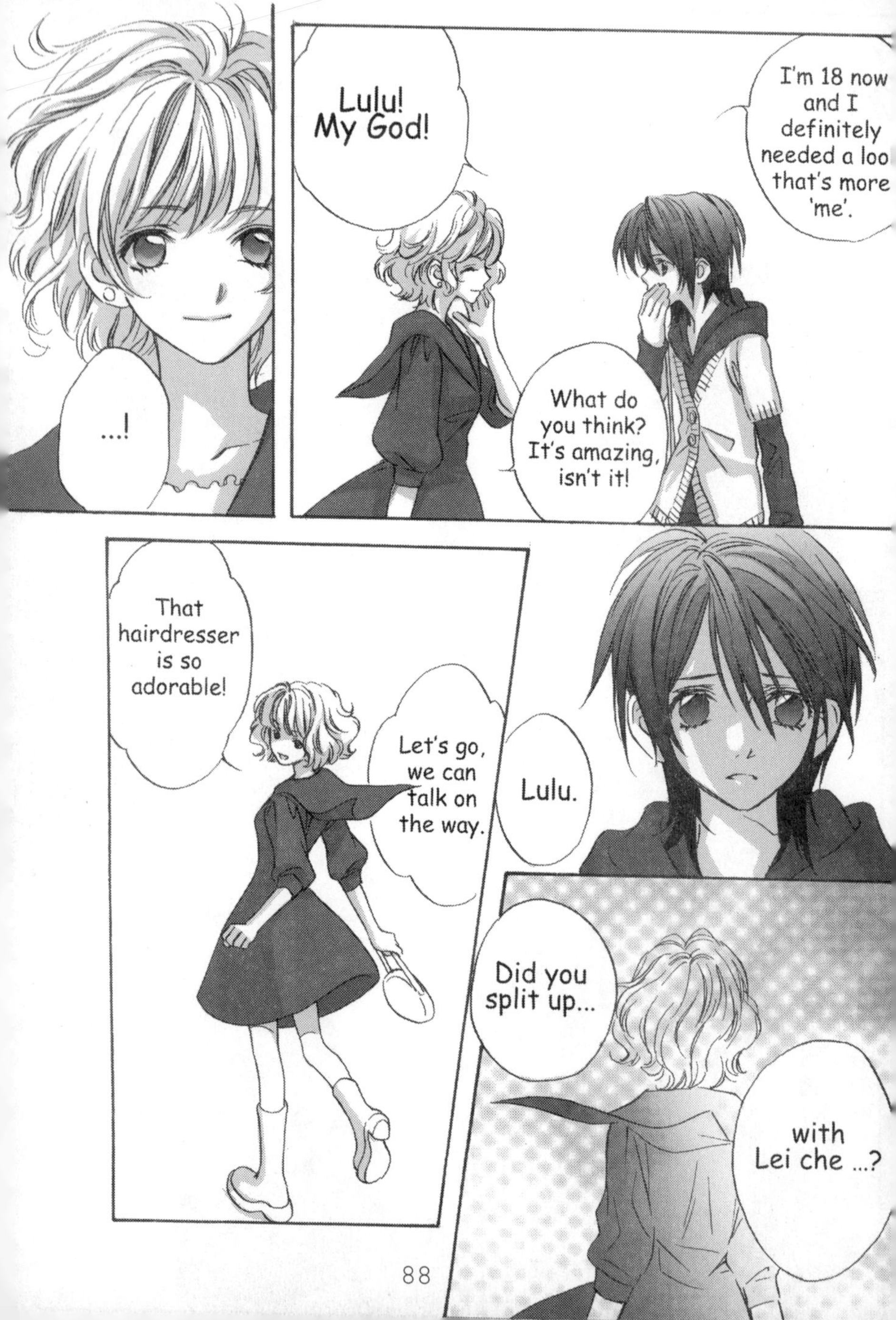
...!
Lulu! My God!
I'm 18 now and I definitely needed a loo that's more 'me'.
What do you think? It's amazing, isn't it!
That hairdresser is so adorable!
Let's go, we can talk on the way.
Lulu.
Did you split up...
with Lei che ...?

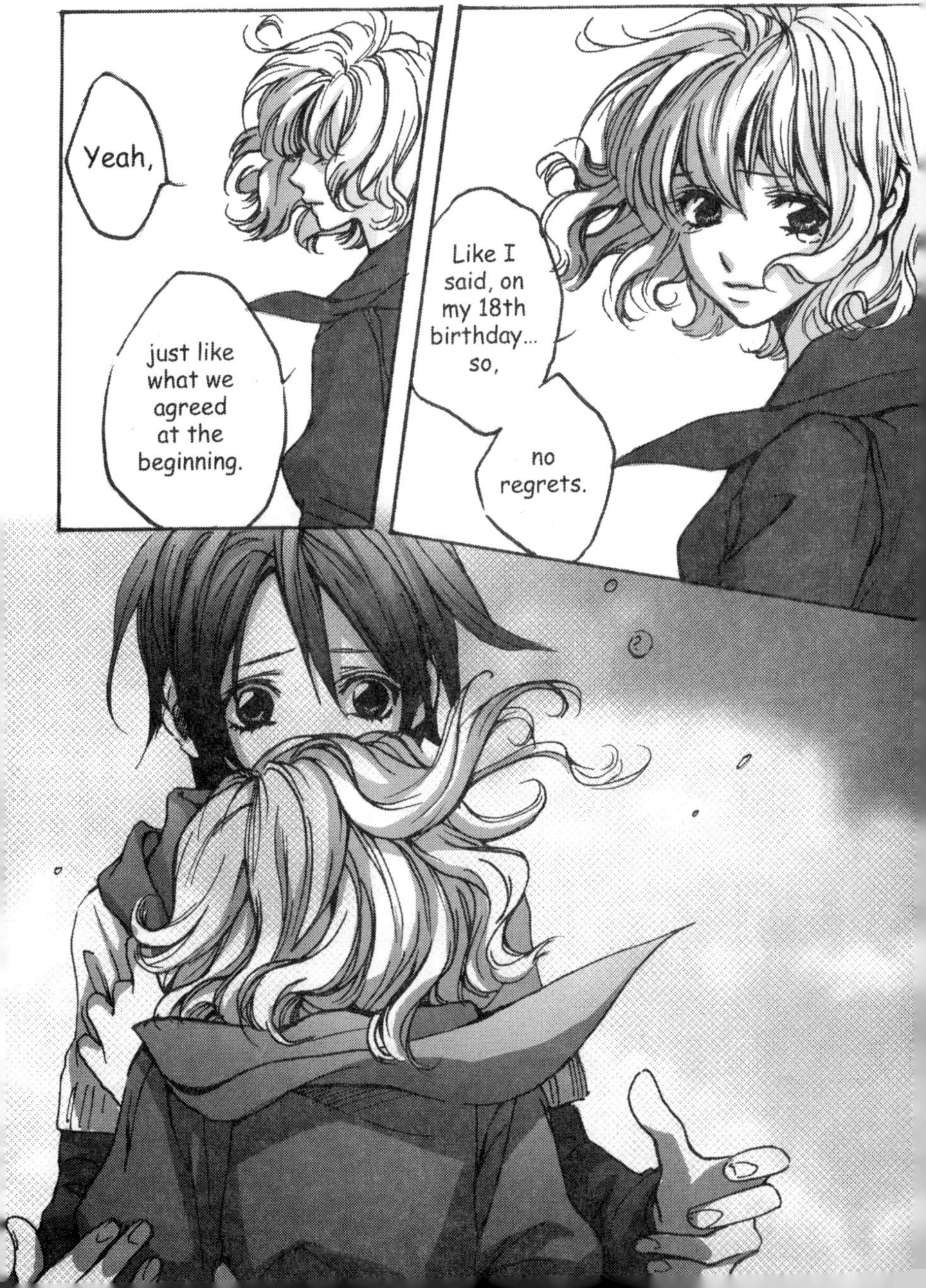
Like I said, on my 18th birthday... so,
no regrets.
Yeah,
just like what we agreed at the beginning.

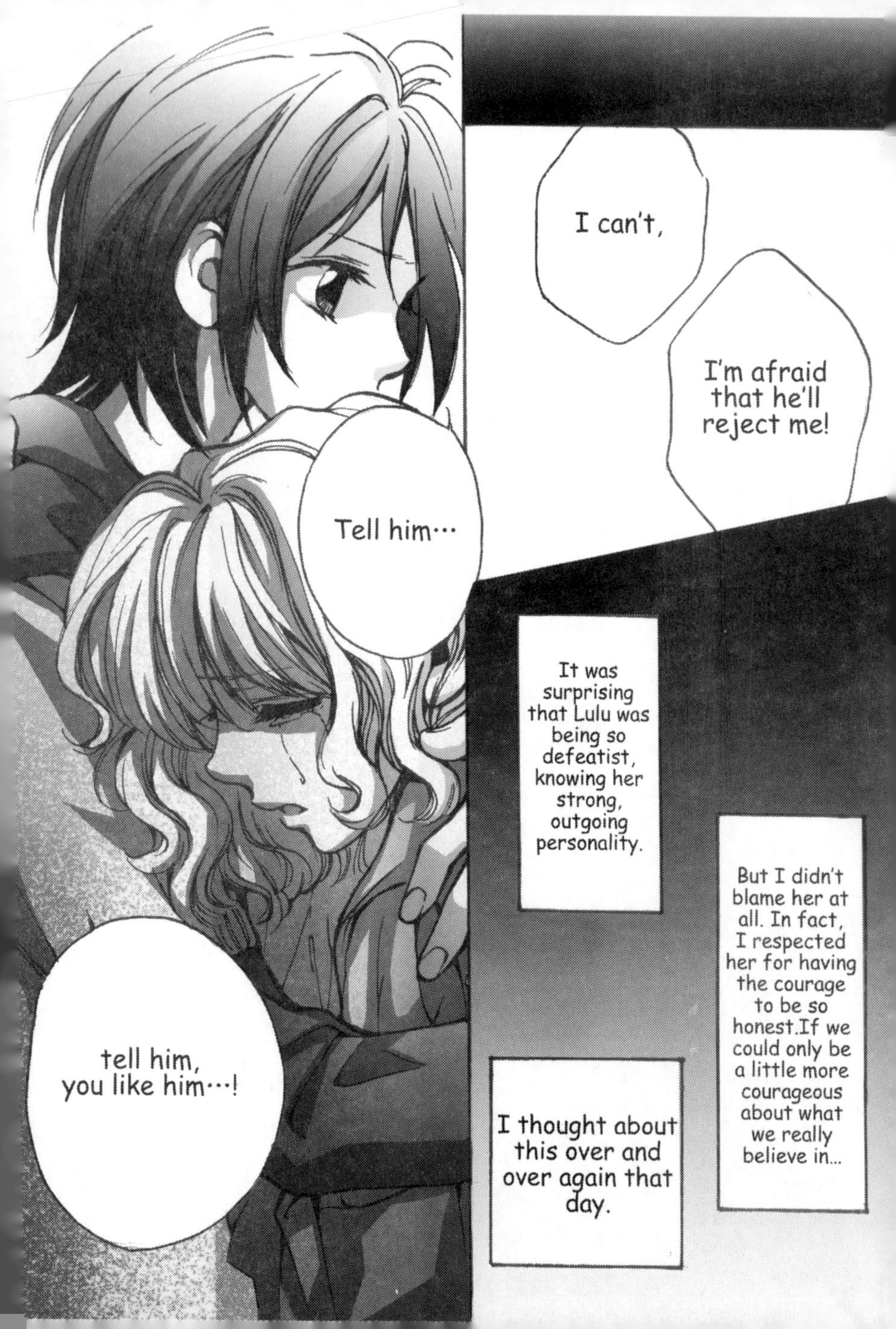
I can't,
I'm afraid that he'll reject me!
Tell him…
tell him, you like him…!
It was surprising that Lulu was being so defeatist, knowing her strong, outgoing personality.
But I didn't blame her at all. In fact, I respected her for having the courage to be so honest.If we could only be a little more courageous about what we really believe in...
I thought about this over and over again that day.

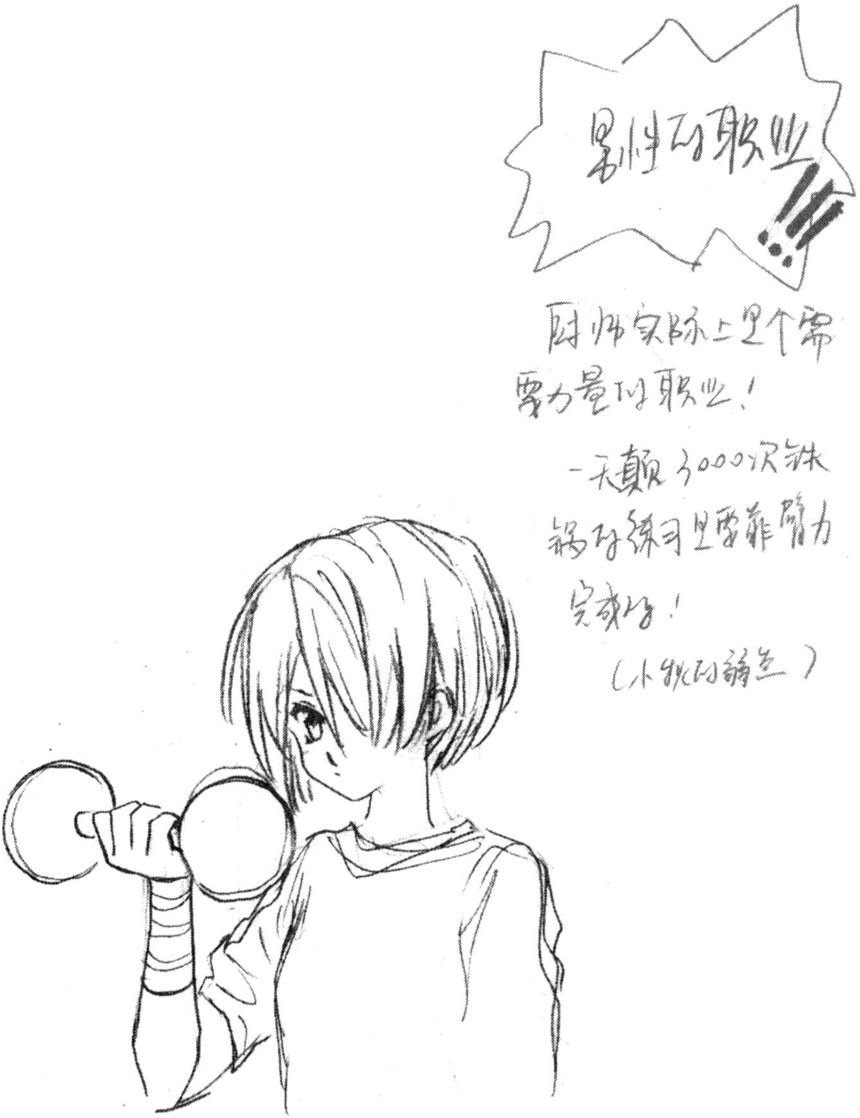
男性的职业
厨师实际上是个需要力量的职业！
一天颠3000次铁锅的练习是要靠臂力完成的！
（小秋的解说）

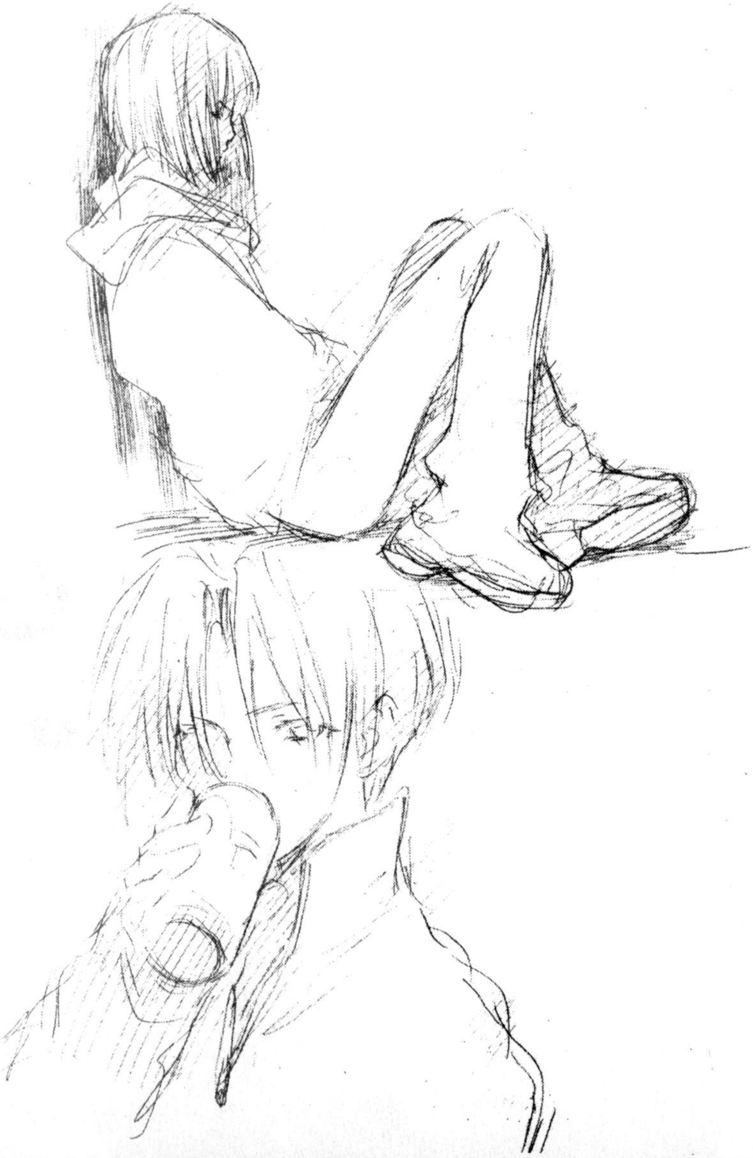

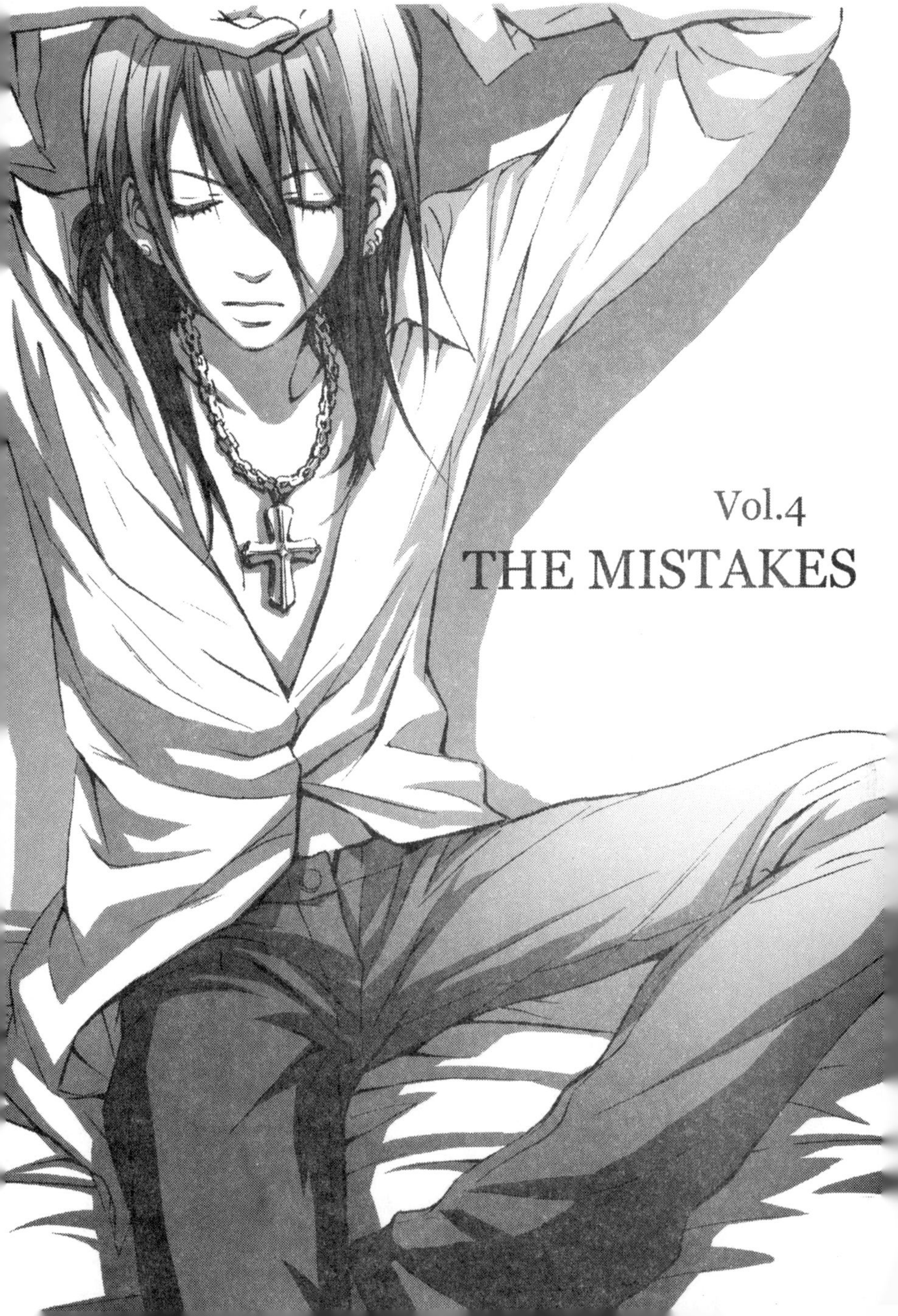
Vol.4
THE MISTAKES

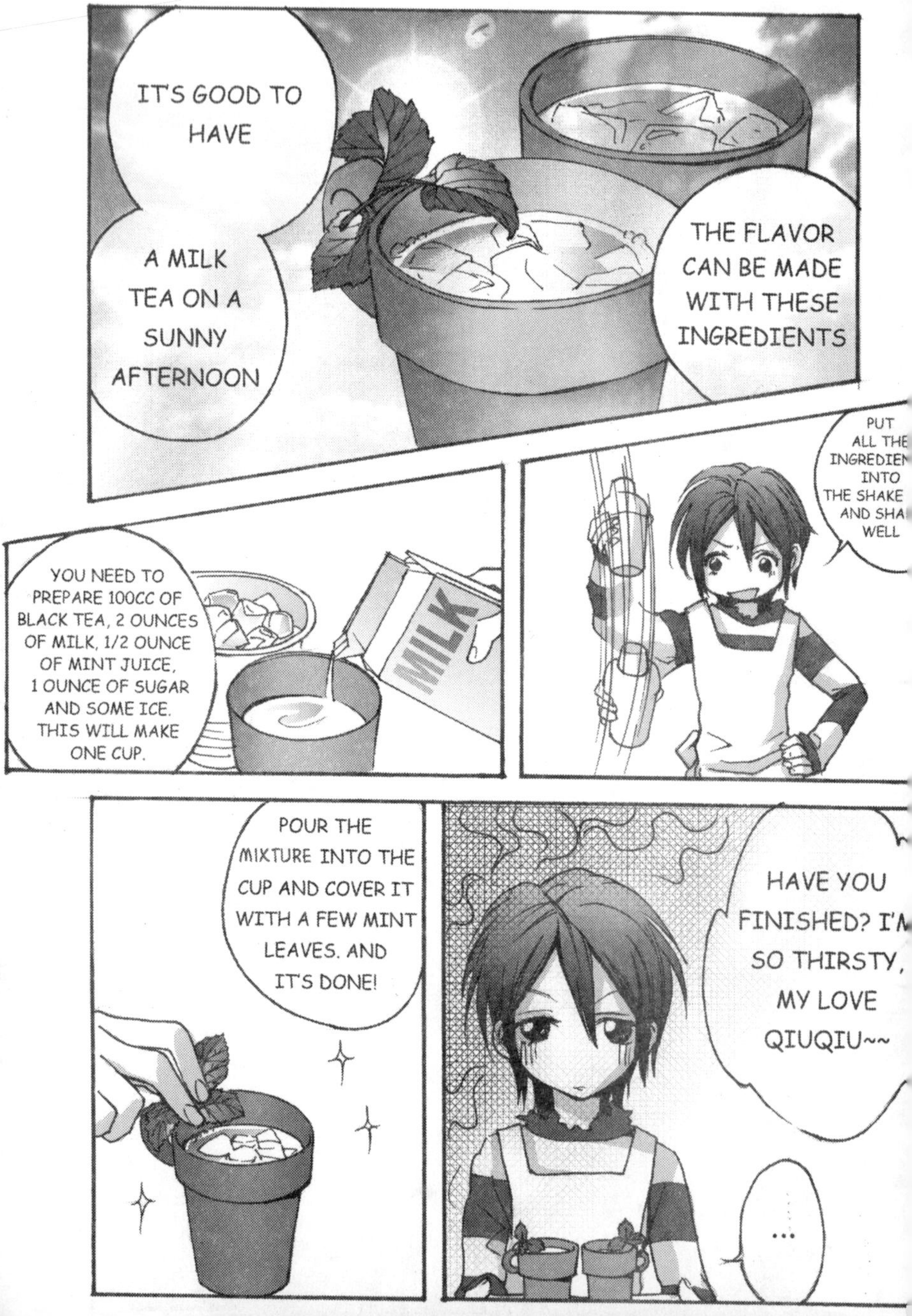
IT'S GOOD TO HAVE
A MILK TEA ON A SUNNY AFTERNOON
THE FLAVOR CAN BE MADE WITH THESE INGREDIENTS
YOU NEED TO PREPARE 100CC OF BLACK TEA, 2 OUNCES OF MILK, 1/2 OUNCE OF MINT JUICE, 1 OUNCE OF SUGAR AND SOME ICE. THIS WILL MAKE ONE CUP.
MILK
PUT ALL THE INGREDIEN INTO THE SHAKE AND SHA WELL
POUR THE MIXTURE INTO THE CUP AND COVER IT WITH A FEW MINT LEAVES. AND IT'S DONE!
HAVE YOU FINISHED? I' SO THIRSTY, MY LOVE QIUQIU~~
...

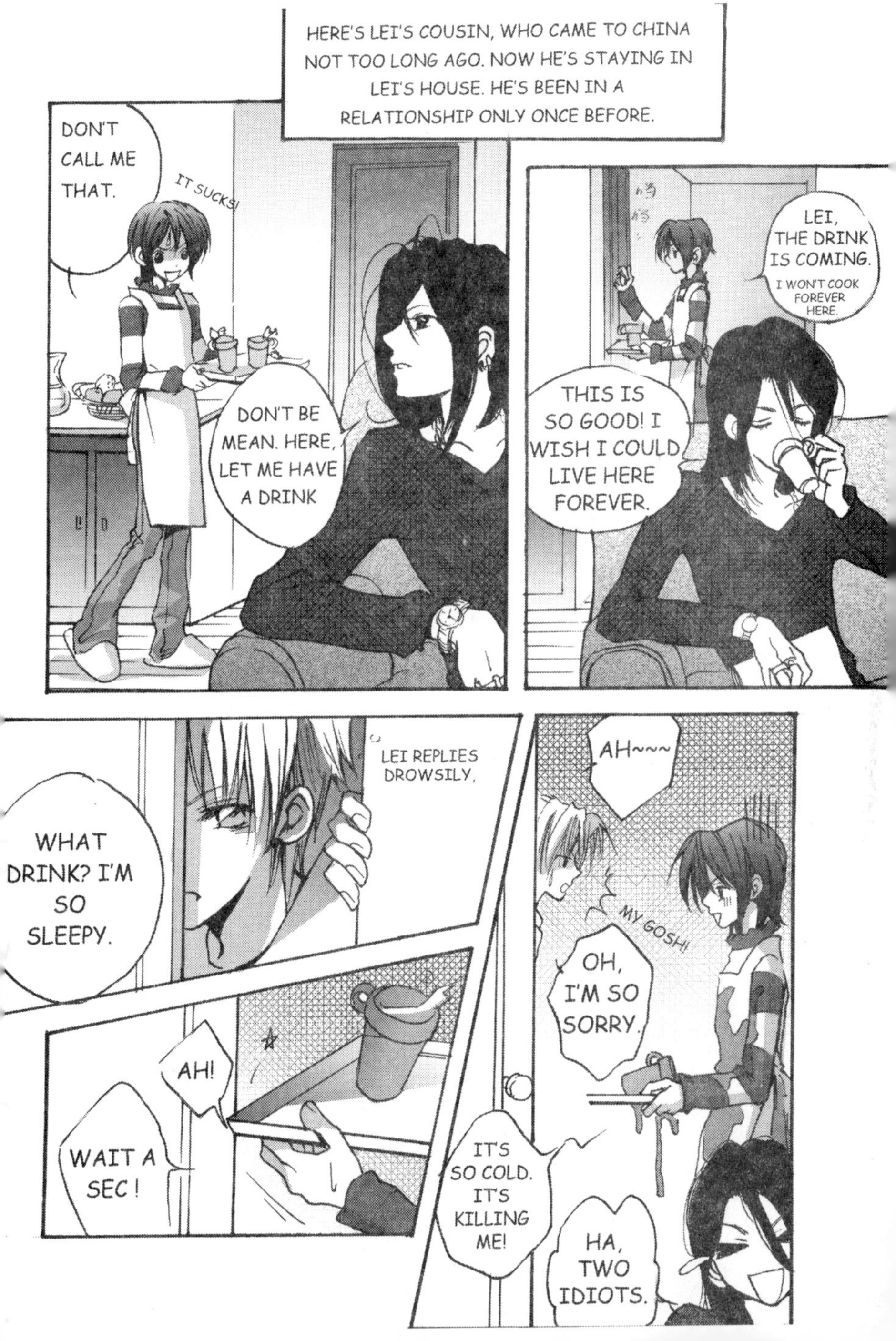
HERE'S LEI'S COUSIN, WHO CAME TO CHINA NOT TOO LONG AGO. NOW HE'S STAYING IN LEI'S HOUSE. HE'S BEEN IN A RELATIONSHIP ONLY ONCE BEFORE.
DON'T CALL ME THAT.
IT SUCKS!
DON'T BE MEAN. HERE, LET ME HAVE A DRINK
LEI, THE DRINK IS COMING.
I WON'T COOK FOREVER HERE.
THIS IS SO GOOD! I WISH I COULD LIVE HERE FOREVER.
LEI REPLIES DROWSILY,
WHAT DRINK? I'M SO SLEEPY.
AH!
WAIT A SEC !
AH~~~
MY GOSH!
OH, I'M SO SORRY.
IT'S SO COLD. IT'S KILLING ME!
HA, TWO IDIOTS.

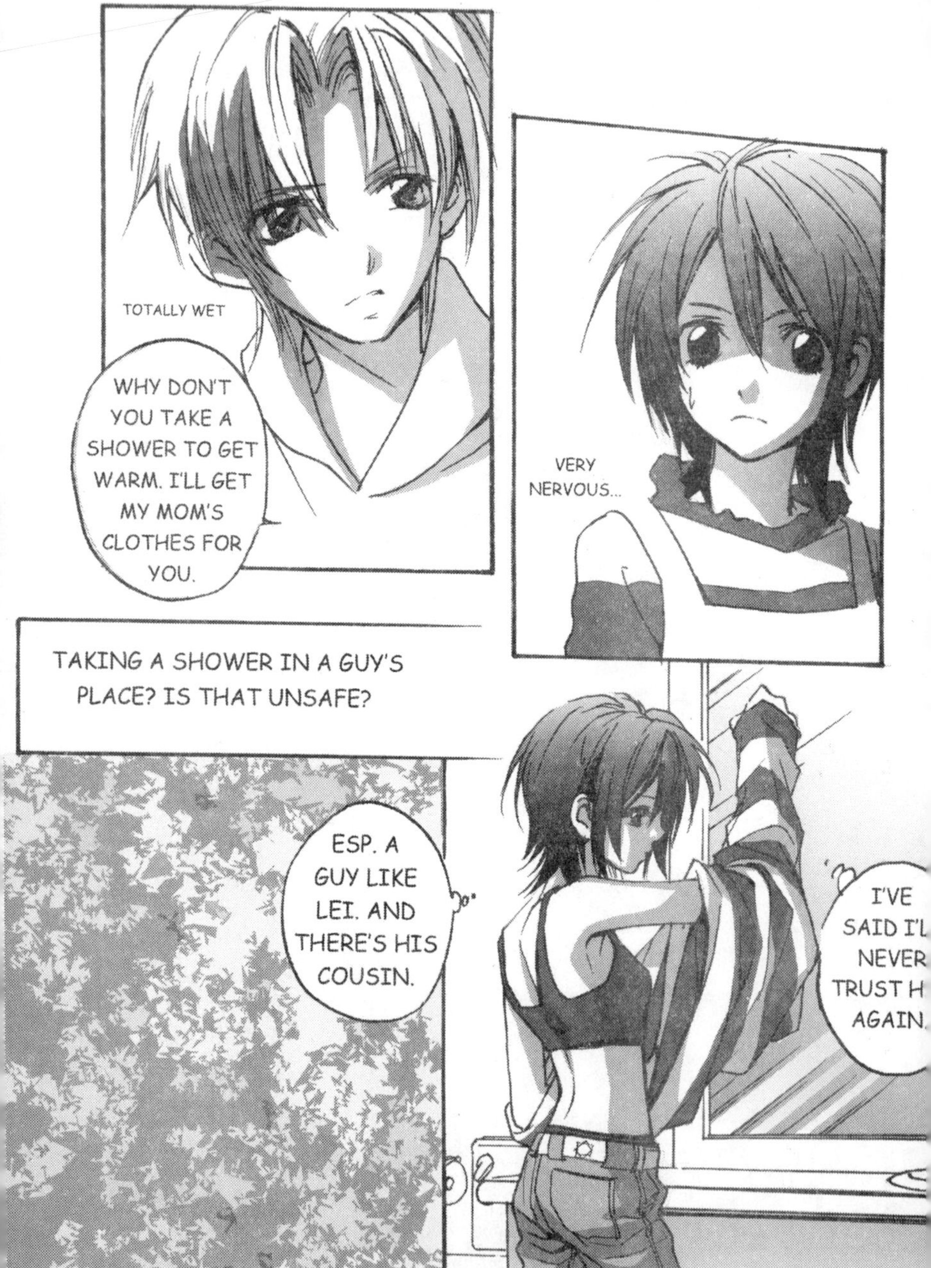
TOTALLY WET
WHY DON'T YOU TAKE A SHOWER TO GET WARM. I'LL GET MY MOM'S CLOTHES FOR YOU.
VERY NERVOUS...
TAKING A SHOWER IN A GUY'S PLACE? IS THAT UNSAFE?
ESP. A GUY LIKE LEI. AND THERE'S HIS COUSIN.
I'VE SAID I'L NEVER TRUST H AGAIN.

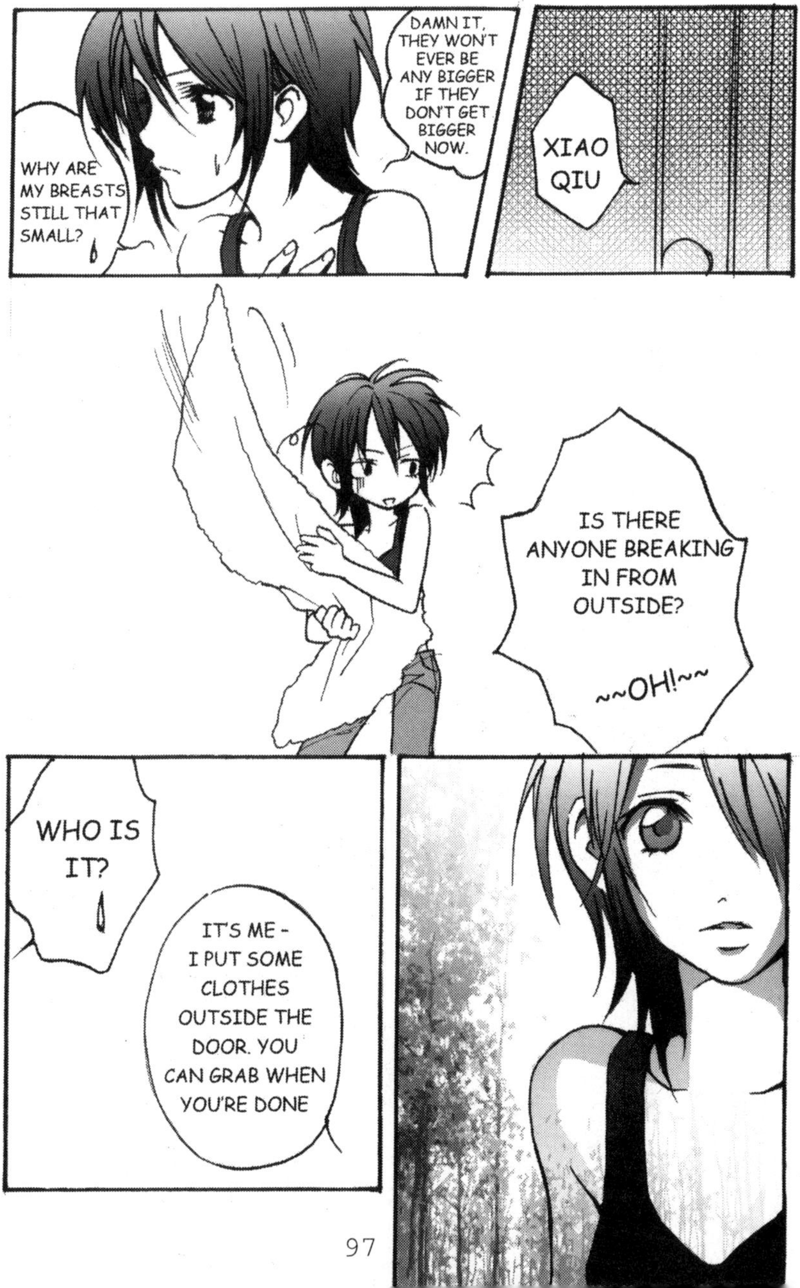
WHY ARE MY BREASTS STILL THAT SMALL?
DAMN IT, THEY WON'T EVER BE ANY BIGGER IF THEY DON'T GET BIGGER NOW.
XIAO QIU
IS THERE ANYONE BREAKING IN FROM OUTSIDE?
~~OH!~~
WHO IS IT?
IT'S ME - I PUT SOME CLOTHES OUTSIDE THE DOOR. YOU CAN GRAB WHEN YOU'RE DONE

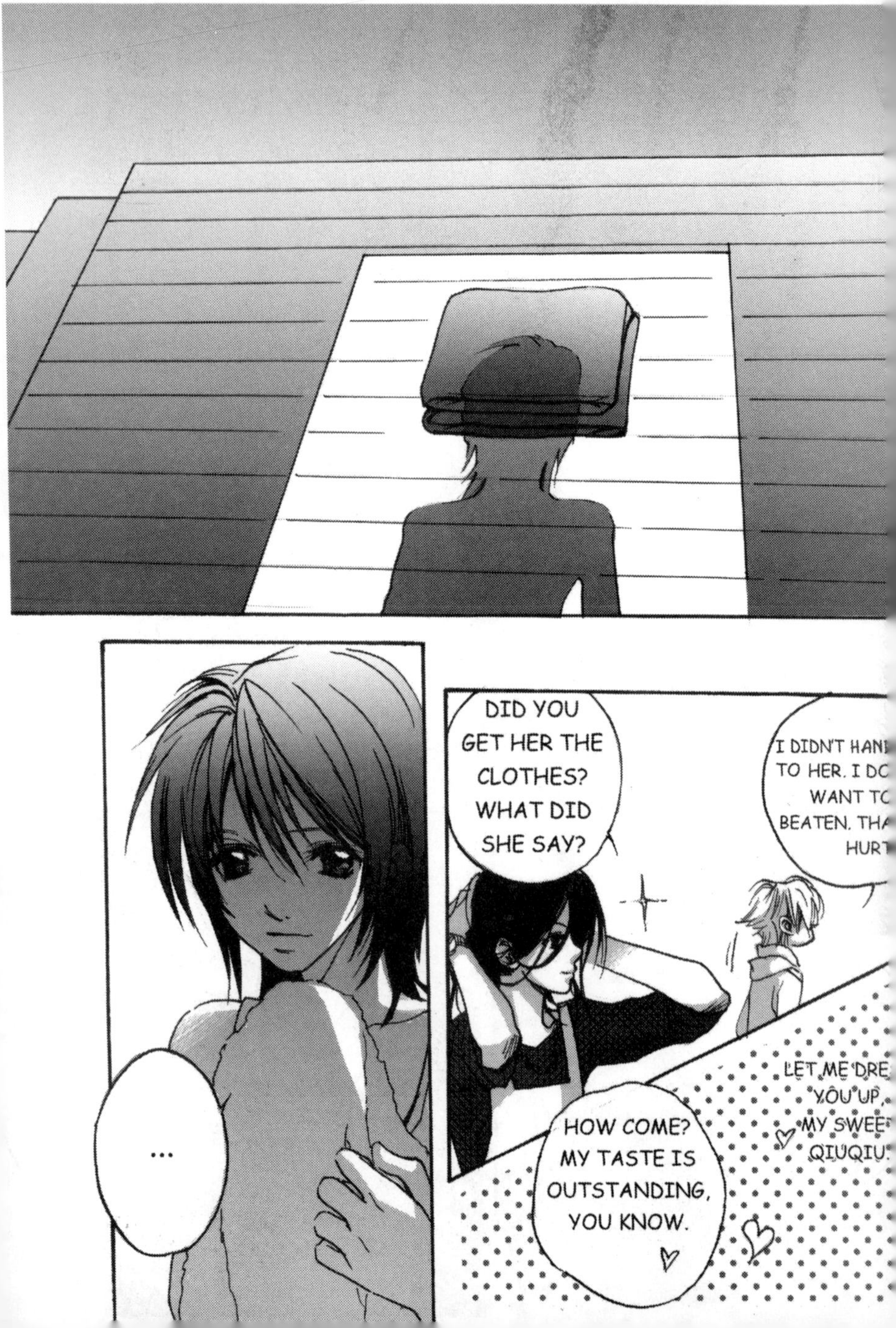
...
DID YOU GET HER THE CLOTHES? WHAT DID SHE SAY?
I DIDN'T HAN TO HER. I DO WANT TO BEATEN. THA HURT
LET ME DRE YOU UP, MY SWEE QIUQIU.
HOW COME? MY TASTE IS OUTSTANDING, YOU KNOW.

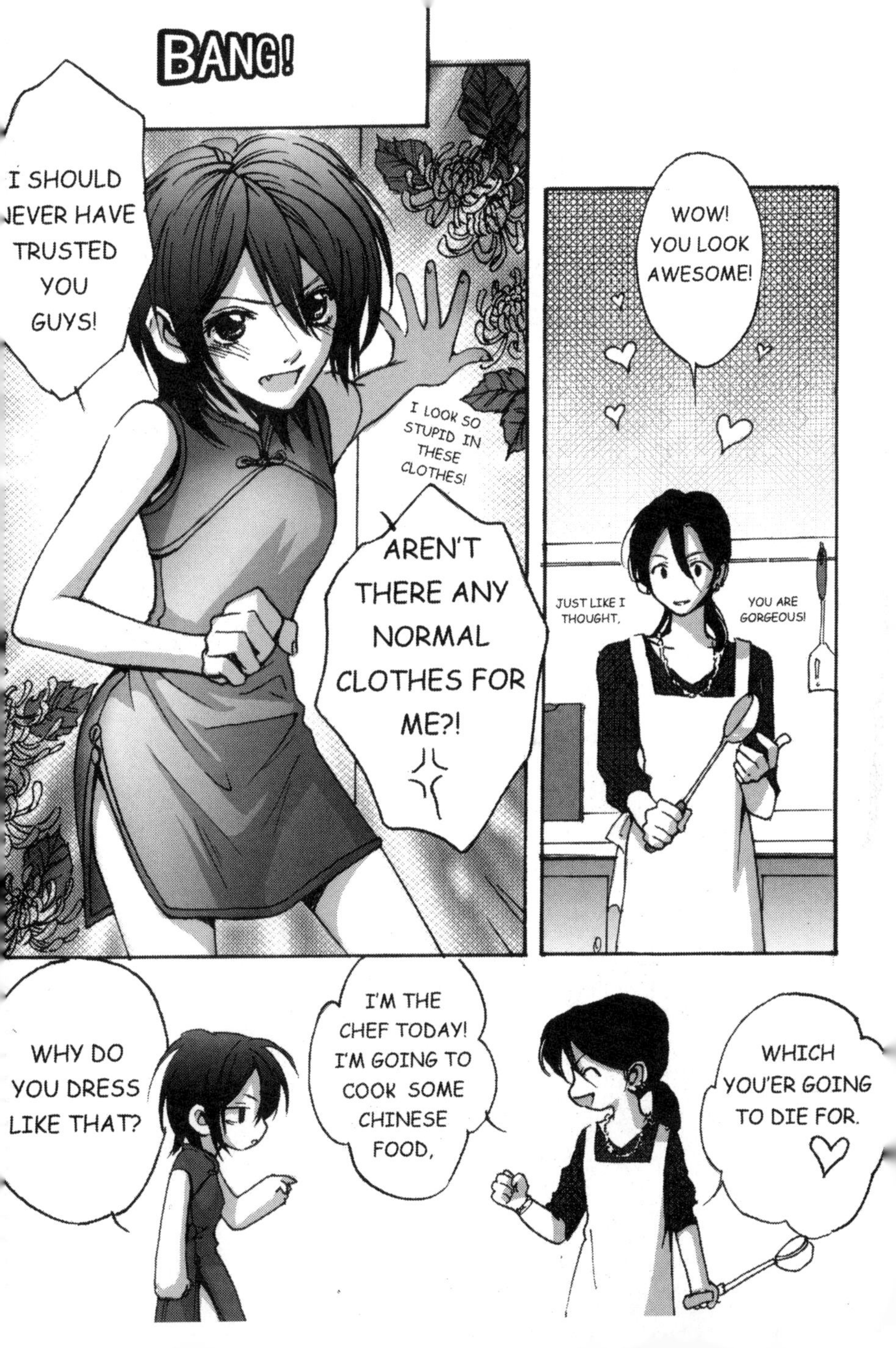
BANG!
I SHOULD NEVER HAVE TRUSTED YOU GUYS!
I LOOK SO STUPID IN THESE CLOTHES!
AREN'T THERE ANY NORMAL CLOTHES FOR ME?!
WOW! YOU LOOK AWESOME!
JUST LIKE I THOUGHT,
YOU ARE GORGEOUS!
WHY DO YOU DRESS LIKE THAT?
I'M THE CHEF TODAY! I'M GOING TO COOK SOME CHINESE FOOD,
WHICH YOU'ER GOING TO DIE FOR.

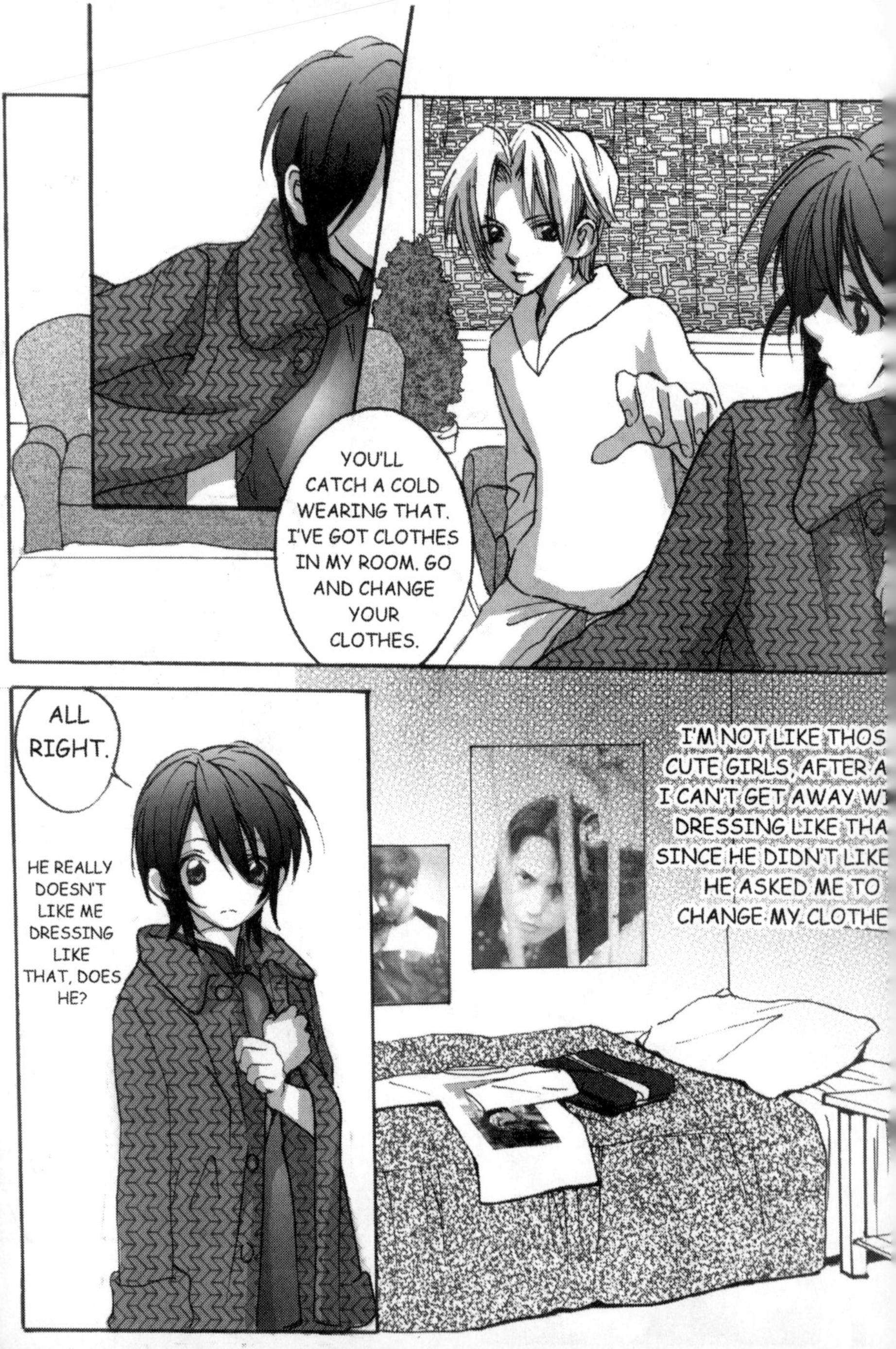
YOU'LL CATCH A COLD WEARING THAT. I'VE GOT CLOTHES IN MY ROOM. GO AND CHANGE YOUR CLOTHES.
ALL RIGHT.
I'M NOT LIKE THOS
CUTE GIRLS, AFTER A
I CAN'T GET AWAY WI
DRESSING LIKE THA
SINCE HE DIDN'T LIKE
HE ASKED ME TO
CHANGE MY CLOTHE
HE REALLY DOESN'T LIKE ME DRESSING LIKE THAT, DOES HE?

RIGHT AFTER ENTERING THE ROOM, SHE REMEMBERED THAT KISS BEFORE. IN SPITE OF HERSELF.. THAT KISS THE HEAT OF HIS BODY, HIS SMELL

LEI'S SHIRT IS A BIT LARGE.

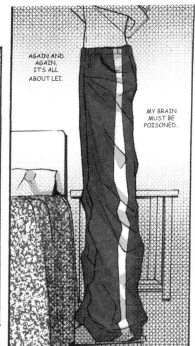

AGAIN AND AGAIN, IT'S ALL ABOUT LEI.

MY BRAIN MUST BE POISONED..

WHY DID YOU ASK HER TO CHANGE? SHE LOOKED GOOD IN THAT.

GIVE ME ANOTHER EGG.

OK

YOU CAN'T SEE IT JUST BECAUSE IT'S SO CUTE.

WHAT? YOU'RE MEAN!

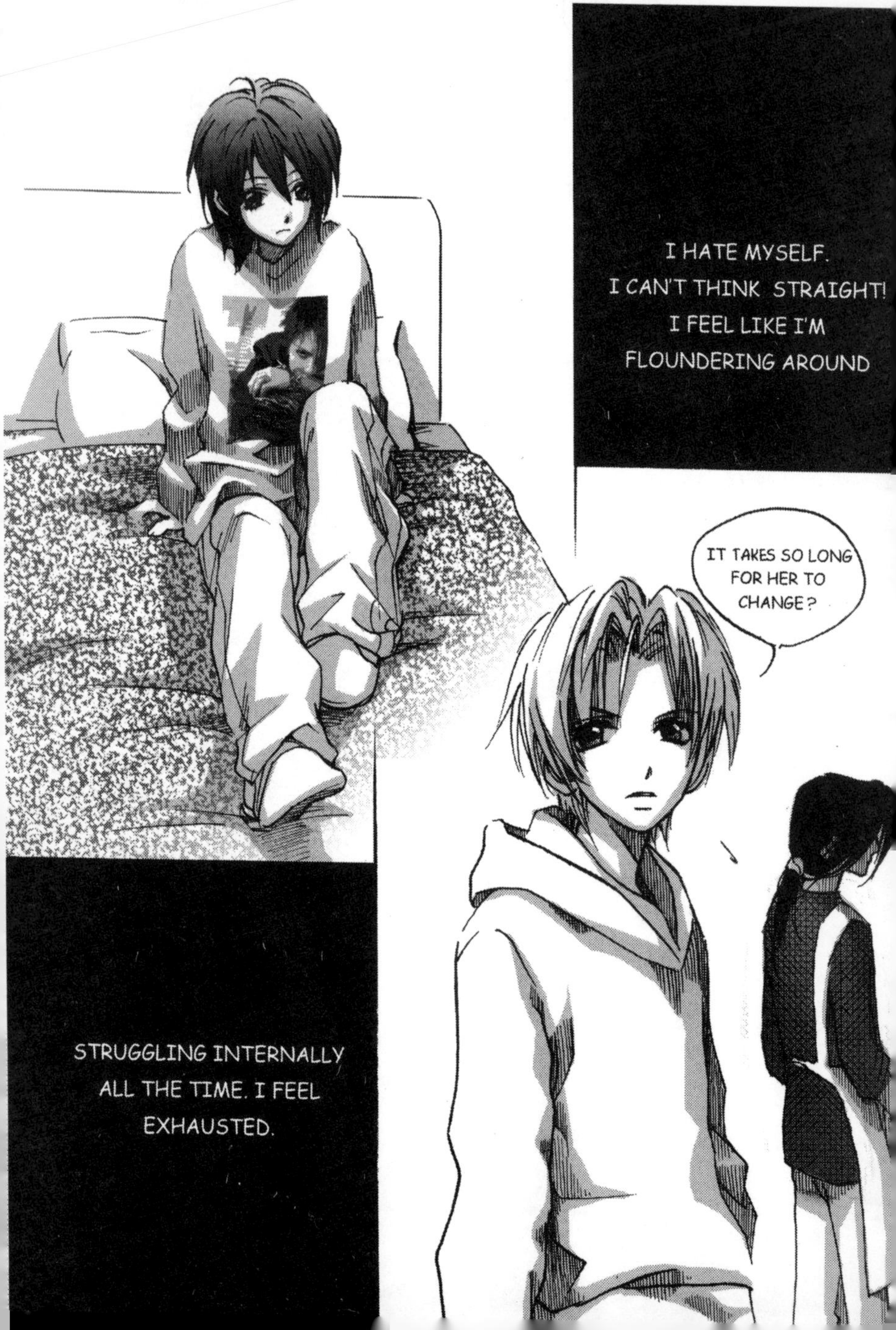
I HATE MYSELF.
I CAN'T THINK STRAIGHT!
I FEEL LIKE I'M
FLOUNDERING AROUND
STRUGGLING INTERNALLY
ALL THE TIME. I FEEL
EXHAUSTED.
IT TAKES SO LONG
FOR HER TO
CHANGE?

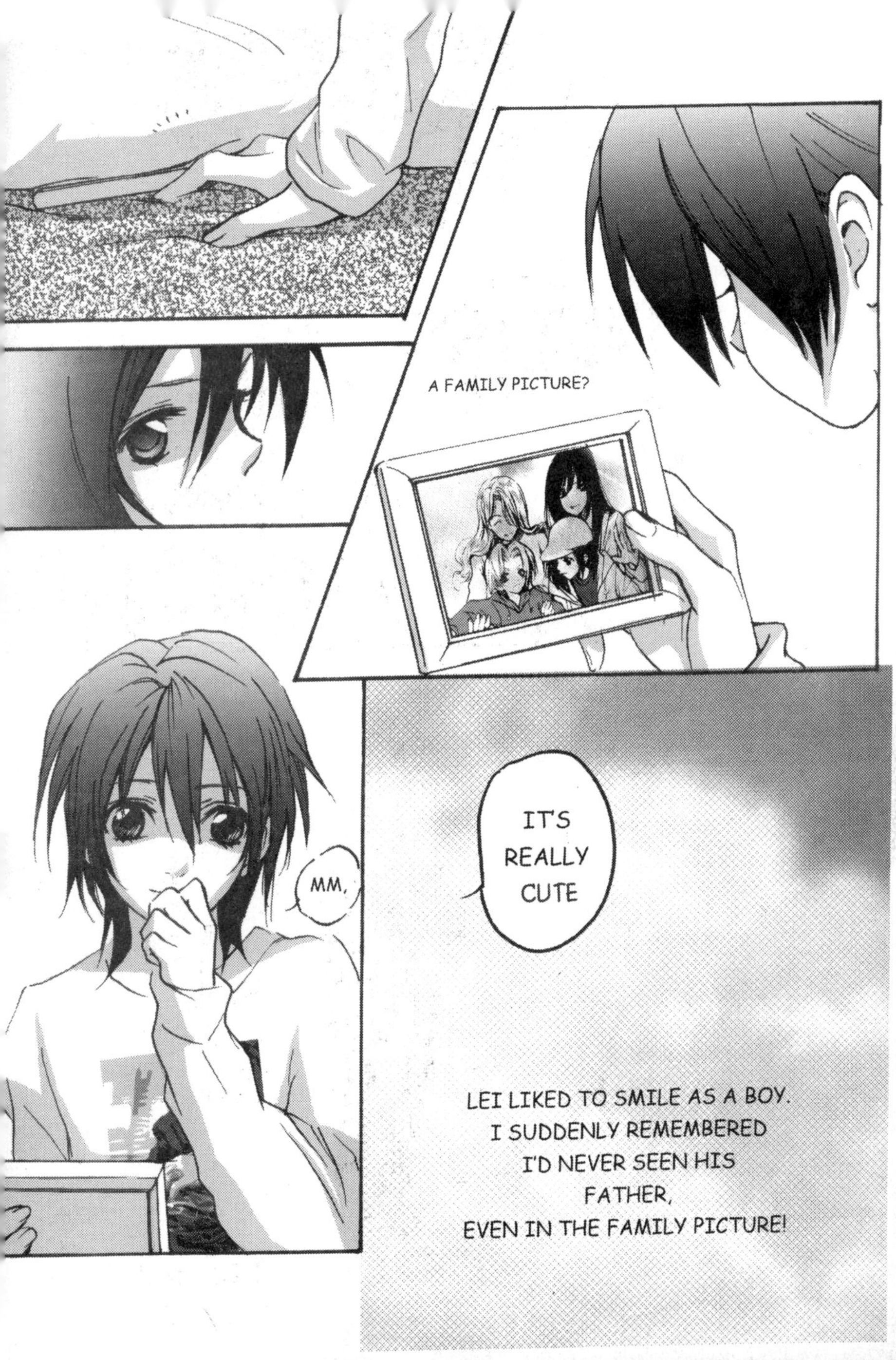
A FAMILY PICTURE?
IT'S REALLY CUTE
MM,
LEI LIKED TO SMILE AS A BOY. I SUDDENLY REMEMBERED I'D NEVER SEEN HIS FATHER, EVEN IN THE FAMILY PICTURE!

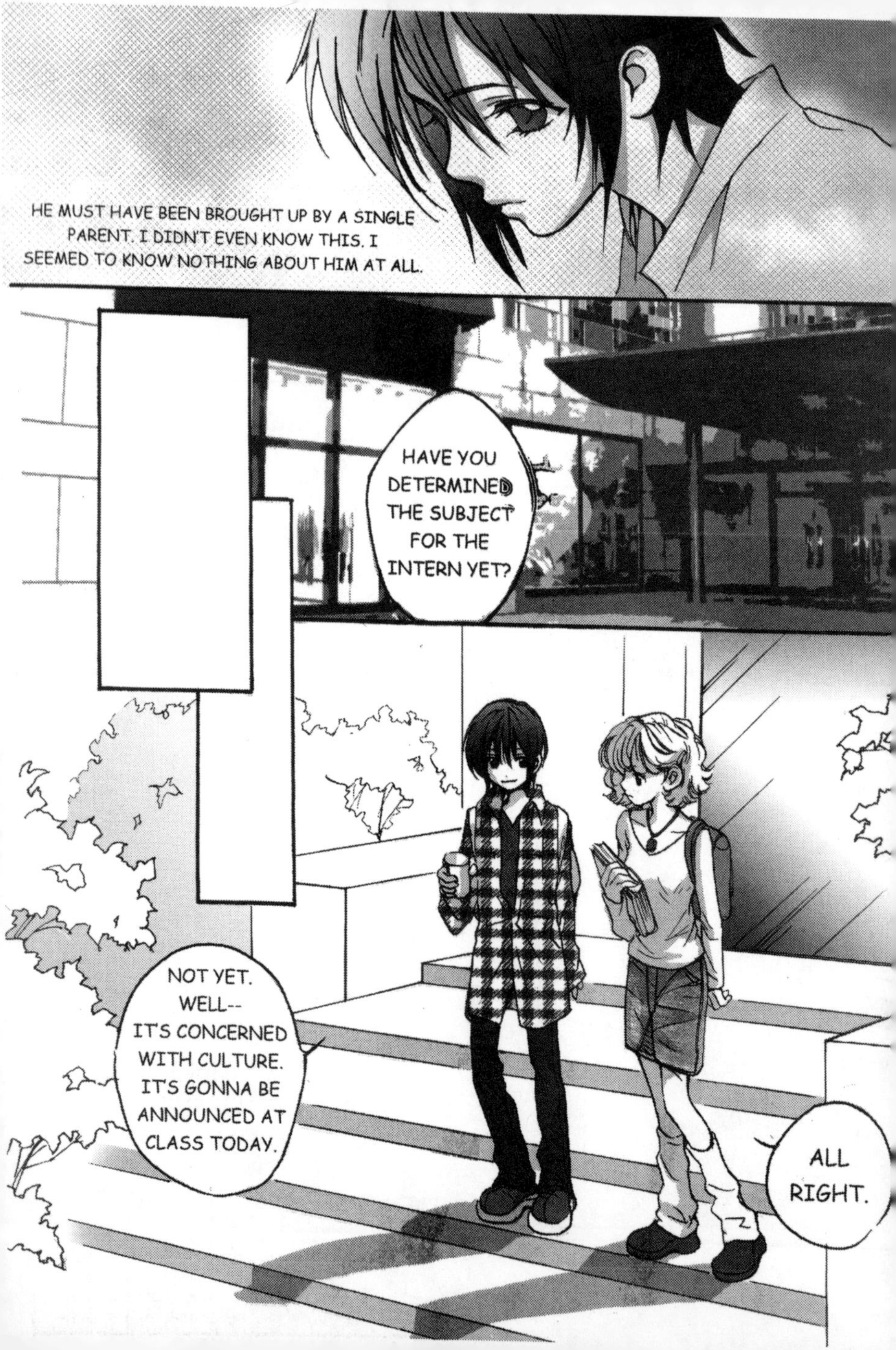
HE MUST HAVE BEEN BROUGHT UP BY A SINGLE PARENT. I DIDN'T EVEN KNOW THIS. I SEEMED TO KNOW NOTHING ABOUT HIM AT ALL.
HAVE YOU DETERMINED THE SUBJECT FOR THE INTERN YET?
NOT YET. WELL-- IT'S CONCERNED WITH CULTURE. IT'S GONNA BE ANNOUNCED AT CLASS TODAY.
ALL RIGHT.

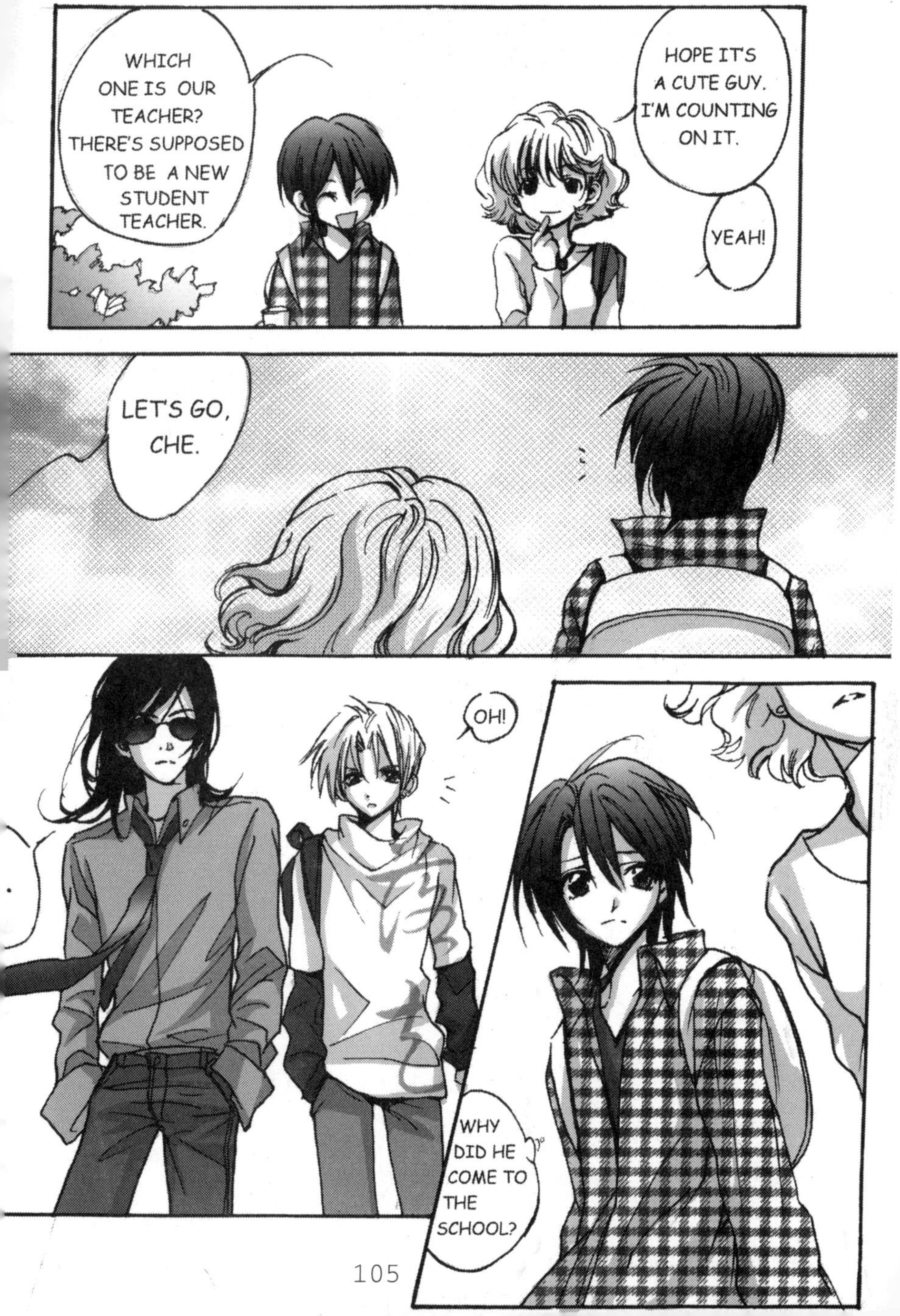
WHICH ONE IS OUR TEACHER? THERE'S SUPPOSED TO BE A NEW STUDENT TEACHER.
HOPE IT'S A CUTE GUY. I'M COUNTING ON IT.
YEAH!
LET'S GO, CHE.
OH!
WHY DID HE COME TO THE SCHOOL?

YOU!

CHE APPEARS UPSET WHEN HE SAW LULU'S HAIR.

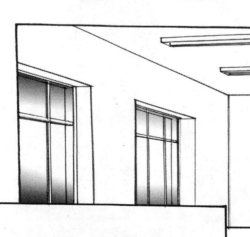

ALL RIGHT, EVERYBODY, LET'S MEET YOUR NEW STUDENT TEACHERS.

I THINK HE CARES ABOUT HER

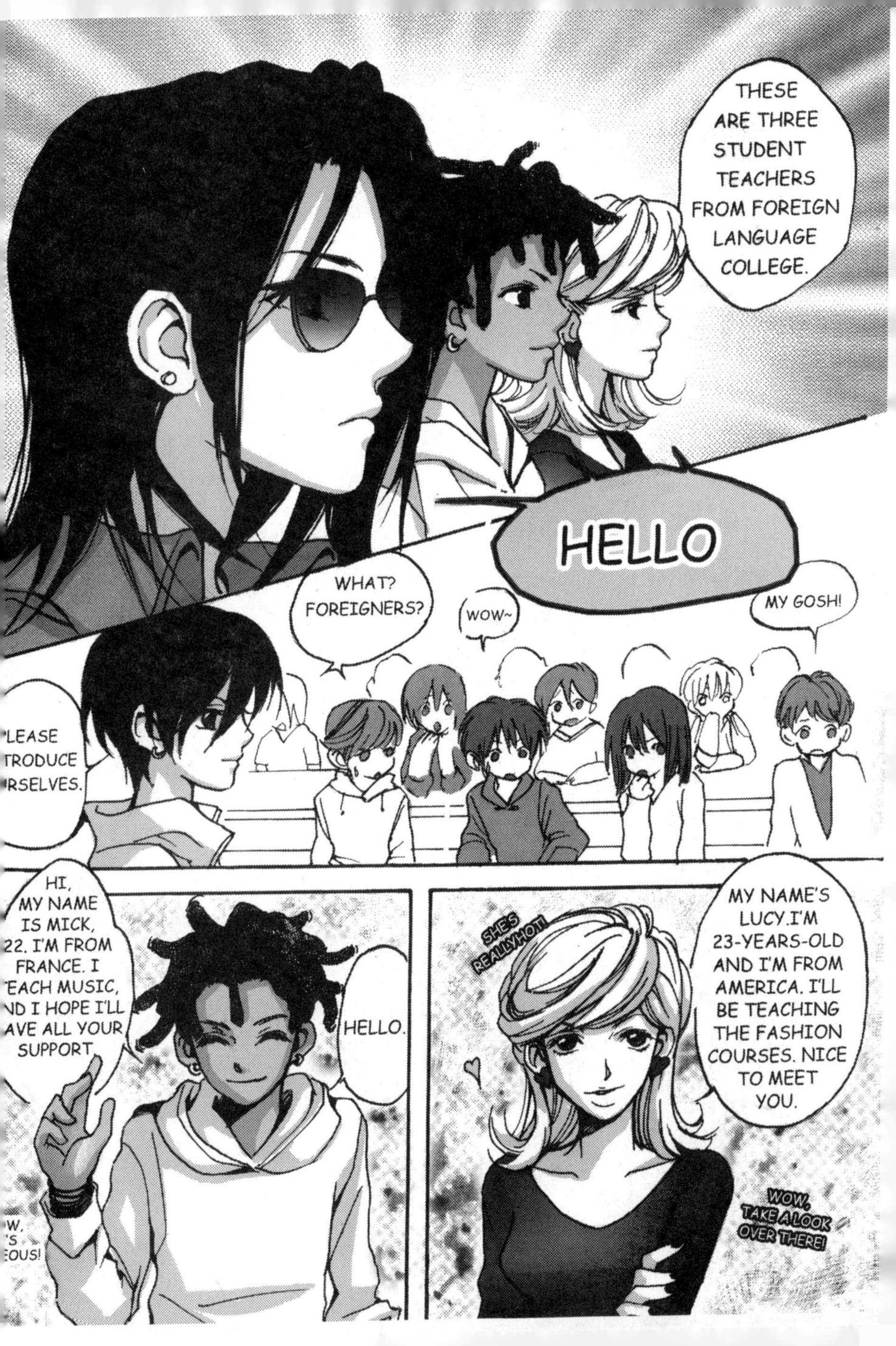
THESE ARE THREE STUDENT TEACHERS FROM FOREIGN LANGUAGE COLLEGE.
HELLO
WHAT? FOREIGNERS?
WOW~
MY GOSH!
LEASE TRODUCE RSELVES.
HI, MY NAME IS MICK, 22. I'M FROM FRANCE. I EACH MUSIC, ND I HOPE I'LL AVE ALL YOUR SUPPORT.
HELLO.
MY NAME'S LUCY. I'M 23-YEARS-OLD AND I'M FROM AMERICA. I'LL BE TEACHING THE FASHION COURSES. NICE TO MEET YOU.
SHE'S REALLY HOT!
WOW, TAKE A LOOK OVER THERE!

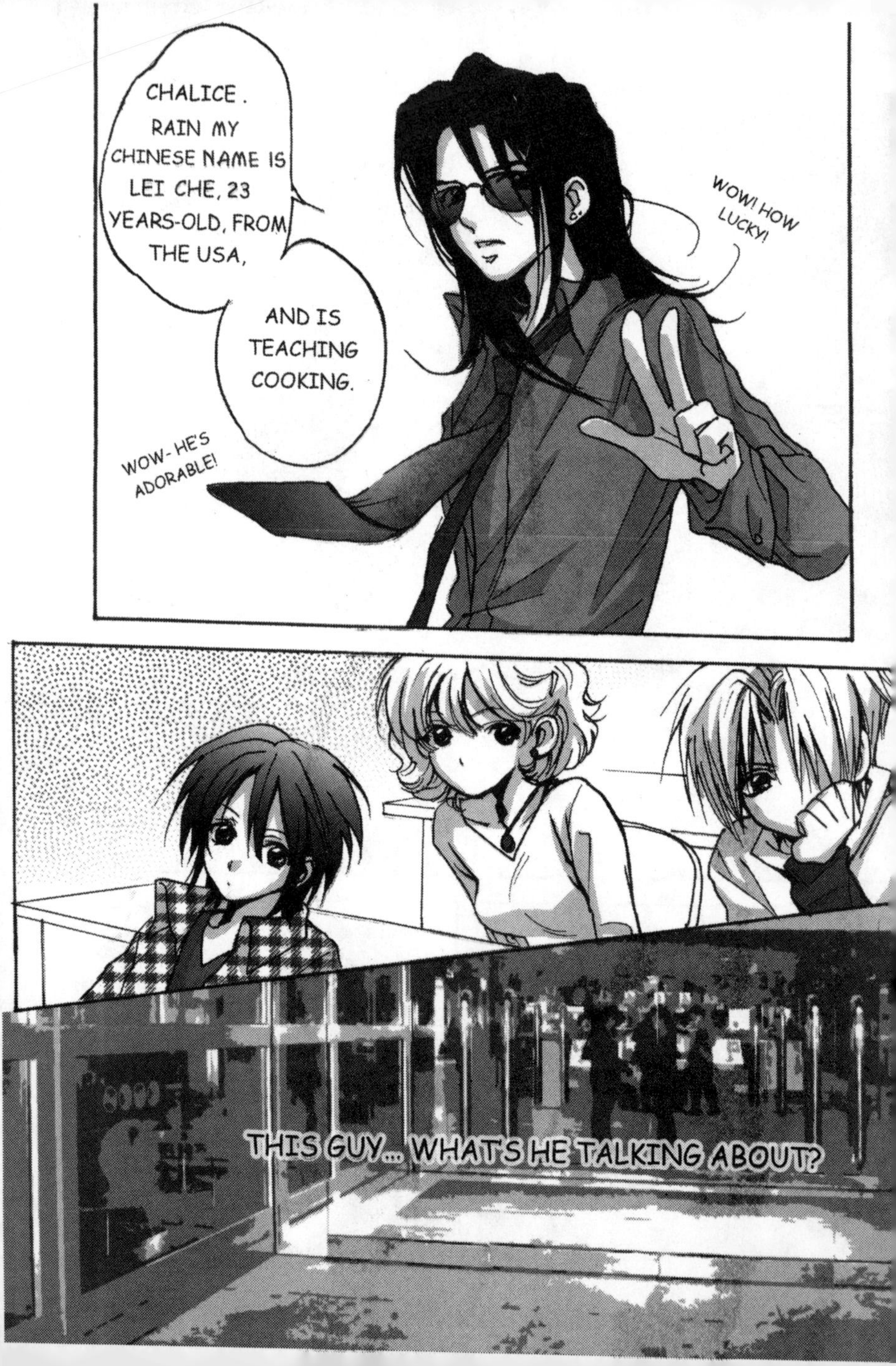
CHALICE . RAIN MY CHINESE NAME IS LEI CHE, 23 YEARS-OLD, FROM THE USA,
AND IS TEACHING COOKING.
WOW! HOW LUCKY!
WOW- HE'S ADORABLE!
THIS GUY... WHAT'S HE TALKING ABOUT?

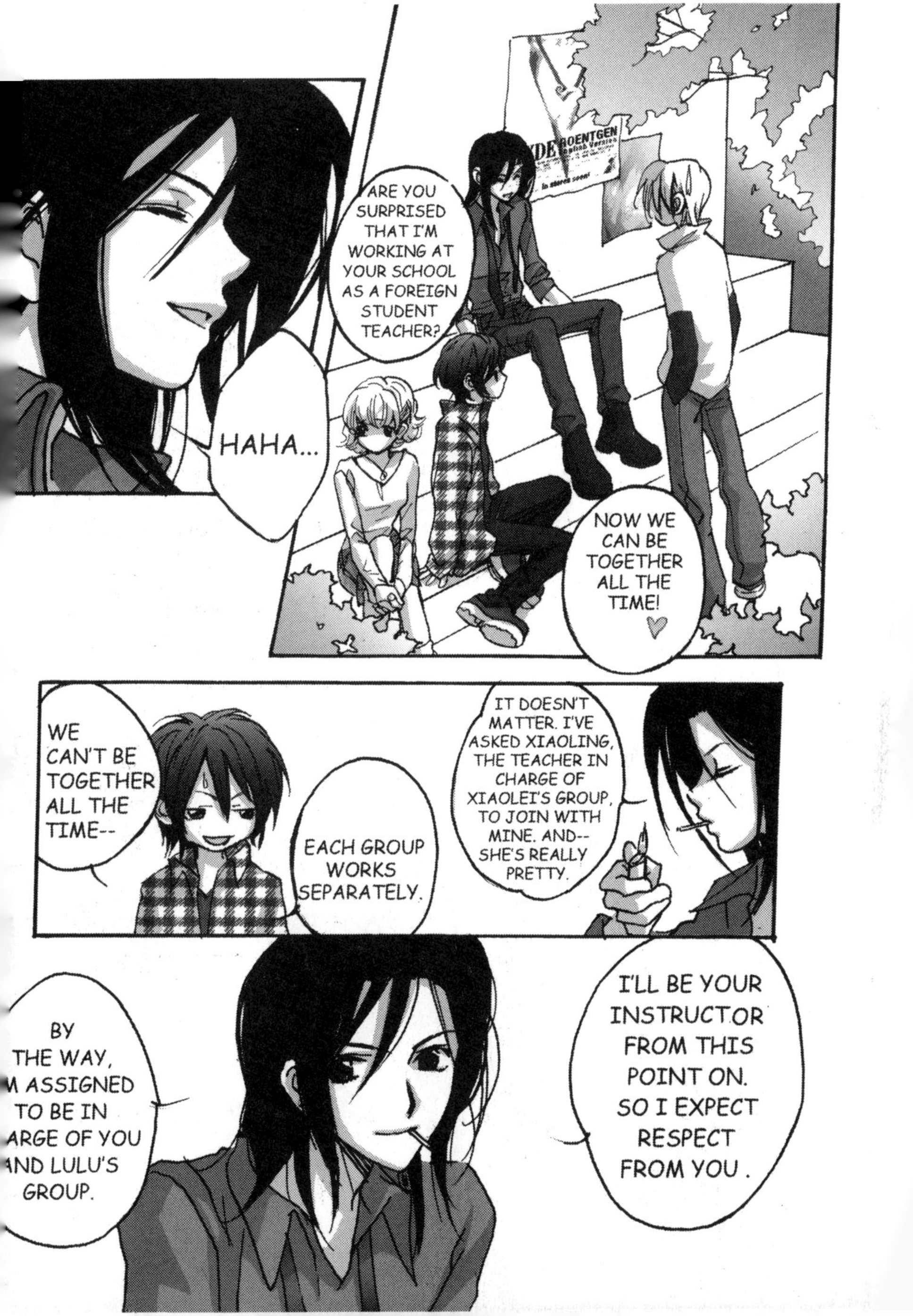
ROENTGEN
In stores soon!
ARE YOU SURPRISED THAT I'M WORKING AT YOUR SCHOOL AS A FOREIGN STUDENT TEACHER?
HAHA...
NOW WE CAN BE TOGETHER ALL THE TIME! ♥
WE CAN'T BE TOGETHER ALL THE TIME--
EACH GROUP WORKS SEPARATELY.
IT DOESN'T MATTER. I'VE ASKED XIAOLING, THE TEACHER IN CHARGE OF XIAOLEI'S GROUP, TO JOIN WITH MINE. AND-- SHE'S REALLY PRETTY.
BY THE WAY, M ASSIGNED TO BE IN ARGE OF YOU ND LULU'S GROUP.
I'LL BE YOUR INSTRUCTOR FROM THIS POINT ON. SO I EXPECT RESPECT FROM YOU .

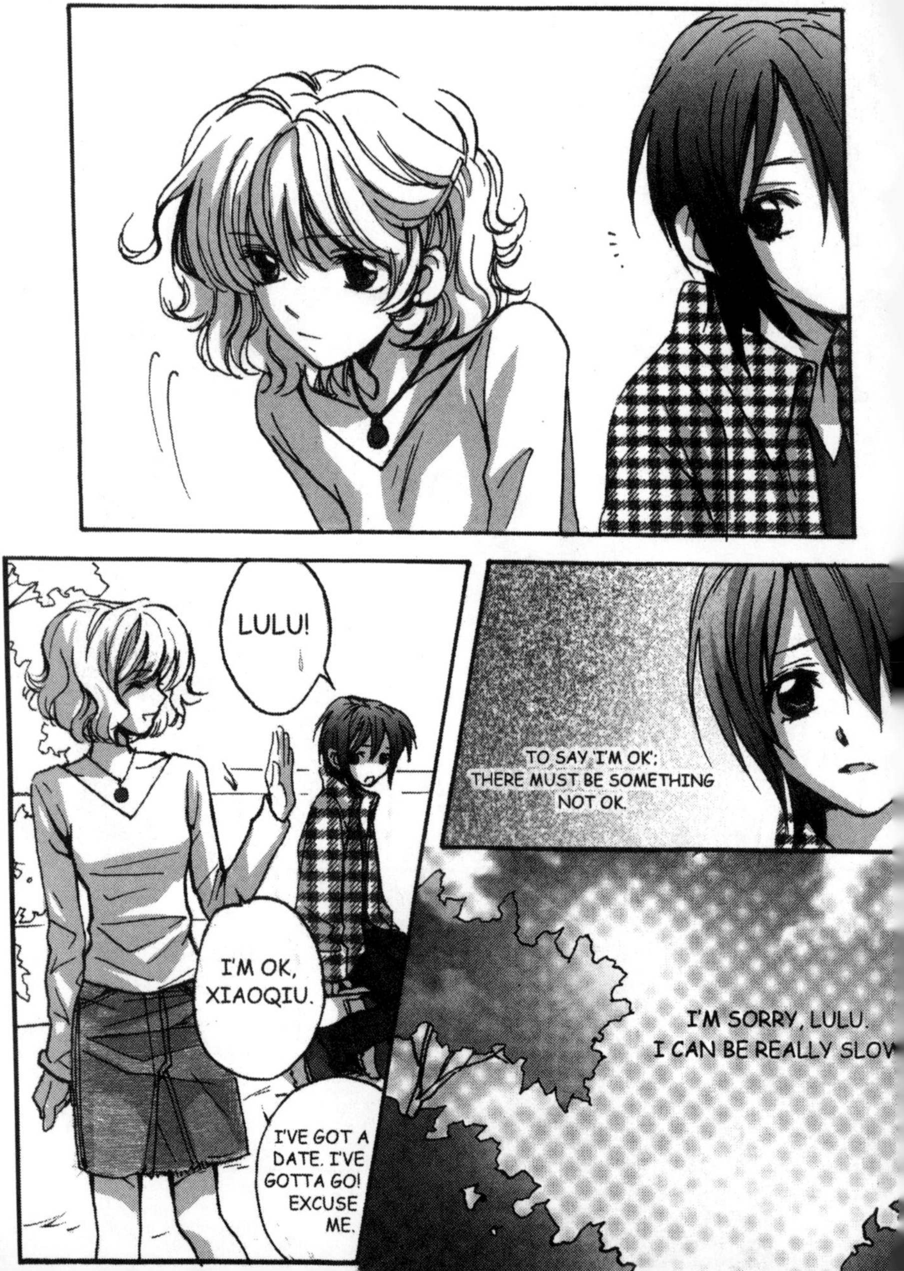

LULU!
I'M OK, XIAOQIU.
I'VE GOT A DATE. I'VE GOTTA GO! EXCUSE ME.
TO SAY 'I'M OK'; THERE MUST BE SOMETHING NOT OK.
I'M SORRY, LULU. I CAN BE REALLY SLOW

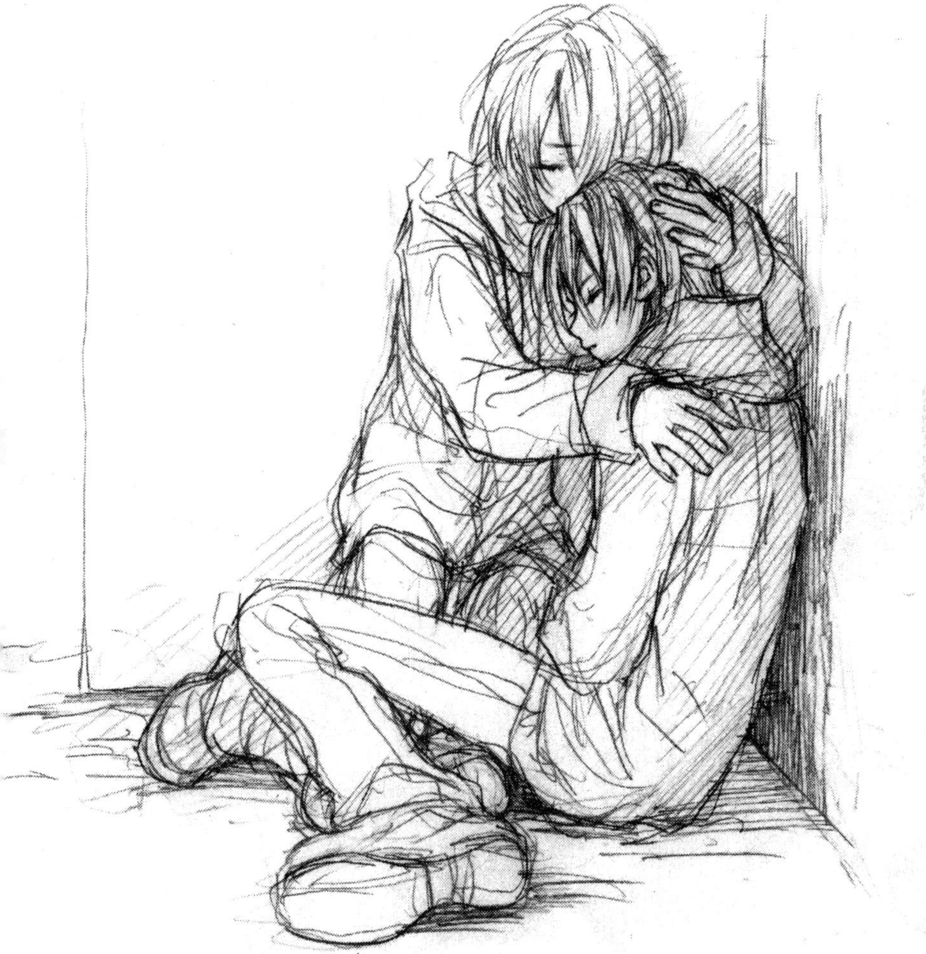

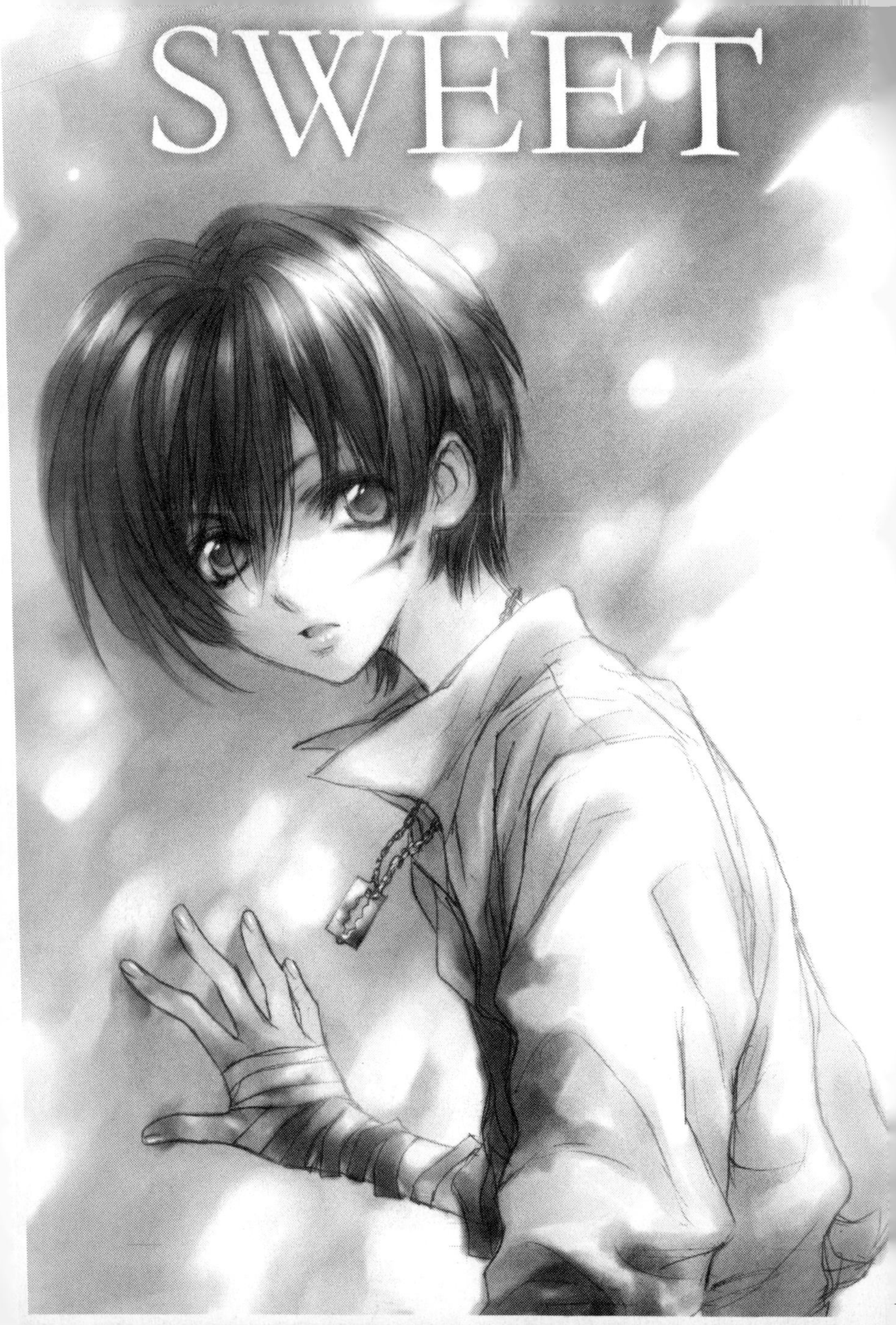
SWEET

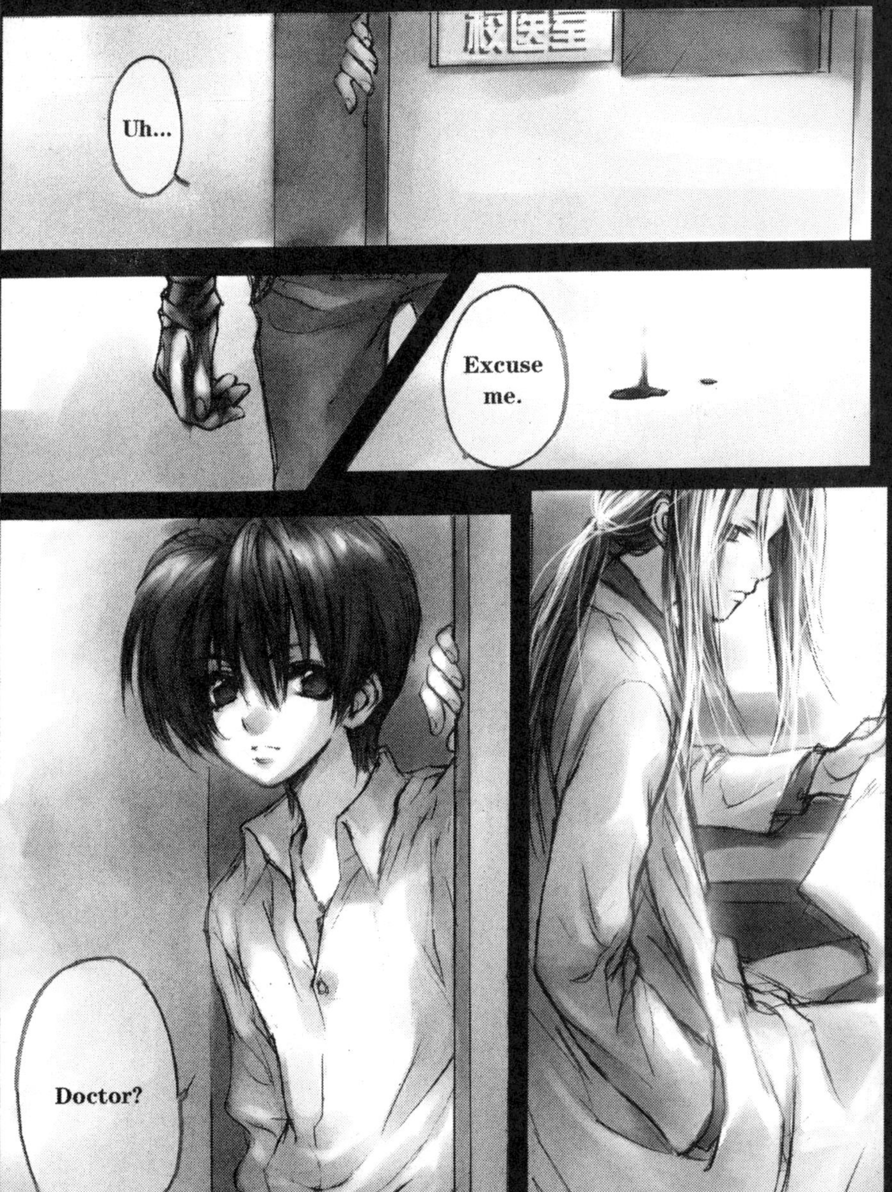
校医室
Uh...
Excuse me.
Doctor?

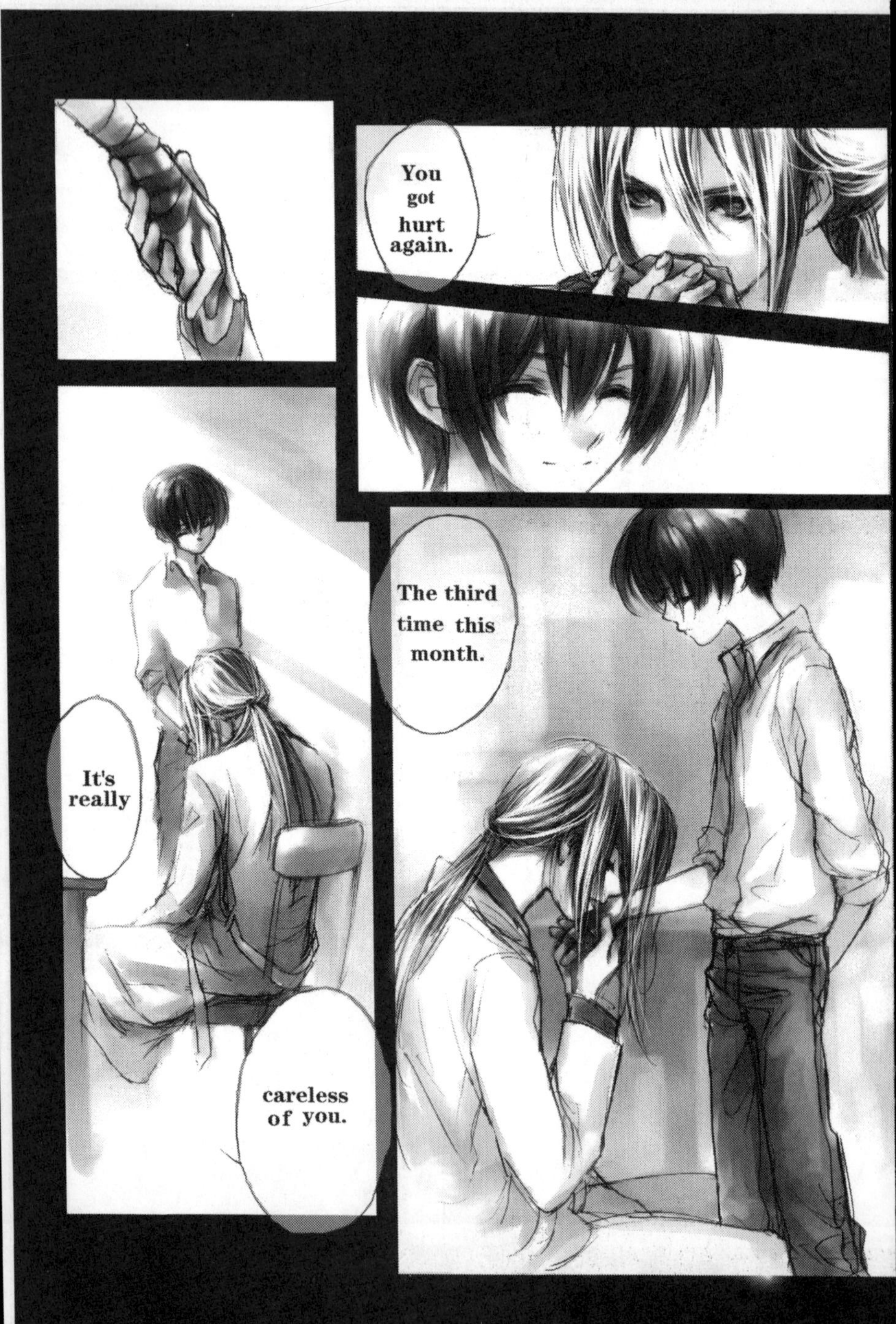
You got hurt again.
The third time this month.
It's really
careless of you.

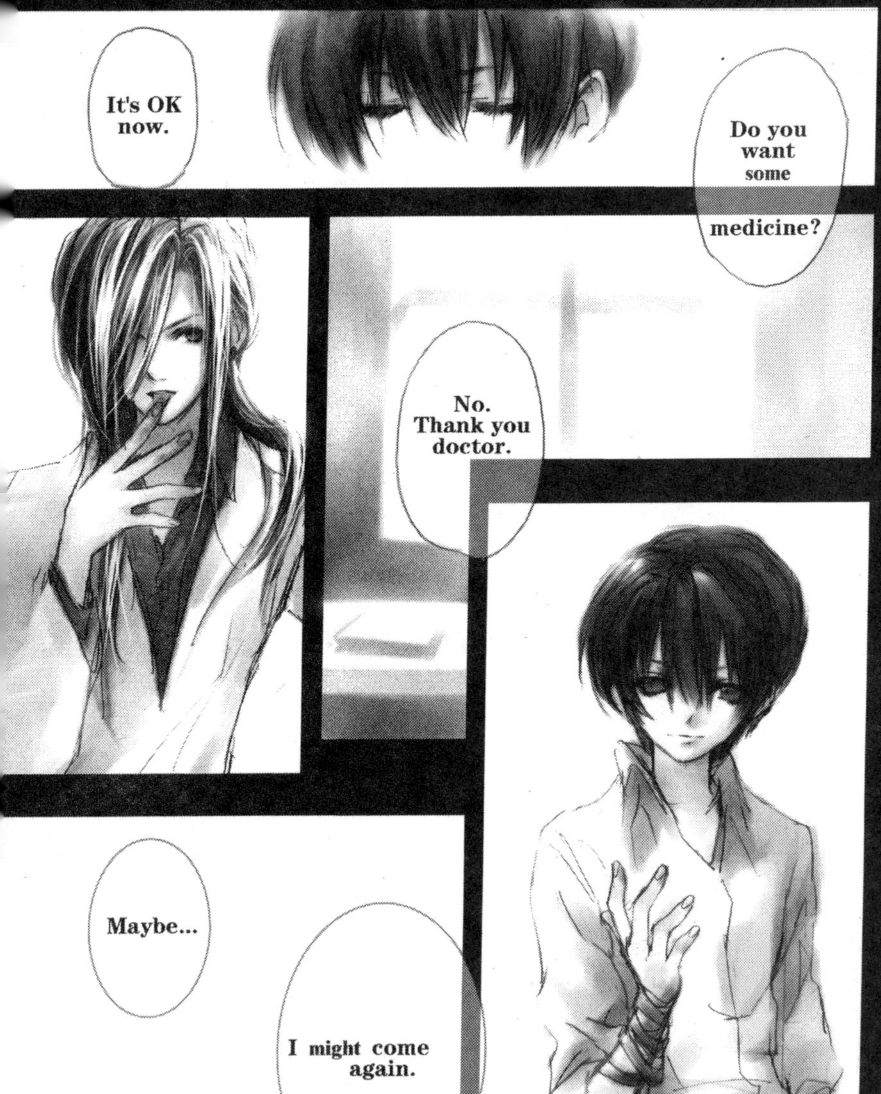
It's OK now.
Do you want some medicine?
No. Thank you doctor.
Maybe...
I might come again.

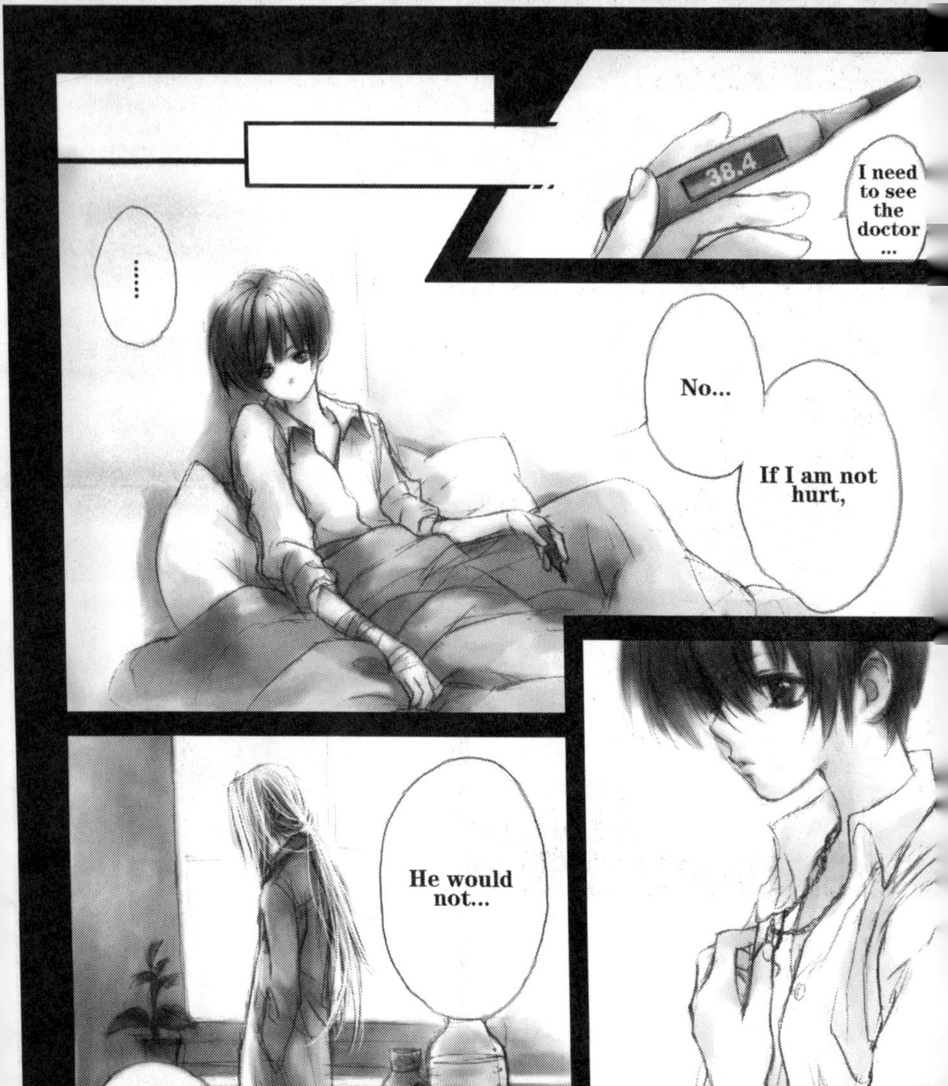
38.4
I need to see the doctor...
......
No...
If I am not hurt,
He would not...
treat me like that.

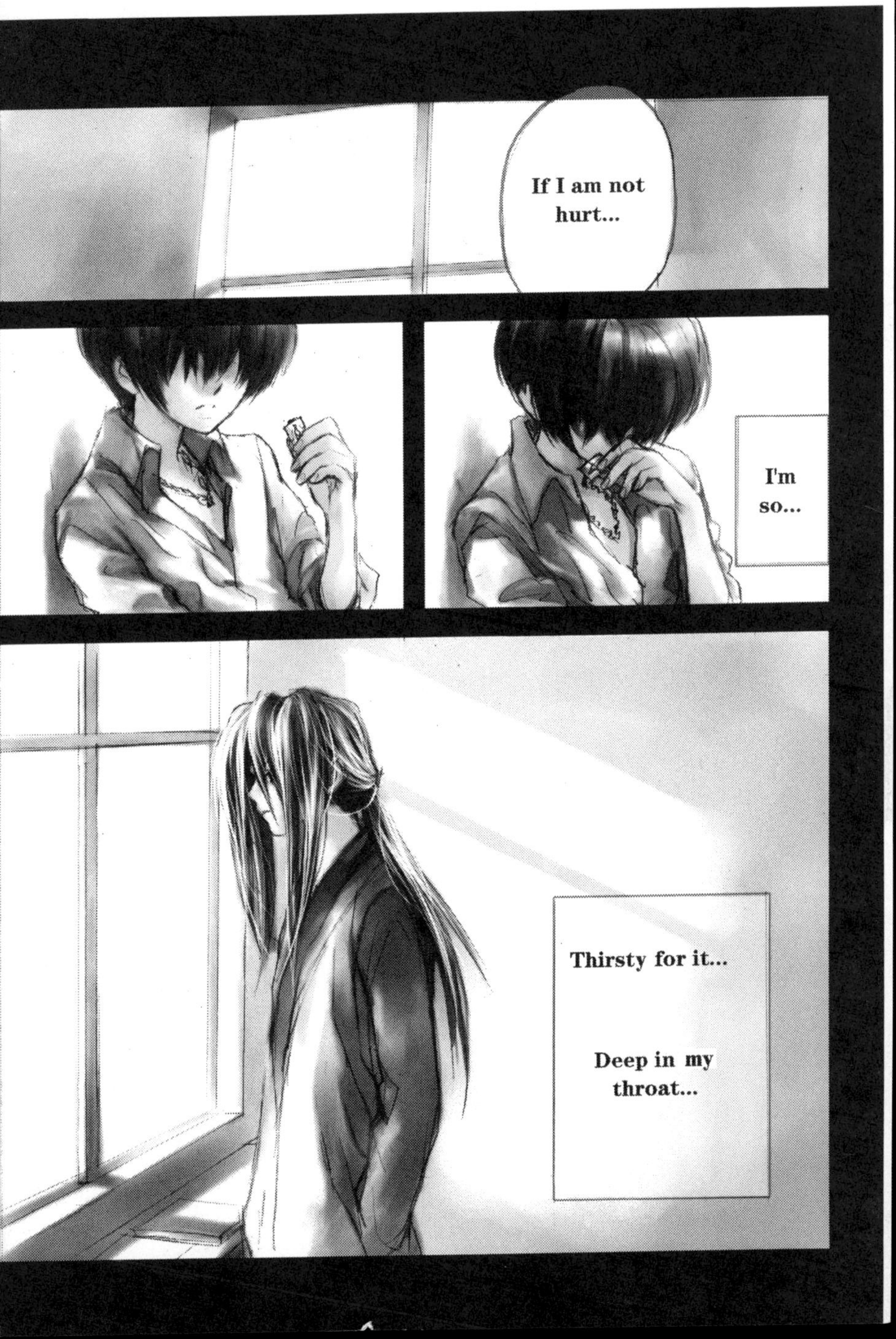
If I am not
hurt...
I'm
so...
Thirsty for it...
Deep in my
throat...

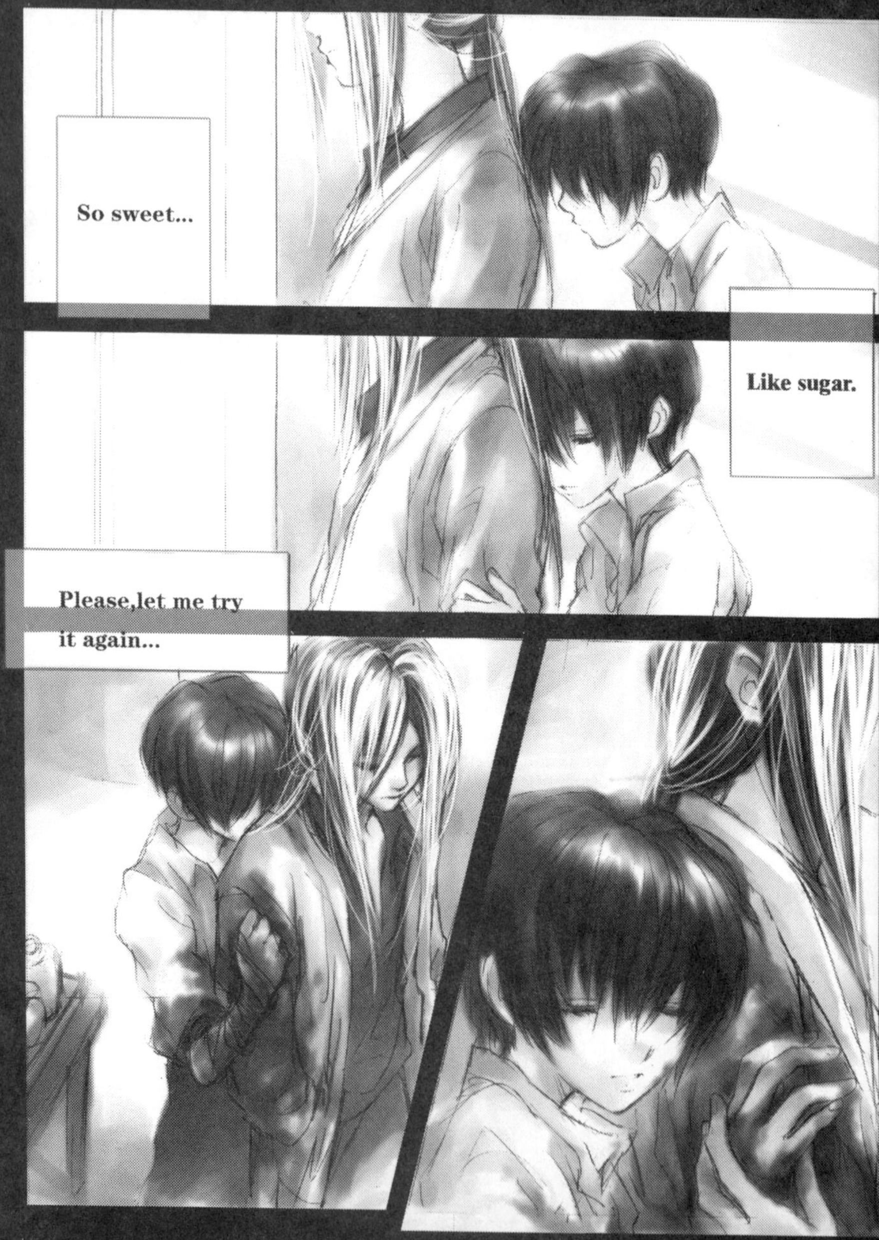
So sweet...
Like sugar.
Please,let me try it again...

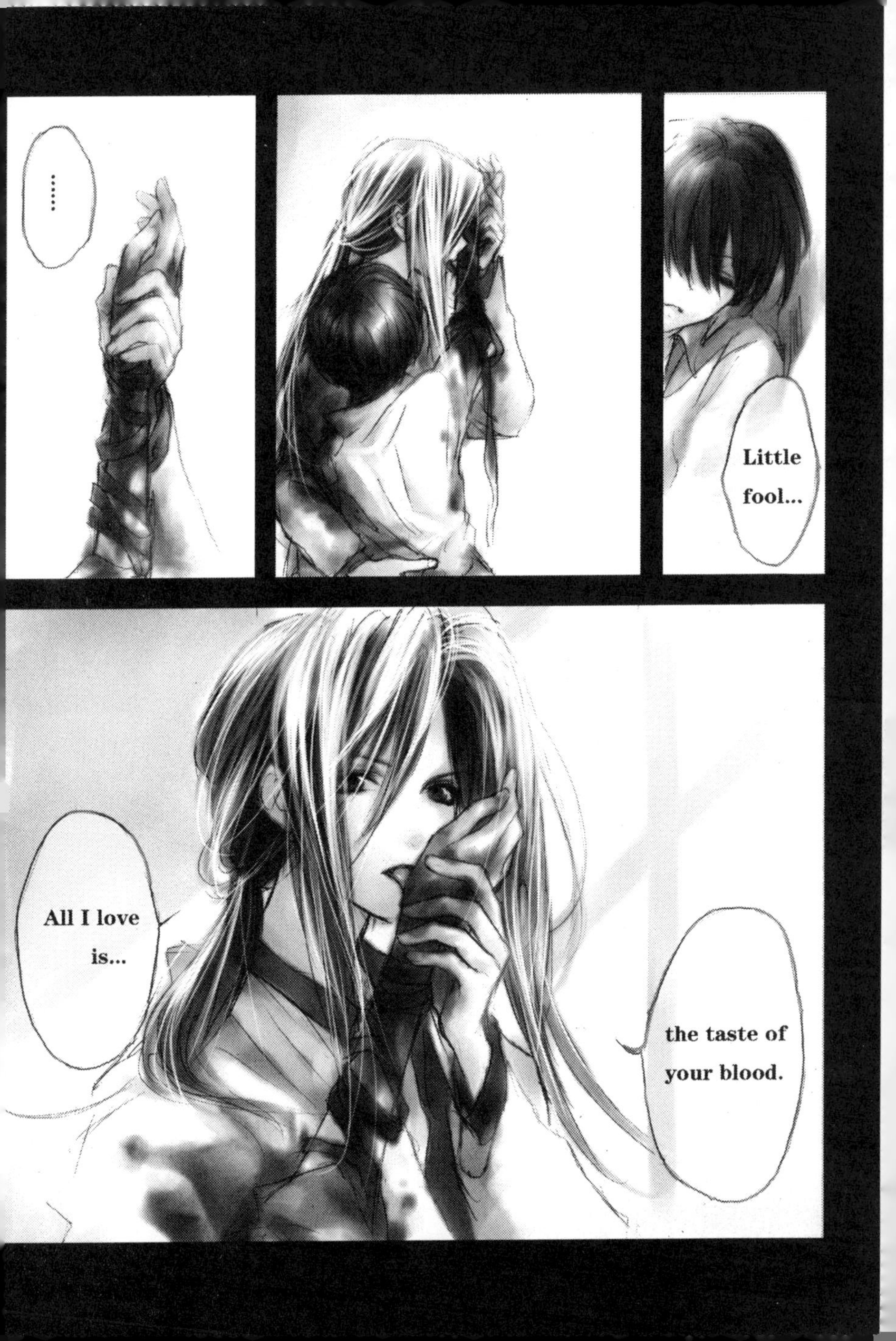
……
Little fool...
All I love is...
the taste of your blood.